A Methodology for Developing and Deploying Internet and Intranet Solutions

ISBN 0-13-209677-3

9 780132 096775

90000

Hewlett-Packard Professional Books

A Methodology for Developing and Deploying Internet and Intranet Solutions

Jeff R. Greenberg

and

J. R. Lakeland

To join a Prentice Hall PTR Internet mailing list, point to:
http://www.prenhall.com/mail_lists/

Prentice Hall PTR
Upper Saddle River, New Jersey 07458

Library of Congress Cataloging-in-Publication Data

Greenberg, Jeff (Jeff R.)
    A methodology for developing and deploying Internet and intranet
solutions / Jeff Greenberg & J.R. Lakeland
        p.   m.
    Includes index.
    ISBN 0-13-209677-3
    1. Internet (Computer network) 2. Intranets (Computer networks)
I. Lakeland, J.R. II. Title.
TK5105.875.I57G74 1997
004'.36'0684--dc21   97-41592
                                                                          CIP

Editorial/production supervision: *Dawn Speth White*
Art design director: *Jerry Votta*
Cover designer: *Scott Weiss*
Manufacturing manager: *Julia Meehan*
Marketing manager: *Miles Williams*
Acquisitions editor: *John Anderson*
Editorial assistant: *Tara Ruggiero*
Manager, Hewlett-Packard Press: *Patricia Pekary*

Published by Prentice Hall PTR
Prentice-Hall, Inc.
A Simon & Schuster Company
Upper Saddle River, NJ 07458

Prentice Hall books are widely used by corporations and government agencies for training, marketing, and resale.

The publisher offers discounts on this book when ordered in bulk quantities.
For more information, contact: Corporate Sales Department, Phone: 800-382-3419;
Fax: 201-236-7141; E-mail: corpsales@prenhall.com; or write: Prentice Hall PTR,
Corp. Sales Dept., One Lake Street, Upper Saddle River, NJ 07458.

Ami Pro, Lotus, and 1-2-3 are registered trademarks of the Lotus Development Corporation. CICS, DB2, and SNA and MVS are trademarks of the IBM Corporation. Communicator and SuiteSpot are registered trademarks of the Netscape Communications Corporation. HP-UX, HP OpenView, HP OpenView/OmniBack and HP IT/Operations are registered trademarks of the Hewlett-Packard Company. Microsoft, Windows NT, Windows, and MS are registered trademarks of the Microsoft Corporation. ActiveX is a trademark of the Microsoft Corporation. Java and Javascript are registered trademarks of Sun Microsystems, Inc. Adobe, Framemaker, and Pagemaker are registered trademarks of Adobe Systems Inc. Puddleduck Press is a trademark of Puddleduck Press Inc. Slinky is a registered trademark of James Industries. UNIX is a registered trademark of X-Open Company Limited. WordPerfect is a registered trademark of Corel Corporation. All other products or services mentioned in this book are the trademarks or service marks of their respective companies or organizations.

Printed in the United States of America
10 9 8 7 6 5 4 3 2 1

ISBN 0-13-209677-3

Prentice-Hall International (UK) Limited, *London*
Prentice-Hall of Australia Pty. Limited, *Sydney*
Prentice-Hall Canada Inc., *Toronto*
Prentice-Hall Hispanoamericana, S.A., *Mexico*
Prentice-Hall of India Private Limited, *New Delhi*
Prentice-Hall of Japan, Inc., *Tokyo*
Simon & Schuster Asia Pte. Ltd., *Singapore*
Editora Prentice-Hall do Brasil, Ltda., *Rio de Janeiro*

In memory of my father, Arnold Greenberg, 1925-1997.

Table of Contents

Table of Illustrations

Acknowledgments

Between this being my first book and a number of unexpected life events, the road from book proposal to final copy has been severely chuckholed. A number of people have been instrumental in making this possible. I hope I've accounted for you all, and to all I thank you for your support. My additional thanks to:

Lindsay, Daniel, and Megan for being supportive and tolerating my years of seclusion, missed opportunities, and, far too often, my being grumpy.

My parents for having encouraged my insatiable appetite for reading.

My parents, in-laws and friends for their encouragement and for understanding why I "wore" a laptop during vacations and visits.

Bill Hewlett, Dave Packard, and the folks at HP for a great laptop, and who helped make this happen, especially Bill Murphy, Chris Caldwell, Amy Cowen, Pat Pekary, and Whit Matteson for his forthrightness.

Carl Kupersmith (*mazel tov!*) for the opportunity, his time, and continuing friendship.

The folks at Puddleduck Press for their web pages and graphics.

The folks at Adobe® tech support for getting me up and running with FrameMaker®, which was used to typeset this book, and out of the clutches of the word processor from hell.

J.R. Lakeland, writer, have a weekend off!

And to the folks at Prentice Hall for their talents and encouragement, and especially my editors, Dawn White for her vision and sense of humor, Patti Guerrieri for the last-minute lifeline, John Anderson for his savvy, Bernard Goodwin for his drive, and Karen Gettman for her patience.

Preface

"Since we happen to be at the beginning, let's begin here."
-J.R. Lakeland

There is an interesting phenomenon today in the computing industry (I mean other than Bill Gates). There has actually been a small rumbling of what could be considered a ground swell to reverse a technology paradigm shift! I've been in computers for twenty years, and I don't recall this happening before. But I'm way out ahead here so let me back up a decade or two.

The late 1980's saw a new paradigm being introduced. The old paradigm was the monolithic computer, and the associated functional but deadly boring terminal screen. The shift was to client-server computing: the use of one computer or class of computers to act as a computing, data, or application server while another computer or class of computers provide client services. An example many people will be familiar with is the typical on-line service where the screen and editing are being provided by your desktop PC, but the look-up data is maintained on the server end. The two applications speak to each other transparent to the user, as opposed to filling in a screen, pressing enter, and waiting (although even that can be client-server in a very loose model).

Client-server computing is meant to put the processing power where it is needed, thus reducing the need for humongous mainframes and allowing the provision of meaningful information to the user like never before. Sounds great, no? Many CIO's believe so, and showed it by 'betting the farm' on client-server technology.

This "ground swell" movement is suggesting that a move back to the mainframe might be appropriate. Why? If client-server technology is so wonderful, why move back to the mainframe? Why even consider shifting the paradigm back with the cost of losing what the shift was supposed to provide, let alone the cost of the reversal? Why do cubicles have signs like:

Mainframes: We're back, and boy are we ticked off!

Aside from the fact that the local mainframe sales representative probably photocopied a stack of them and left them around, what would lead to the display of these signs?

There is a perception that the client-server paradigm isn't working. I agree to some extent, but not for any reason that would have me advocate people returning to mainframes, the 'art' of 80-column JCL, and data in the form of reams of green-bar paper instead of information.

Let's not lose sight of the Internet earthquake, and the aftershock of Intranets. Lest we forget, both are examples of client-server technology, and there's not a darned thing wrong with it. There are ongoing issues with the application side of client-server technology, but before I discuss the cause and solutions, let me expand on the symptoms of the issue.

Symptoms

- the technology is expensive to manage
- the applications are expensive to develop
- payback is lacking

Frankly, these symptoms were common long before client-server technology. The inference is that client-server technology itself is the cause of these symptoms. Untrue.

successful after being implemented. Plan well; don't stumble when the paradigm shifts.

I hope you enjoy reading A Methodology for Developing and Deploying Internet and Intranet Solutions.

JEFF R. GREENBERG
MANAGER, TELECOM SOLUTIONS SUPPORT PROGRAM
HP PROFESSIONAL SERVICES ORGANIZATION
ATLANTA, GEORGIA
MAY, 1996

Foreword

In the wake of the widespread client-server migration of the late 80s, mainframe computing is a distant memory for many companies. As dumb terminals were replaced by desktop PCs, the centralized information model of the past gave way to more efficient, localized repositories of information available when and if needed by the desktop user. For those visionaries who migrated early, the client-server paradigm promised empowered users and self-sufficient terminals. More importantly, the crash of one system wouldn't mean the whole company had to stop and wait for the reboot to complete.

The unparalleled growth of the Internet and the World Wide Web has shown client-server technology at its most successful. When you log onto a web page, you are requesting information from a server. However, when you log off, you are still sitting in front of a fully functional machine. It is surprising, then, that despite the perception that the Internet, intranets, and extranets must be viewed as cornerstones for tomorrow's Enterprise computing, many are heralding a return to Mainframe systems.

The widely discussed Network Computer (NC) is, after all, an updated model of the dummy terminal. The thin client may be functional for the home user and for certain applications in the corporate world, such as 3270 terminal replacement and other task-oriented applications. But, for the corporate world to disregard the technologies advanced by the Internet and once again adopt a centralized information repository can only be viewed as a step back.

When initiated, managed, and deployed correctly, enterprise-wide implementation of client-server technologies yields an open computing environment designed to keep up with constantly changing and diversifying computing needs. The negative ramifications of a system unable to adapt to change or accommodate job diversity within the company can not be understated. Just as today's companies could not survive without an Internet presence and an intranet for streamlining internal processes, a computing environment unable to meet the various demands of a business moving at Internet speeds can not take your company into the next century. A strong client-server environment, especially one which takes advantage of, and builds upon, Internet and intranet technologies, can provide the foundation for your company's computing future.

Whether overhauling your own enterprise's client-server environment or implementing a large-scale client-server environment for a client, success or failure will fall on the shoulders of the lone project manager. Thrown into the middle of a mission-critical enterprise-wide technology transition, the project manager will need a solid and proven road map that will take the team, the company, and the solution from the initial planning phases to deployment. The best road maps, however, have often been tested and sharpened by experience as well as planned after careful surveyance of the terrain to be covered.

Faced with a mission-critical project in a world where businesses change with lighting speed, the assigned project manager doesn't have the time to construct a road map through trial and error. For successful development and deployment, there is little room for mistake. A Methodology for Developing and Deploying Internet and Intranet Solutions details a road map for initiating and implementing an Inter- and Intranet client-server migration. Greenberg's years of experience have given him insight into potential pitfalls, solutions, and strategies resulting in his approach to development and deployment. When you're ready to move your company into the next century and join the ranks of successful client-server organizations, you want to do it right. Greenberg's sample case study in A Methodology for Developing and Deploying Internet and Intranet Solutions provides tried and true techniques and strategies designed to sharpen your project management skills when it counts — before the project begins.

William J. Murphy
Director, Internet Programs
Hewlett-Packard Company

Introduction

> "If you don't have the time to do it right the first time,
> when will you have the time to do it over?"
> -Anonymous

> "It costs less to do it right than it does to fix it"
> -Jeff R. Greenberg

The quotes above summarize the premise of this book, which discusses technology implementation, the Internet and intranets, client-server technology, infrastructure development, and advanced project management. Whew! Boiled down, it discusses the issues faced in trying to plan and manage the implementation of new technology on a large scale (although most of the principles apply to small-scale implementations too), and although it focuses on technology, most of the methodology introduced in the book can easily be used with any major process change, even if it's not technology-based. Specifically, it will

- provide a baseline definition of client-server technology.
- describe technologies, services and associated products that complement client-server and Internet technologies.
- create a case study business for deploying client-server technology, Internet, and intranet technologies.
- show how to determine and develop the infrastructure needed for the new technology.
- Identify potential implementation pitfalls and how to overcome them.
- Reveal methods for successfully planning and managing such

implementations.
- Establish the criteria for defining a prototype, pilot and test plan.
- Show the support that is necessary during and after the implementation.

As has already been mentioned in the Preface, the Internet and intranets are examples of client-server technology. This will be explained in more detail as we progress, but for now let's accept that as a given, and thus, throughout the book, when the term 'client-server' is used it will be inclusive of the Internet and intranet, while 'the Internet' or 'intranet' will be specific to those technologies being subsets of client-server technology.

Client-server technology is the '*du jour*' technology for the 90s, but not in the sense of it being a passing fad. For a company to be prepared to compete into the next century, it should have, or be planning to have, client-server technology as one of its foundation technologies.

The adjective 'foundation' was chosen specifically, since a house is a convenient analogy. If a house is built on a foundation that was rushed, at the least there will be expensive repairs later on, at worst, the house will fall. Similarly, if the house is completed without having the necessary infrastructure (wiring, plumbing, and so on), the cost of making it usable will be prohibitive. The same ideas hold true with the implementation of a client-server enterprise.

There are very few facets of information technology as consistently misunderstood and misrepresented as client-server technology and enterprise technology implementation, and here we're dealing with both! Client-server technology is neither easy nor inexpensive to implement successfully. This is especially true on an enterprise-wide basis where, by definition, the entire company will be touched.

'Success' is a subjective term, so I'll define my usage to be as follows:

When the implementation is complete, the customer is positioned to realize the return on its investment and the benefits from the implementation.

Enterprise technology implementation is very often one of the largest impact phases of a company's existence, and all too often the most underplanned. Often this is a reality based on structure: The IS department is normally a cost center, and as such the budget fought for is jealously guarded for staffing and hardware. The planning process and success of the implementation lay in the hands of the project manager, and very few skillsets are as misunderstood and underestimated as project management. Sure, you can buy a book on project management or take a course or two and you'll know how to read a project plan, perhaps create one, and know how to recognize at some point that you're in trouble (assuming you've kept the plan up to date), but there are many more subtle skills necessary to succeed that aren't taught, many of which are used throughout the book.

As the technology used as an example in this book represents a recent major paradigm shift, we ought to define that before moving on.

par•a•digm n. 1. An example serving as a pattern or model

Over the last thirty years, the paradigm, or model, has been the 'mainframe shop'. There are some exceptions, and with the advent of the mini-computer, permutations. Usually the mission-critical applications within a company reside on a mainframe. So in a typical company, the base IT technology and infrastructure are the evolutionary result of a foundation laid twenty to thirty years ago. Introducing new enterprise-wide technology is shifting the paradigm, and with very few exceptions, the people managing this existing technology have never had to ride the crest of a paradigm shift. Upgrades, yes, add-on equipment, yes, tweaks to the original infrastructure, yes, but not the enterprise-wide rollout of new technology and its supporting infrastructure. With that general lack of experience and the risks, why would any CIO want to?

The reason should be that there is a business case that is undeniable. Although they, understandably, wouldn't step forward to admit to it, most CIOs facing an undeniable business case and the daunting challenge of a paradigm shift are caught between a rock and a hard place. They launch an internal paradigm shift with trepidation and a concern for their company (and their job). Why their company? Because an undeniable business case translates to mission-critical, a situation that assures that failure will be noticed and will cost more than the sum of its parts. Thus a shift must proceed and must succeed, and the responsibility sits on the shoulders of the project manager, who is typically the person in IS who was doing the least at the time, is seldom a volunteer, and, unfortunately, is seldom really qualified for the role.

Most project managers aren't afforded the opportunity of sitting down and developing a plan and then starting the implementation. Too often the project is underway without the plan, and the project manager is asked to develop the plan 'on the fly.' We'll look at this 'opportunity' later. The biggest challenges to a project manager in implementing new technology are not the mechanics of project management shown above, but:

- getting your arms around the project.
- keeping your arms around the project.
- understanding what you have your arms around.
- knowing when to let go.

We'll discuss these topics throughout the book in a look at what I call 'project psychology.' A lot of the concepts are gray and abstract; the more abstract they are, the more explanation I'll try to provide in the hopes that by the end of the book you'll be armed and ready to take on the challenges of project managing a client-server enterprise implementation.

Here's what you will find in each chapter.

Chapter 1

In the first chapter we'll set up the business scenario for the rest of the book. We'll meet the project manager and some of his co-workers, be introduced to the client and their key players, look at the solution and its driving forces, and put together a proposal (the portions germane to the book) and initial project timeline.

Chapter 2

Developing the proposal will be the key to this chapter. Along the way we'll look at how to move from a Work Breakdown Structure to a draft timeline, and the cornerstones of a low-risk proposal such as roles and assumptions.

Chapter 3

It's time to launch the project. We'll look at an internal project kick-off, where roles are nailed down and the scope of activity is validated. Also discussed are refinements to the time line, project team interviews, steering committee, project communications, and the full kickoff meeting. The chapter also covers some of the political realities of cross-organizational implementation and how that translates to the selection of a steering committee and core project team members.

Chapter 4

Phase One. The investigation begins as does the software development cycle. Approach papers are published and the Phase Two project plan is developed.

Chapter 5

Phase Two. When writing a screenplay, one of the more popular methods of proof-of-concept is the two-page screenplay – the theory being if the plot doesn't work in two pages, it certainly won't in 100. The same holds true for implementation. The main reason for a prototype is that if the concept doesn't work in prototype, it won't work later. Of course money can be thrown at a failed prototype to make it work, but the decision should be made beforehand whether this is acceptable, not while under fire. This chapter also covers prototyping the software solution.

Chapter 6

The primary concept of cookie-cutter proliferation is that the implementation be planned and executed correctly once, and then reused without additional overhead. This chapter leads the reader through some of the complex set of issues that need to be addressed before deployment. Topics include site readiness, data transfer, user education, and software releases.

Chapter 7

Infrastructure is quickly becoming as overused a term as state of the art; nevertheless, infrastructure is fundamental to the success of an implementation. If the organization, tools, and network are not in place to support a client-server environment, it's time to get the checkbook and a lot of fire extinguishers ready.

Chapter 8

Quality control and testing are key to any success, yet this process is often trimmed down because of time constraints, politics, or the expense of extra equipment and logistics. The irony is that the cost of implementing without the quality control can quickly overshadow the cost of testing. This chapter covers one workable series of unit, system, alpha, beta, and user acceptance testing. The Phase Three plan and pricing are developed and proposed.

Chapter 9

Phase Three. Staging the equipment can make or break an implementation, especially in the case of remote installations with software or hardware from various sources. This chapter covers the logistics of staging, preparing a sterile system from which to create a staging tape, the staging process, and uses the success of the HP Field Integration Center as an example.

Chapter 10

The pilots (yes plural (introduce a new set of logistics and issues because (1) everything, including the proliferation plan and staging, needs to be tested, and (2) there are issues related to such seemingly trivial things as site selection, testing method (parallel, tangential, or perpendicular), and application regression.

Chapter 11

With everything else under our belt, it's time to throw the switch – but WAIT! – there are issues related to proliferation despite the cookie-cutter approach. Topics include the proliferation command center, support hand-off, ramp-up and ramp-down of resources, and switch-over.

Epilogue

The project postmortem, where final hand-offs and sign-offs are done. And the wrap-up party, where recognition is given to the team members.

Chapter 1

In this chapter we'll create an implementation business case to use in the case study throughout the book. I'm going to take the approach of using a composite of many situations I have experienced. We're not going to present a diary, so some issues may jump out as appearing staged or farfetched (as they tend to do in real life).

One of the factors that most consistently steps in the path of a large implementation being successful is company politics. If you're nodding, good, but if you're scratching your head, thinking "politics?" or worse, thinking "we don't have any politics in our company," you might be in for a rude awakening when you find yourself in the 'crash dummy' seat.

> pol-i-tics n. (used with a sing. or pl. verb). Maneuvering within a group to obtain control..

The politics within a company are often debilitating and counterproductive. They are sometimes the result of the organization structure, sometimes the personalities of unit managers, and sometimes an inheritance that results in "the way things are done" without anyone remembering why. These politics have, actively or passively, such a large potential for a major impact, directly or indirectly, on a project, that I'll be focusing on them often during various stages of the book, just as you will need to during various stages of the planning and implementation. With that in mind, I'll shortly build us a small corporation, complete with politics, but first let's talk about the target audience.

A project's manager comes from one of two places, inside the company or outside. When forming a mental picture of the project details, getting your 'arms around it,' the two have different information available to them during the formative period of the project due to their standing, among other things. This information bias in turn has a tendency to bias the 'gut feel' impression of the project's scope that the project manager needs to form, and usually needs to form fairly quickly. After all, there is a point preceding the start of a project where the decision needs to be made to 'go' or 'no go.' There are "show-stoppers" that can cause a project to be shut down in midstream, but those are severe land mines. Once a project is chartered and the requirements documented, it should be full steam ahead.

An internal project manager may have less freedom of decision, and we'll discuss this more later, but there is always at least a mental, if unspoken, decision as to whether the project makes sense. We'll begin to discuss the mechanics which lead to the 'project manager presumptive,' being able to comfortably and realistically form this opinion, in the next chapter, so for now let's acknowledge that this need exists, and to fulfill the need there is a period of 'squirreling' that occurs, where you scurry around and gather all the information that you can.

This scurrying wears different faces in various methodologies, but is typically called a requirements or needs analysis. This is a book on deployment methodology, not consulting methodology. The logical phases of the project will not be pigeonholed to fit a given consulting methodology. Nor will every aspect of project delivery be covered — the discussion of employing a consulting methodology throughout the life cycle of a project would need more than one book to do it justice. So if you're going to say, for example, "Functional decomp wasn't covered," fire away, but the purpose here is to get you around the gotchas of delivering a technology implementation project by way of a deployment methodology, not to teach project management or a consulting methodology.

Though this is a technical book, the discussion of impressions and thoughts will be used. An attempt could be made at presenting the perspective of both an internal and contract project manager, and tell you to pay attention to whichever applies to your situation and ignore the other, but that really doesn't work and leads to unnecessary confusion. An example of this is the 'Trial of the Century' that's occurring as this is being written. It seems that every day the judge is telling the jury to 'disregard that last statement.'

It's not really possible to disregard something. The internal and contract project managers will each have some information that the other doesn't. If both are provided with the instruction 'but disregard this if you're an internal PM,' the goal here, which is to accurately simulate a project environment, will not be reached. Even though the two project managers have different information, the contract project manager usually faces a larger need for discovery and more issues than does the internal one.

So to cover as much material as possible we'll be using a contract project manager in our case study. If you're an internal project manager, the additional information you glean from this book will provide you with more insight when you're dealing with contract people.

1.1 THE PROJECT MANAGER

Daniel Pratt is a project manager with the Hewlett-Packard Company (not really, so don't try sending him e-mail) in the Professional Services Organization. He has been approached by a HP sales representative, Megan Cobb, to join her on a customer visit.

The customer, Mid-Central Telephone, wants to purchase systems for each of their operations centers, a potential multi-million dollar deal, and Daniel has been identified by his manager as having the skill set necessary to scope the resulting engagement.

One factor that encourages a successful implementation is having a qualified project manager, 'qualified' being the key. This encourages success, but it's not a guarantee; certainly, having an unqualified project manager is asking for trouble. I wouldn't recommend an unqualified project manager on any large project, let alone one that involves new technology and multiple sites like we'll be talking about.

So what are the prerequisites to being a qualified project manager? Probably everyone asked would offer a slightly different answer. Mine is: experience, experience, experience, and an ability to understand the issues and their impact on the overall strategy. Being able to develop and work from a Gantt chart is a fundamental requirement, but only one. I liken the course skills of a project manager, project plans, etc., to the financial analysis skills of a manager; it can be delegated to someone else, and once delegated, the matters remaining are what define the skill of the manager.

So here is Daniel on his way to the customer. Is he a qualified project manager? Does it matter? After all, at this point he's only been asked to scope the opportunity, not to manage a project. Well, here's where I go out on a limb.

TIP ☞   The only hope a project has of being successful, of fulfilling its reason for being on-time and within budget, is if its manager has his or her arms around the big picture.

The best opportunity to get your arms around the project is in the scoping phase, before there is a project *per se*, well before the implementation begins, hopefully before there exists a project plan, but definitely prior to its being "written in cement." So yes, his being a qualified project manager does matter, because if this opportunity turns into a project managed by someone else, its being scoped properly is a necessity.

Daniel's professional background is a composite of technical and project management experience. Following is his professional profile, the document that he presents to prospective clients as a résumé towards a contract (as opposed to employment, which would call for a résumé with a different emphasis).

Daniel M. Pratt

Daniel specializes in helping customers implement technology projects by developing project plans and managing the execution of the plans, especially when the implementation involves multiple sites. He has been with Hewlett-Packard for nine years and has over 20 years of experience as a computer consultant and project manager.

During college, Daniel worked as a disk jockey and there learned about working with the public and the media. While completing his undergraduate degree he worked full time as an application developer. After graduation he worked as a Systems Analyst with a consulting firm and managed the development of custom systems on HP and mainframe technology for Fortune 500 firms.

Daniel consulted as an independent for a number of years, specializing in designing and developing custom applications to run on HP equipment. During this time he developed a methodology for successfully rolling out the technology and applications to multiple sites, which he is currently involved in publishing.

As a Senior Systems Analyst for a large chemical corporation, Daniel was responsible once again for implementing new technology and systems into multiple locations. This time the venue was Europe, and during this multiyear implementation Daniel learned a great deal about multinational implementations and localization.

Daniel joined HP in 1986 in the U.K. He worked on a multiple site implementation, wrote a systems security application, and then joined HP's European Customer Response Center to provide technical support to HP's European and Middle-East country response centers. While there he also developed and managed a number of programs designed to improve HP's customer satisfaction worldwide.

Joining HP in the U.S. at the end of 1987, Daniel worked with several large manufacturers and retailers to develop and execute multiple site technology implementation plans, rolling out over 1,000 systems in the process. He is a trained and experienced project/program manager, and keeps his software development skills honed. Daniel graduated with a Bachelors of Science in computer science from Oxymoron University.

Daniel's profile shows that he has extensive project management experience, usually resulting in skills that come only with time ('usually' because, let's face it, some people's sponges are already full when they stick them in the water). He has also planned and managed projects that introduced technology.

Assuming that these were successful, that would indicate Daniel's ability to understand the inherent issues at a strategic as well as a tactical level. This is a jump from statement to conclusion, but for now consider it a 'leap of faith' from you that an understanding of the strategic issues is imperative; we'll expound on this later.

Daniel has other experience that can be useful as well, depending on the circumstances. Often the introduction of technology involves migrating existing applications or developing new ones, and with his software development background he'd have an understanding of the relevant issues. Also, he has experience with multiple-site implementations, a type of implementation that brings with it its own issues. His experience of working with the media and the public can be useful when dealing with the end-users and the change management that will need to take place with them, which will also be covered further in this book.

TIP ☞   A project manager must possess a technical understanding of the issues sufficient to understand each managed task and its impact upon the project.

We'll find out more about Daniel as we develop our case study. Right now he's sitting in the passenger seat of Megan's car, on their way to the customer's office, reading some background information (I envy those who can read in a car — one sentence and my stomach is shot for the day).

1.2 THE CLIENT

Following is the blurb of introductory information on the client provided to Daniel (their organization chart is outlined in Figure 1-1).

> Mid-Central Telephone is a privately held company that provides local toll service throughout the mid-central U.S.. The company has its head office and sales office in Otumwah, Iowa. It was formed in 1977 by its president and CEO, Scott Ralston. The company posted $520 million in revenues for the last fiscal year with 11 percent net profit.
>
> Averaging a 3.25 percent IT budget, MCT relies primarily on their in-house mainframe for their IS needs. Each operations center has an old HodgePodge 250, with a proprietary operating system, which is used for customer service applications and the normal back-office accounting and personnel functions.
>
> The entry of formerly long-distance-only carriers into MCT's market as a result of the Communications Deregulation Bill is expected to result in MCT losing an initial 20 percent of its customer base. As a result, MCT has had to have a comparable across-the-board layoff.
>
> MCT wants to decentralize their service order functionality via client-server technology to allow for better responsiveness and more immediate information. They also want to give their customers the ability to see an electronic "face" to the company and to have a better method of disseminating information throughout the company.

Following his initial visit, Daniel came away with the following three categories of information about the company:

- corporate organization — with a focus on the CIO's staff
- client's current expectations
- a list of his initial concerns

We'll look at each of these in order, as they all play an important role in the early stages of the project.

1.2.1 MCT Corporate Organization

Mid-Central Telephone

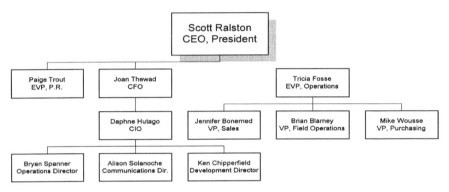

Figure 1-1 MCT Organization

1.2.2 Initial Client Expectations

Ken Chipperfield, the Development Director, wants the service order applications to be client-server with a GUI front-end and a relational
stored-procedure back-end. Naturally, he would like his staff to develop
the applications, but he's accepted the fact that this isn't viable; his staff
was reduced and the existing mainframe applications need to be maintained.

There is no current thought on the best method of providing the
consumer information. Ken and his staff are leaning toward a series of
custom client-server applications, but experience heartburn whenever
they discuss how to approach designing the applications and associated
data engines to allow the flexibility and information immediacy desired,
particularly because they have no background in the technology.

Daniel has some ideas. He tells Ken about a group in Hewlett-Packard called the Telecom Software Solutions Program (TSSP), a group that specializes in developing and maintaining software solutions for the Telecom industry. This group has the infrastructure and processes in place to allow a quick and effective response to Ken's needs. He also has an approach in mind for the "electronic face" that MCT wants to develop. Daniel would like to develop a proposal for a complete solution. Ken is eager to see Daniel's ideas.

The discussion turns to project organization. MCT will make its staff available for the project, and Daniel will provide the project management with MCT providing a project 'liaison' in lieu of a joint project manager — again, staff availability is limited due to the layoffs. Daniel asks Ken what his thoughts are on the logistics necessary for deploying the solution. Daniel understands the complexity, the deployment being more complicated than the development, but wants to see what Ken's take is. As he thought, Ken has never been at the helm of a major technology/application deployment before, having always managed development for existing mainframe technology. Ken does have a gut feeling based on other deployment, but Daniel spends time discussing the complexities that they'll face, not the least being the infrastructure. Daniel also lets Ken know that the support infrastructure for the new technology and applications can be outsourced to the TSSP group as well, and that he'll account for that in the subsequent proposal.

There are a number of items that Ken hadn't brought up, so Daniel did. These are expectation items that will help form a more solid foundation in the relationship. The information is also necessary to put together the proposal pricing.

TIP ☞   It's easier to take a turn in the road when you understand the need before the turn, than after it.

There is a likelihood that changes will need to be made to some of the points during the course of launching the project, but any changes that cause a significant impact can be addressed via standard change management. Following are the items that should be on your expectation checklist when scoping an engagement.

Daniel's initial engagement is a requirements analysis, but the following information will also be relevant during the subsequent project.

How often are formal meetings required between you and the client?

Defining this expectation is a limiting measure, but an upper and lower limit need to be set. Too many meetings offer no more than an too few. If the time frame of the project is not severely compressed, one meeting per week should be sufficient, perhaps with more at the project's beginning and home stretch.

At what location will the meetings be held, and for what duration?

Setting the location will serve to set the expectation that a meeting place will be required, and when coupled with the meeting frequency will allow you to determine the cost of attending the meetings (should they be somewhere that will cause additional travel expense, for example if the management site is different than the project site). Setting a goal for the duration can be touchy to approach, but here again you don't want to get a group of people together and hear that you only have ten minutes of their time, nor do you want them to expect a half-day from you (for example if the project status is to be discussed as part of an overall IT status meeting each week). If graphing the length of a meeting against its value, the line begins to curve downward in value at some point. The length varies depending on the type of meeting, but a good rule of thumb for status meetings, where there is one activity being discussed, is one hour.

How often are you expected on-site, and for what duration?

This is another item used for determining costs to include in the proposal, but can also avoid sticky moments later. Often the client expects to see you whenever there's something on their mind, which translates to 8:00am - 6:00pm Monday through Friday. There may be no need for you, other than their expectation, to be on site that often, and there may be every reason not to be. You might have internal or third-party items that need addressing one day per week. You might not want to travel Sunday night and Friday night so that you can be on site Monday morning and Friday afternoon. Negotiate this expectation up front, or at the minimum make it an explicit part of the proposal. Keep in mind though, it's tough to keep the momentum of a project going if you're not on site, even if you're not supposed to be. If people come to see you and you're not there, they'll sooner go on to something else than attempt to track you down, especially if the visit would have resulted in a benefit more to you than your visitor and they were just being helpful.

Another consideration, one that, as you'll see later, pertains to our business case, is whether some or all of the services are to be delivered remotely.

What turnaround time is the client expecting on questions, on complaints?

The management of any project can be a daunting task. Often the project manager (PM) and technical lead(s) are working 60+ hours per week. Despite your best efforts, you might not be able to juggle informal requests for information with a turnaround of better than one day, but the requester could be expecting an answer within an hour or two, perhaps immediately. If their expectation is not met, you can be sure they'll tell someone that you're not being responsive. So understand the expectation up front, and then reset the expectation that with each new requester expecting a turnaround of x, you will do your best to respond, but that because the critical project issues come first, a turnaround of 2x or 3x is not unlikely.

What tool is to be used for the project plan — and do you have exclusive write access?

The client might use a specific project management tool and want you to use it too, even though you're more comfortable with another. You might end up having to use both, which is never pretty. One package should be used as the primary creator of the time line. If the project is sufficiently large to warrant various project leaders needing to electronically update subprojects, you need to determine how that will happen. You don't want them updating your master plan directly, so you can import their changes, but if one subproject's update on Monday morning ends up impacting another due to cross dependencies, you will have to provide the resulting update to the impacted project leader on Tuesday morning in such a way that you avoid negating any changes he's made in the interim. If this need arises, you will have to define the timing, that is they update their subplans while you leave the master alone, then you take their subplans and update the master while they're 'frozen', then you provide them with the new subplans.

What medium and format is to be used for progress reporting and deliverables (how often are progress reports desired)?

Does the client want daily status reporting? Should it indicate progress, issues, ratio of hours booked to milestone progress? Is it going to be done on their e-mail system? (does your tool for generating status reports tie into that system?) Do they have an electronic bulletin board application where updates and correspondence will be stored? Do you have access to these systems when you're not on site? Make certain that their requirements can be met with the tools you will have at hand and the times you will have access to those tools. If they want electronic versions of your deliverables and status reports you will need their software if anything beyond vanilla formatting is involved — don't depend on the import filter of their software or the export filter of yours!

What will be the communication protocol between you and the client organization, and what will the content be?

Does the client want you to keep their entire organization updated with some form of newsletter? On the other end of the spectrum, do they want you to avoid updating their people at all except for a primary contact? Defining who you can and can't talk to about what will determine what additional effort might be required, or whether you need to mumble a 'no comment' whenever someone asks you how it's going.

What change management process will be used, and who will approve the changes?

There will be changes, and to avoid denials and finger pointing down the road you will need to use a change management process. The process needs to be defined. Perhaps all changes go onto a change form, but $0 changes will be automatically approved while all other changes need to go before a panel. The process definition will define the effort required and the expected turnaround. Beware a stringent approval process unless you have guarantees that the process itself won't cause substantive delays to the project.

What access will you have to the various players in the client organization?

You will potentially be dealing with a large portion of the organization chart. If you're going to have to schedule appointments a week in advance every time you need to talk to someone, you'll either need to improve that scenario or expect each task to be encased in large periods of idle time.

During what hours will you have access to the client site?

If a day is running long will your team need to leave the site anyway because you're not allowed to stay after hours without an escort, and escorts get paid overtime? If you want to get an early start, will you have access? If you work on weekends or in the evening, does the air conditioning (or heating) stay on? If you go out for dinner and return, will you find yourself locked out? Are there certain activities you will not be able to do at certain times? I had a crew of people laying cable in a series of television studios. They'd be forced to stop work, sometimes every fifteen minutes, for periods of thirty minutes to an hour. If you have a need to do something under, over, or at people's desks, will this be allowed during the day? If not, will your team have access at night to all the areas that they need to?

Will you (and the team, if applicable) have a secure work area at the client site?

It's a pain to have to take every document out with you in the evening because you don't have a filing cabinet to lock them in, or to not be able to leave your laptop computer on your desk when you go to lunch because your door doesn't lock. You will often need to have private conversations and phone calls, difficult if you're relegated to a cubicle. The PM should have an office, and the team a 'War Room' in which white boards and flip chart sheets can be safe and secure. These requirements need to be enumerated in the proposal.

1.3 INITIAL CONCERNS

After your first meeting, you should take the opportunity to draft a concerns list while things are still fresh in your mind. Even if you've taken copious notes, they won't necessarily reflect your emotions, so document your concerns and feelings while making your notes. One method is to put symbols next to entries. A check or a happy face for something good, an exclamation point or a frown face for a concern. Taking a look at Daniel's list it will start to reveal the process that should be used for developing a list of concerns.

1. How will success be measured? Ken's idea of success is that the systems get installed at each operations center, but how the economic buyers of the project view success can be substantially different, and that raises further questions, the answers to which will provide an answer to this one.
2. What critical success factors does this project fulfill? If there is no success that the company considers critical fulfilled by the

project, then it might not have the visibility, sponsorship and leverage that is needed for its success.

3. What ongoing support happens when the project ends? Unless there will be no continuing use of the project deliverables, someone is going to maintain them once the project ends. Often this will be a warantee period, but even then the support could be provided by individuals who were not part of the project. A handoff from the project team to the support team needs to be assessed, and is very often a task that falls through the cracks.

4. Are the client's initial expectations resettable? If the client is espousing their view of the landscape, and you sense that that view might be inaccurate for one reason or another, there will be a need to address it. The best time to do that might not be at the current meeting though. You could embarrass the manager, or embarrass his staff if they were the ones responsible for initially setting his expectations.

5. What commitment is there from the MCT organization? Is this a "well, if we have to" project, or is there backing from the user community and the parts of the organization which are critical to success?

6. Is this good for my company and me? After considering the risks, the political climate, the time and resources available, the decision needs to be made. If you're not the one to make the decision, you certainly need to advise them.

If you're looking at the list thinking that it's a bit lean, you're correct. At this point Daniel and we are considering only the strategic issues — those that really ought to be resolved prior to beginning work on a project plan. Let's consider for a moment why this is so important.

Picture being in the woods and following a map. You're going to travel ten miles from beginning to end. The map says that you're to follow a course of 27°, but because your compass isn't calibrated correctly, the course you actually follow is 28°. By the time you walk the ten miles you're going to be very far off course. The same holds true for a project. If the strategy that the project is based on is flawed or misidentified, it's better to discover that at the beginning than at the end. Identifying such weaknesses prior to developing a project plan is not absolutely essential, but from the point of view of the project manager, one plan is enough anguish without having to redo it. So let's resolve the strategic issues first, then we can add some fat to the concerns list.

1.3.1 In Search of the Vision

Daniel has promised Ken a proposal. There are many facets to a proposal, and one is that the proposal is a statement of "I know what you need." Even if what is being proposed is "a study," then you're saying that, at this stage, within the context of this proposal, is that the client needs a study. Does Daniel know what MCT needs? No, not really. He may have some ideas, perhaps a very clear vision, but not enough to propose a solution and its associated price. And let's be clear about this — MCT, not Ken the Development Manager, is the client. If Ken rides shotgun through to the last day of the project, nodding his head in agreement all the way through, and at the end MCT is not satisfied with the results, Daniel's in trouble and won't be able to hide behind Ken, not even if Ken is identified in the contract as the 'official' client project manager. In that case, MCT might lose in court, but Daniel's company would lose face and a client.

You might be thinking that if Ken did a good job of explaining the engagement that Daniel should be able to proceed, that the project charter and requirements analysis Daniel wants to do are not a necessity. Not really, and Ken's agreement to delay so that these documents can be produced shows it. Ken's looking at this from the level of a manager, but the driving force for a project of this size, a paradigm shift, comes from above him.

There are business issues that the project should address. You might ask, "Is it possible to meet the objective of the project without meeting objectives defined by the business issues?" Good question. Yes. I'll give a quick example, and then we'll go get the information. Note that since there was no project charter or requirements analysis done, there is no request for proposal (RFP) or request for information (RFI) here; the customer has not produced a document that lays out their technical and functional requirements. Therefore the intention is to produce those documents. The proposal will need to include these findings as a definition from which to move forward, and as an indicator to MCT that their needs, at that level, are understood.

Some of you might remember the television show "Superman" from the late 50s. Well, it has been shown in reruns ever since. There was an episode with Superman's friend Professor Periwinkle. It seems that the professor had fulfilled every alchemist's dream and invented a machine to create gold. So let's say that the objective of the project was to create a machine that can invent gold. *Voila!* Well, almost. As it turned out, to have $5,000 worth of gold come out of the machine, $10,000 worth of platinum needed to go in (the Professor wanted to make gold, not a profit). Now, they didn't go into a discussion of corporate objectives in the show, but it's a safe bet that a 200 percent cost of sales wasn't one of them! This is also an example of the project being successful (his invention worked) without there being true success.

In order to better understand where to get this information from, let's take a look at a tool that is used in positioning many Hewlett-Packard service engagements, the HP Information Technology Service Management (ITSM) Model (shown in Figure 1-2).

The HP ITSM Model can be a bit cumbersome to look at the first time, but upon inspection you will see that it lays out a services scenario quite well.

Ken is asking Daniel to put together a proposal which addresses several boxes in the model. The issue in moving forward here is that even if the project were conceived for the right reasons, there is still the danger of its being implemented in such a way that it fails to fulfill the business objectives in part or in whole.

Who then is the best person to provide Daniel with the information needed to succeed? Ken might seem to be the logical person because he's the contact, but Daniel doesn't think he is for the following reasons:

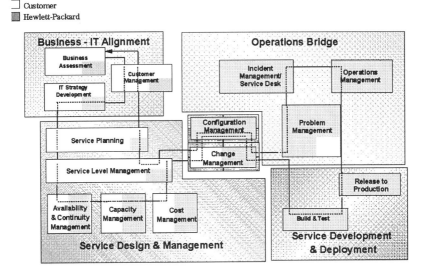

Figure 1-2 HP ITSM Model

- Ken is levels removed from the best source of that information.
- Ken has a focus on the project, and might unconsciously overlook anything that indicates that the project might not make sense as defined.
- Daniel doesn't know how much Ken doesn't know, and Ken might not either for that matter.

That last point needs some more explanation. There are two levels of ignorance: knowing that you're ignorant, and not knowing. If I ask for directions to somewhere (my wife asks me to point out that this is purely hypothetical), I'm doing it because I realize I'm ignorant of that information. If the route is dependent on whether I'm walking or driving, and I don't know this, then I won't ask — an example of not knowing what I don't know. Frequently, not knowing what you don't know can be easily overcome if someone else volunteers information and doesn't come back later with the dreaded, "...you didn't ask." You can't depend on this though, and generally the best way to not end up in this situation is to take nothing for granted.

There's a reason that I use so many analogies. I use them in presentations and conversations as well. It's very easy for two people to hear the same information, and draw different conclusions on what they didn't hear (because it wasn't said). Implications can come back to haunt you, so you must be very careful when setting expectations. An analogy shifts a person's focus away just long enough to give them a jolt of curiosity, and also offers an opportunity for them to confirm or contradict what it is they thought you were saying. Very often when I use an analogy I receive back an, "Oh are you saying...?" which means that, through the analogy, the listener may have discovered an assumption to be inaccurate. The whole business of project management and your success at it hinge on clear expectations.

TIP ☞   Set expectations correctly the first time – then set them again for good measure!

There is every possibility that Ken has been made aware of his company's Information Systems (IS) strategy and business objectives. After all, he's a high-level manager, and very often these items are published and passed on, or covered in planning meetings. Let's look at the possibilities set out in Table 1-1.

	Ken understands strategy	Ken accurately relays information
Scenario 1	Y	Y
Scenario 2	Y	N
Scenario 3	N	Y
Scenario 4	N	N

Table 1-1 Expectation Setting

In all but the first scenario you will be in worse shape than when you began, because you will walk away thinking you have your course laid out and be starting off pointing at least a few degrees in the wrong direction.

So what if Ken offers to let you read the company's IS Strategy and Business Objectives as documented? Better, but things change, sometimes even while the ink is drying. Not only that, but there's always the possibility that you'll interpret the text differently than it was intended — if it can happen with the Constitution and the Bible, it can happen here. Also, what if the need of the customer would necessitate a change in that strategy? No, the best bet is to get the information straight from the horse's mouth. And in this case the horse is the CIO.

Daniel needs to ask Ken to arrange that meeting — there's no sense starting off on the wrong foot by doing an end run here. Convincing Ken that this meeting is necessary might not be easy. And if there was a layer between Ken and the CIO, it could get downright messy explaining to multiple people that you need a clear message untainted by interpretation, but do it you must. Let's be completely clear about this. A project that involves a true paradigm shift on an enterprise-wide scale is a gamble up to and including the CIO. If the premise <u>seems</u> sound, and the project is a failure, guess who goes first? Don't take no for an answer. With the amount of money being gambled (not just the project capital, but the loss of business that results if it's not successful), there should be an hour of executive time available to get the information you need.

TIP ☞   If you absolutely cannot have access to the right people in order to understand the business issues that drive the project – give thorough consideration to running in the other direction.

Daniel needs to handle any objections Ken might have as well as do some expectation resetting.

1.3.2 Resetting Expectations

Few enterprises of great labor or hazard would be undertaken if we had not the power of magnifying the advantages we expect from them.

--Samuel Johnson

The need to reset expectations often happens early on, and that is the case here. Ken has asked Daniel for the proposal to contain a project plan. This is not unusual, although sometimes it takes a different form: the client wants the proposal to account for the planning <u>and</u> implementation. Before Daniel can reset Ken's expectations, I need to set yours. The process of planning this type of implementation can take from one month upwards. And in order to develop a plan there needs to have been preliminary detailed information gathered, and until you have a plan in front of you that shows how long the implementation will take and what resources will be required, there is no way to effectively determine the cost of the implementation. What this means is that the initial proposal should only account for the implementation planning, not the implementation. The result of the implementation planning is that you will have two deliverables, the plan and an implementation proposal.

The method Daniel will use to reset Ken's expectations accordingly is the HP ITSM Model. There are other views of HP's methodology that focus and expand on engagement delivery, such as the Custom Project Life Cycle (CPLC), but the HP ITSM Model is well suited for a client presentation of this kind. By taking Ken through each block in the model, Daniel should be able to get a nod from Ken as to the process making sense. Having done that, Daniel can move on to explaining that each box in the model is dependent on those around it. From this plateau, he can then explain that he can't approach, for example, IT Transition Planning without having sufficient understanding of their business, IS and IT stratagem, and that the IT Transition Plan needs to be in place before the scope of delivering the implementation pilot and deployment can be understood and priced.

This is all fairly logical, and we know that Daniel's not trying to pull a fast one here, but these issues don't always play solely to logic — remember the politics. Ken might simply refuse to allow the vendor past him. He might be shielding his manager because he feels it's necessary or because his manager told him that it is, or he might feel that he's protecting his own job, not wanting his manager to feel that Ken can't handle the situation on his own, the latter probably being true if Ken isn't willing to explore the possibility of a meeting before saying "no." Should you be left with no avenue of obtaining what you feel to be essential information, consider no bidding.

TIP ☞   On the front end of a project it might
            seem like you were able to get start-
            ed without what you felt was essen-
            tial information, but watch out on
            the tail end!

Daniel shows Ken the ITSM Model, and after much discussion gets Ken's buy-in as to the sequence of events. It's then time to hit the nail on the head. Ken is talking about the project proposal once more, and states he would like to see a proposal with an initial project plan in two weeks.

Daniel flashes the "time-out" signal. "Ken, I understand your need for speed, but is there a published project charter and requirements analysis?"

"No, we really don't have time for that level of depth. I understand the requirements, as does my team, so ask us whatever you need to know and we can go from there."

"Ken, are you saying that your people have done the footwork but just haven't documented the findings?"

"Well, no. They understand what we need to accomplish, but they haven't done what you would consider a formal finding."

"Well Ken, this raises some concerns that I need to share." Ken crossed his arms. "The type of project we're talking about here stands to impact just about every box on the corporate org chart, right?" Daniel continued, "So even if we had enough information now to piece together a project plan, which we don't, I'm not comfortable that the precepts upon which the project plan would be based are shared by the user base. Will you succeed if their needs aren't met to their satisfaction?"

Ken's arms unfold. "Okay, bottom-line this for me."

"Sure. I think to be successful we need to know that the aims of the project are congruent to the needs of the interested parties. I believe the only way we can come close to assuring that is by doing a project charter and requirements analysis before we put together a project plan."

"Time?"

"One month."

"Okay. Your point is well taken. I think we can afford to delay a month if it will avoid bigger delays or failure later."

Daniel did an excellent job of making his case (allowing us to have subsequent chapters). He went on to explain the audience he would need for some of the study, and Ken did set up a meeting between Daniel and Daphne Hutago, the CIO; he'll have thirty minutes.

1.3.3 Mapping the Organization to the Project

It might seem a bit early to be giving consideration to the players from MCT who will be participating in the project, but that needs to happen immediately to some extent. There are two items in particular to be concerned with at this point:

- Is there management buy-in from critical organization areas?
- Are the project team members already chosen?

We can see from the organization chart that Ken has a number of peers. Further discussion reveals that they have little exposure to the project at this point. This is certainly something that will need to be remedied. The organizations under these people are critical to the success of the project. Again, it might seem a bit premature to want to meet with these people, as we haven't been awarded the business yet, but a short meeting with each is warranted just to get a feel for whether any show-stopping issues are lurking in the wings. I'd recommend meeting with them each in their own office, one-on-one, as it is there where they'll feel the most comfortable (each in their own castle) and therefore possibly more inclined to "open up."

I'd certainly avoid meeting with them along with Ken. There's no way at this point to be certain of the relationship he has with them, or what the resulting dynamics might be. There is a chance that they might open up more with Ken, someone they know, in the meeting, but there's more of a chance that they will open up less and offer fewer "off-the-record" comments.

As for the project team, if it has been chosen and etched in stone, give considerable thought to whether it will suffice. We'll touch on the formation of a project team later, but in this stage we want to have an understanding that at the least we'll be able to choose what departments are represented in the project team. Shoot for the top, though — and that is to be able to interview people from MCT for inclusion on the project team. Daniel has requested this, and Ken has agreed in principle — in principle, because naturally he only controls the destiny of his own staff and can't be certain that the priorities of this project are sufficient to include any and all staff that might make sense regardless of their current assignments.

1.3.4 What's In It for Me?

This last issue might at first appear to be trite, but you only get one go-around in life, and what moves a project manager forward from one project to the next is reputation. Taking on a project that has very little chance of being successful is akin to professional suicide, because no matter what qualifications, caveats, or concerns were voiced or written by you at the onset, if the project fails it will be (as far as anyone else is concerned) viewed by history as your fault, and will be branded between your eyebrows for some time to come.

Ken made it clear that he was going to be available only on a limited basis, so this project was definitely going to fall on Daniel's shoulders. What always needs to be considered is the possibility of your initial concerns not being resolved satisfactorily. If the answers to the preceding questions indicate that this project either can't be delivered successfully or, having been delivered successfully, will not fulfill its causative goals, will the impact on Daniel's career be acceptable compared to the impact if he turns down the assignment.?

Risk has to be considered. There is a very real possibility as well that Ken might stick a feather in his cap and call it macaroni and move on to other things before an inherent failure is discovered, leaving Daniel to absorb the fallout. If the risk is high that the project will not go well, then is the business worth the risk and his reputation? If so, all Daniel will have to worry about is the depression and sleepless nights that accompany it. This is a very subjective topic and I won't pretend to understand how everyone else should weigh the applicable factors, or even how they decide what is applicable. I will discuss items I feel deserve consideration as danger signals, and let you know what I would do — bluff, play your hand, fold, walk, or run away. If I raise the flag for you, you can then decide whether it applies or not. If I don't raise the flag at all? I once heard that one type of mosquito bites, but is silent. The other type of mosquito makes noise, but doesn't bite — so if you hear the whine of a mosquito you're safe — but if you hear nothing...!

Daniel does have concerns, but there are some things in the "plus column." Ken has arranged meetings with his manager and his peers for Daniel. This shows that he's willing to do the right thing without giving too much consideration to appearances and politics.

Ken's also agreed to the project team interview process, which shows again that he's willing to do the right thing. In addition, although Daniel hasn't heard it from the horse's mouth yet, it's a good bet that MCT is betting the farm on this project. This latter point doesn't pave the way for success on the face of it, but favorable things can roll downhill too.

Daniel also sees a great deal of potential for additional revenue in providing MCT with the client and employee information solution. With all this activity beginning and direction-setting conversations to take place, this is a good time for Daniel to start a project notebook.

There are five essential pieces of equipment that a PM needs.

- A PC that is powerful enough to run project management, word processing, and presentation development software.
- A pocket calendar — you want to be able to schedule appointments no matter where you are without having to write it down on a scrap of paper.
- A tape recorder — as long as people will allow it (assure them that the tapes are reused once you transcribe your notes), you'll be able to pay much closer attention to body language and comments at meetings if you're not having to write everything down.
- A journal — use a lab notebook, the hardcover bound notebook that pages will not tear out of (you always throw out something you need later) and use it for all your notes instead of scraps of paper.
- A project notebook — this will start out as a three-ring binder, but will probably bloom into multiple binders with one dedicated to the hardcopy of e-mail messages.

1.4 PROJECT CHARTER AND REQUIREMENTS

The meetings all went very well, in fact, the meeting with Daphne Hutago lasted twice as long as was slotted — always a good sign as long as no one is screaming. Let's take a look at what came out of these meetings, because this information will help build our 'gut feel' for the proposal as well as reference material for the project charter and requirements document.

1.4.1 The CIO

The key to a successful meeting with the CIO is preparedness. This is your opportunity to access the person who is at the helm in the context of your issues. The CIO is in the pivotal role of taking the mission critical objectives of the company, as defined by its management, Chief Executive Officer (CEO), Chief Operating Officer (COO), CFO, and so on), and mapping that into IS and IT strategy. The resulting strategy should aid in moving the company closer to meeting the original objectives. This can be a massive responsibility considering the requirements demanded by competition in the marketplace, and by the continuing paradigm shifts in technology (which allow the computer equipment manufacturers to deal with their own competition in the marketplace). No wonder the typical CIO changes jobs after about two and one-half years. So, we can guess that Daphne Hutago, the CIO, has a full plate, and thus rare opportunities to focus on this project despite its overall importance. We have to make the best use of her time.

We'll need to assume that this meeting might be the only one of its kind, that we may never again get on Daphne's calendar. So how do we come out of our half-hour with the information we need, and not be faced with the dreaded, "I forgot to ask . . ." situation?

My wife is a big "list person." Sometimes she even makes lists of the lists she needs to make. This meeting is pretty much a one-on-one; an agenda would be much too formal and pretty pointless as there's only thirty minutes. You'll need to be in control; you're the one who needs the meeting in the first place.

Remember that a CIO spends a fair amount of time lobbying quite effectively for their organization's needs. The last thing you want to do is get the CIO on a soapbox and watch your time fly out the window. The best tool for you will be a list of the items you need to resolve with a check box beside each. That way you have immediacy in the ability to sense where you are with relation to the time allotted.

A palmtop PC can be a superb tool in this case. It's small enough to sit at the top of a pad without being disconcerting. The To-Do screen allows you to check off each task. Just about any electronic organizer of this size will make your job easier here.

There is the possibility that Daphne is not a succinct person, and that time will run out before all the information can be gathered, so the checklist should be ordered by priority. As the meeting progresses the information remaining to be gathered will be less important to you than what you already have.

Now that we're clear on how we need to gather the information, let's step back a minute. We need to remember that this is still a pre-sales environment. Daniel is moving towards a proposal. He hasn't been awarded the business yet. There are two reasons that I'm raising this. The CIO might

- want to know how much this is going to cost.
- be reluctant to part with some information.

Let's look at the latter point first. Daniel isn't marching into Daphne's office asking for some trivial information. The mission-critical business objectives of a company along with its IS and IT strategy are pieces of information that define years in advance how that company is going to approach doing business. No, it's not like walking into the Coca-Cola Company and asking to see the '7x' formula, but it's not the office supplies budget either. Daphne might have a very real issue with sharing some of this information with Daniel. Until the business is awarded, Daniel's company is not even a vendor, and Daphne might have a problem with sharing the information with a vendor. Daniel will have to account for this at the beginning of the meeting when he states his objective. One bit of fine-tuning that can be done to the list to help us through this potential pitfall is to note under each item the minimum information with which we can move forward.

The former point might seem trivial, but it's not. The CIO has a clear need to understand the impact of the project, and the fact that the price will be given along with the proposal will not necessarily assuage the question being posed. If it is, alluding to the price being given at a later date will probably not be a satisfactory answer. Yes, you and I (and Daniel) know that we're going through this information gathering exercise so that we can put a price to the engagement. The CIO knows this too – but might still ask. Your 'out' ties back to the latter bullet, so let's work on our opening.

We need to concisely inform the CIO as to why we need this information. We understand that this is a massive project, technologically and logistically, and that because of its potential impact on the company in cost, resources, and benefits, that it must dovetail directly into the IS strategy, which is driven by the company's objectives. I find that a useful analogy in this instance is the laying of track. We know we have one station, the IS strategy, and that the track leading to it is coming from the business objectives. We know we have another station, and track leading away from it to the horizon.

The question is how this project lays the track between the two stations, and that depends on what we want to achieve. If we consider the track to be the implementation of the technology, then as long as it's laid properly it will be usable. But let's say we lay it end-to-end in a manner that supports a high-speed express train, but the strategy calls for a freight train with sidings along the way where we can add and remove cars. Or let's say that we lay it with the sidings and many switches to other tracks to accommodate the transfer of cars, and the strategy calls for an uninterrupted high-speed bullet train. Unless we understand the objectives and strategy, we might not implement the project in the manner best suited to support them. This could lead to rework, and rework by its very nature eats directly into the return on investment. A loss of ROI is something a CIO can relate to very well. The manner by which we approach this project can affect the pricing, and that's why it's not possible to offer a price at this point.

I should mention that in some circumstances it might be worthwhile offering up an 'order of magnitude' price if you have one. If your order of magnitude is way off from what the CIO is contemplating then this might be a good time to understand that. You'll need to weigh the potential gain of validating the order of magnitude against the pitfall of playing part of your hand early in a competitive situation, especially if you're not the CIO's preferred vendor. Since this deal includes a substantial amount of hardware, and Megan is probably hard at work obtaining acceptable discount schedules, and since the hardware cost might dwarf the services cost, an order of magnitude price is probably not appropriate at this time.

We've discussed the opening. The next item to consider is the information we're looking to obtain. I recommend focusing on the IS and IT strategy points. We have to be aware of the time we have. If necessary, we can take one of the strategy points and delve into the business objective that drove it.

Here then are the pieces of information provided by Daphne.

- The solution needs to be Open; that is it should leave MCT in a position where other vendors can be used to provide equipment so long as they adhere to the same industry standards.
- Each operations center will have an application server feeding the clients.
- The server and client hardware, OS and networking, need to be 99 percent Open, so that the vendor and technology can be changed at any time with minimal effort.
- The application architecture will be client-server and, preferably, object-based.
- The implementation impact at each operations center needs to be minimal.
- There must be a way for customers to receive electronic information on available services and products in a manner that provides immediacy and inclusion.
- Training must be provided to all users and support personnel.

Paramount to Daphne was that the major deliverables of the project, and the project as a whole, contributed to the bottom line of the corporation. The contribution could be quantifiable (increase in sales, decrease in cost of sales and/or expenses) or not (increase in customer satisfaction). To address the former, there would be workstations placed in the customer service area, the special orders desk, and the credit desk. This was a strong mapping point between the business strategy and the IS strategy: MCT was vehement about the importance they placed on customer satisfaction, and this permeated every facet of their operations through to their advertising.

Daniel requested and received an important commitment, that Daphne would deliver a "Call to Arms" speech at the project kickoff meeting; the importance of this being that it gives Daphne an investment in the project's success. It might seem early in the process to be asking for this because the deal hasn't been won, but there might not be another opportunity to have a meeting with the CIO prior to then and the commitment is important enough for Daniel to bullet in the proposal.

Important information has been obtained here with regards to how we might approach the implementation. We'll take a look at this when we put together the proposal, and throughout the implementation planning.

1.4.2 The Operations Director

Bryan Spanner is the Operations Director. He is responsible for infrastructure, of which IT is a part. His people are responsible for operations center construction, cabling, power, and so on. The first thing he mentioned to Daniel is that, except for inferences to this project made at Daphne's staff meetings, this is his first exposure to the project. Wave the red flag.

TIP ☞   The Operations group typically is
               the most critical to the success of
               the implementation, and the last
               consideration of the project's spon-
               sors.

Daniel let Bryan know that he considered the operations group crucial to the success of the project, that he would make sure that they were well represented on the project team, and that he'd like to keep close contact with Bryan; he scored points and got Bryan's initial buy-in. In conversation he discovered that Bryan's people are run ragged, and that of the key individuals who can bring absolute answers to the party, few would be available full-time for the project. After all, they had to keep the facilities operating.

Bryan made it clear that he had been employee number thirteen, "my lucky number," and that he contributed to the company growing from its first office to the present size "long before they brought in consultants." Wave the yellow flag.

TIP ☞   There is frequently an almost caste separation between the operations and development (or systems) groups due to the nature of the work and the background from which people enter each: professional and vocational. This is a social problem with which you may need to deal: treat each instance of it as unique, it can be smoothed from levels above, but not resolved.

Daniel also got the following information from Bryan:

- a typical operations center layout;
- a map showing the operations center locations, and;
- a list of the groups under Bryan's control.

Daniel later created a list showing each high-level implementation focus, and put a check next to each item that the operations group would be concerned with. The results are shown in Figure 1-3.

✓ Site environmentals
✓ Site wiring
✓ Network
✓ Backup/Recovery
✓ Operations
✓ Help Desk
   Education
   Software Development
✓ Pilot Testing
✓ Staging

Figure 1-3 Operations Involvement

The list makes it evident that the Operations group will play some role almost across the board. Most of the issues surrounding the implementation involve infrastructure, which is what the Operations group represents. Daniel will be well advised to ensure that the project budget will contain funds for infrastructure issues. A peek at the organization structure might help here. Certainly, if there is a manager responsible for infrastructure reporting to the Operations director, then you know that infrastructure issues are taken seriously. If the Infrastructure manager is a first-level manager, infrastructure might not be high on the priority list. If there's no Infrastructure manager on the organization chart, it doesn't necessarily mean that infrastructure doesn't have any priority; the responsibility can be rolled up into a different title or combined with other responsibilities.

The operations center layout will be of use during the implementation planning, but knowing that it is 'the operations center layout' as opposed to 'an operations center layout' will aid in putting together the implementation proposal, as will knowing the locations of the operations centers (as it affects logistics).

1.4.3 The Communications Director

As the Director of Communications, Alison Solanoche has control over the company's internal voice and data networks, including those of the operations centers. Daniel discovered that Alison had less knowledge of the proposed project than did Bryan.

TIP ☞   It's not unusual for those you would consider to be key players to have little detailed, advanced knowledge of a large project; their relevance will be-come apparent as soon as the project begins.

Alison's group seems to be working on maintaining and extending the current infrastructure (an activity she mentioned in passing with a wave of her hand — it might as well have been holding a red flag) and investigating technology futures as they apply to communications (during which discussion Alison became very animated). When Daniel asked if Alison thought there might be capital budget for infrastructure in the project, she told him that MCT is running smoothly on the current infrastructure thank-you-very-much. Daniel had thoughts to the contrary, but decided that that discussion was best left for another day.

Daniel received a network diagram, as well as an understanding that the physical infrastructure necessary for each operations center was not in place and would need to be part of the implementation (the current systems in the operations centers did not extend out of the back room, while the new design called for workstations in various places).

Some additional questions were raised by Daniel as to the protocols being used. The connection between the operations centers and the mainframe is currently SNA (System Network Architecture), LU6.2. The post-project protocol of choice for the operations centers is TCP/IP.

With information in-hand, it's time to put together the first proposal for MCT. And that means that it's time to craft a 'straw man' solution.

Chapter 2

It's time to craft a solution for MCT. Again, we don't have all the information necessary to define a complete solution, as much of that information will come from meetings that can't take place until the project begins, but we can define enough of it to put together a proposal.

I can't emphasize enough the importance of this period in the process. Here is where the structure of the implementation will be formed in the project manager's mind, and this picture and the understanding of its content is critical when moving forward. Far too often this process is de-emphasized (typically by the proposal being a last-minute cram) in favor of the 'doing' — the implementation itself. If you see that happening, try to get everyone to put the brakes on.

If you're a project manager taking on someone else's plan, you need to spend time with them to understand, really understand, their 'picture.' It's not something that translates well in documentation. It's almost visceral. All the assumptions that are built into the plan, and many are implied, are done so as a result of this 'picture' and further refinements of it (it will be modified daily, even if the documentation is not).

TIP ☞ The project manager's conceptual picture of the project is not unlike the film director's of the film. It, above all other documentation, is what drives your direction of the project from day to day.

The other reason that this process is important is because with a very large project the client is more likely to put the proposal under a magnifying glass. If conceptual issues are challenged (as opposed to pricing issues), very often the sales rep's eyes will glaze over and they will turn their gaze at the project manager, a magnetic effect which seems to draw everyone else's gaze as well. So the project manager needs to be prepared to discuss the issues, and the best way to be prepared is to have that conceptual picture in their head. Waffling at this point is not going to give the client a warm and fuzzy feeling, after all, if the project manager doesn't have a firm grasp of the flow, who does? And a true grasp, true grasp, of the concept will allow you to respond quickly to questions without having to ponder each one while everyone stares at you.

There have been a number of small meetings between Daniel and the co-workers so that he could get their technical input toward defining the solution (the nice thing about a story is that the author can say "one week later" and save you from having to read most of the boring details). Defining the solution at this point is necessary for two reasons beyond needing to propose it: there needs to be a price developed based on the resources necessary to implement the solution and this is the time to validate the implementation conceptually, and fitting the pieces together at a high level provides an opportunity to play 'Devil's Advocate.' I'll introduce the cast of characters now, but their entrance cue will be a bit later in the book.

- Lindsay Coffee, a networking consultant, will design the network layout for the operations center environment as well as the front end to the MCT mainframe, and give consideration to performance and network capacity planning.
- Mike Thewuss, a client-server architecture specialist, will plan the capacity for, and design the operations center front-end and development platform architectures.
- Amber Darling, a systems support specialist, will assist with integration, implementation support, disaster recovery, ongoing support, and obtaining a third-party for cabling the operations centers.

- David Wolfen, an education specialist, understands the training necessary for IS staff and end-users and the options for providing it.
- Marguerita Bass will provide the expertise for planning back-up, recovery and disaster recovery
- Pam Jogger will get into the nitty-gritty detail of operations planning and network and system management
- Claudia Culbiens will focus on high-availability
- Al Ferreman is an Internet/intranet specialist with the Telecom Software Solutions Program
- Joules Disney is a senior consultant, and will be the technical lead should the proposal be accepted

These people have worked together before and form a cohesive group, which is of extreme importance when cramming on a proposal. There isn't time for people to learn each other's body language. They need to be comfortable enough with each other to qualify dissent (and there was some) and move beyond it to an agreement.

Not that everyone has an opinion on every topic, although there are people who seem that way, but in this type of solution the spheres of expertise overlap, an example being the client-server specialist being concerned with the network design. There is one thing in common regarding each person's piece of the solution: at this point it's at 10,000 feet and holding. Each person will need to spend time on site (they were given the opportunity to ask questions via phone) once the project begins to quickly nail down the details.

Not having the details necessary to plan the implementation is of some concern, and will affect the pricing and assumptions of the proposal. We'll take a look at that shortly. Daniel needs to do a number of things first. He needs to take the team's input and lay out the following:

- what the draft solution looks like;
- who provides each piece of the draft solution;
- what needs to be accomplished in the scoping phase;
- what expectations there should be on both sides;
- issues and concerns;

- what the implementation may look like and;
- who will be responsible for each piece of the implementation.

Having done that, he can move on to a high-level time line, assessing risk, defining the proposal's scope of work and assumptions, and finally, the pricing.

Before we do any of that, we need to consider the approach we're taking. It's apparent that there isn't sufficient information available to nail down the scope of the entire project. The steps necessary to pull off the implementation, as well as the duration and cost of each, are a function of the information that surfaces during the planning. With that being the case, we might seem to be limited to two options: fix-price the project with a SWAG (Scientific Wild-Assed Guess), or propose the project as time and materials.

Actually, there's a third option, and a good thing, too, because the former option would probably end your career, and the latter would probably end your chances of winning the business. The third option is a three-phased approach.

- Phase One — Develop the requirements and high-level design.
- Phase Two — Design the solution and develop the implementation plan up to and including a prototype (the definition of 'prototype' is very important, and is covered later) with one of the deliverables of this phase being a fixed-price proposal for the second phase.
- Phase Three — Develop a prototype, construct the solution, deploy, and implement.

This way you're not going to lose your shirt and your job on a blind fixed price (or outrageously overcharge the customer), and the customer's exposure for subsequent phases will be pre-defined in each preceding phase, and thus limited. This first phase can be looked at as an extended requirements definition.

I don't want to give the impression that selling a requirements definition is an easy thing to do, because it's typically a very hard sell. My advice is the same here as it is in many other areas of similar exposure: If you're not quite on the same page as the customer, or the customer (economic buyer) is not quite on the same page as the end user, it's easiest to find out early, and fixing it then will cost much less than later.

This is the option Daniel will take, and so the solution definitions, hardware, software, and services needed for the next phase, phase 2, should be considered budgetary 'place-holders' at this point, as they will be fully defined and nailed-down during the first phase.

2.1 THE WORK BREAKDOWN STRUCTURE

One of the best tools I've found for approaching a proposal on project services is the Work Breakdown Structure (WBS). Project Managers are familiar with this as the first step in assembling a project plan, as well as for an ongoing reference during the project. I find that visualizing the project's flow is important to me when putting fingers to keyboard to describe it, albeit at a higher level, in a proposal. And what better visualization tool than a WBS? If one already exists for the project, use it. If not, this is a great time to put one together at the milestone level. Some people don't need to do this in order to visualize the project. Perhaps it has something to do with my being a lefty.

The WBS for the MCT project was assembled by Daniel, after which he solicited feedback from the team. The reason he did it that way as opposed to a group effort was that only a high level was required, which is at least one layer of abstraction away from technology concerns sufficient to warrant a group effort. Frankly, the caliber of individuals that make up the team put them in constant demand, and thus hard to assemble at one time and Daniel wanted to avoid doing so for a nonessential reason.

The project is divided into phases and subphases, the reaching of each being a milestone. There will be technology milestones within phases as well, but our scrutiny doesn't need to involve those until we take the WBS down another level. We're interested in mapping the first two phases of the project at this point, investigation through prototype.

Many of the project management software packages allow the identifying number of each WBS item to be entered with the associated task for reference purposes, but don't actually provide a way of creating the WBS. In a group environment, a white board or flip chart paper taped to the wall (use masking tape — it's gentle on the wallpaper) provide a good means for development. I prefer large 'stickie' paper, one for each WBS entry, because they can be pasted to the wall and easily moved around and regrouped, making it easy for everyone to see the flow (much easier than a white board with arrows running everywhere).

In working alone, be it to generate the WBS from scratch or from the results of a group meeting, most high-end word processors like WordPerfect®, Microsoft® Word®, and Ami Pro® work well.

Let's take a look below at the WBS that Daniel developed, down to the second level. The WBS can go many levels deep (ours goes one or two more levels).

TIP ☞   If you are responsible for managing each task on the WBS, don't include detail lower than the level at which you want to manage.

The Work Breakdown Structure

I.   Phase One
        A.Engagement kickoff
                1.Define open contract items
                2.Document suitability of project management
                        assumptions
                3.Ready the workplace(s)
                4.Distribute an engagement guide document
                5.Requirements Study
                6.Phase 2 Proposal
II. Phase Two
        A.Build client side of project team

1.Define cross-functional requirement
2.Spread the word
3.Hold interviews
4.Selection meeting
5.Team kickoff
B.Scope the software development and testing plans
        requirements
1.Incorporate development plan into overall project plan
2.Define means to incorporate infrastructure
    requirements into software design and vice-versa
3.Review application and data architecture models
4.Define development platform requirements
5.Document testing methodology
6.Implement development platform
7.Gold Master[1]
C.Design the solution
1.Data design
2.GUI design
3.Middleware linkages design
4.Infrastructure design
D.Scope the requirements for Phase 3
1.Publish an approach document
2.Document the need
3.Define and document client requirements and
    alternatives
4.Define infrastructure requirements in each focus
5.Document deployment requirements
6.Create Phase 3 proposal

You'll find that many of the verbs beginning each bullet are the same. Though the WBS is not the place to create literature, the meaning behind each item should be as clear as possible. In a given situation there will be a need, and that need will be assessed. The requirements to meet all or part of the need will be defined, and then the definition will be documented. A solution can then be developed. Where 'document' is used above, it is assumed (and will later be verified) that there has already been a determina-

---

1. Media containing an application image from which copies (CDs, tapes, etc.) are created; a Phase 3 time-frame milestone.

tion of the definition, and that the definition needs to be documented and perhaps adapted to fit the current context or focus.

The terms above tie into activities which are universal to projects. The HP ITSM Model, Figure 1-2 on page 26, is used to position engagements to the client, but one of the methodologies used to deliver the engagement is The Custom Project Life Cycle (CPLC).

Having seen the top levels of the WBS, we'll see a brief description of each subphase.

Engagement kickoff

The first step in the project is to get it rolling. There are a few things that normally need to be done to accomplish this, and in this case perhaps a few extra as well, due to Daniel not having all the information needed to plan the full project. An internal kickoff meeting would be a good start.

The proposal will spell out assumptions with regards to interaction and project management issues and communication, but finalizing this with the customer is a good idea. Readying the work area(s) will be necessary — and sometime nontrivial as we'll see later.

Build client side of project team

The major hurdle in launching the project is to have a project team, so making sure that all parties at the customer site who could potentially be contributors are aware of the project and the upcoming interviews is important. Once the interviews are held and the team selected, a formal kickoff meeting will come next.

Scope the software development requirements

One of the critical items in this project is the development of the client-server applications. Return on investment for the project will be questionable if there are no applications running on the hardware. For many reasons that we'll discuss later, immersing the project team into understanding the software requirements and preparing the development environment are critical path items.

The development plan (and let's hope there is one) for the applications needs to be incorporated into the overall project plan. The development and testing platforms need to be configured and provided too. There

are many tasks in here, testing, documentation, and contractor selection
to name a few, that we'll cover more fully, but for now let's understand
that the goal of this entire subphase is to develop a "gold master" media
that has the end-user application environment in its "final form" ready to
be integrated with the hardware. Also keep in mind that this subphase
might span our Phases 1 and 2.

Scope the requirements for Phase 3
    Getting the project rolling and making sure that the application de-
velopment environment is in place are critical tasks, but they're not the
only reason Daniel and his team are at MCT. They're there to do an enterprise deployment, and they need to fully understand the requirements
and issues involved in this, with respect to the MCT's particulars, so that
the deployment can be planned, priced and delivered.

TIP ☞   Infrastructure, not deployment lo-
         gistics, will be the critical path in de-
         ployment of new technology,
         except in the rare cases where the
         new technology can use infrastruc-
         ture already in place.

    Are you surprised? Go on, you can admit it. I was the first time.
'New technology' is the key. Sure, if you have fifty sites with a Series X
computer and you deploy a Series X2 to each of them, chances are the deployment issues will be the critical path. However, if you're going to deploy new technology, technology that represents a paradigm shift for the
customer, you'll find that the issues are primarily ones of infrastructure,
and the resolution of the infrastructure also needs to be assessed to plan,
price and deliver Phase 3.

Prototype model

My definition of this activity will probably be controversial to some, but that aside, a prototype is the final activity of Phase 2. The success and design of it will lead us down many parallel paths of activity in Phase 3.

Create Phase 3 proposal

There will be cost associated with developing the deployment plan and executing it (boy, will there ever!), so a proposal that lays out Phase 3 along with a high-level plan and the associated cost to the customer for our services will be an essential deliverable of Phase 2.

2.2 THE DRAFT SOLUTION

There are several components that make up the solution. Let's take a look at each one so that we can become more familiar with the big picture. A project manager has no lack of issues on his hands and not very much free time. It's essential that the solution be so familiar to him that he understands the concepts of it backwards and forwards, and thus can focus on the issues as they relate to that big picture and not have to spend time discovering where the pieces fit, or, worse, be blind-sided by an issue due to a lack of understanding.

TIP ☞   Any point, any illustration, any piece of technology, any task which is 'fuzzy' to the project manager represents potential danger and should be solidified with someone who can provide a coherent explanation.

Remember the three-phase approach. Each heading in the solution definition will be subdivided into Phase 2 (planning and development) and Phase 3 (implementation). The latter items are included in the proposal to show the direction we plan to take technologically and logistical-ly, but not as a firm definition, configuration, or cost.

The Computers The Computers

There are four requirements for computers in the solution we'll be proposing. Let's take a short look at each of them.

- A UNIX® server at the corporate offices will be used as a front end to the mainframe. This server will pull information from the mainframe, and have that information available to the applications. This system will also act as an Internet server. Depending on the high-availability solution, there might be a need for another server.
- A small UNIX server will be installed at each operations center. This system will act as a client to the corporate front-end server, and also as a database server and intranet server to some of the operations center workstations. There will also be four 'operations center systems' installed at the corporate office. I don't want to jump ahead at this point to discussing the project strategy, so take my word for it that they'll be needed.
- UNIX workstations have been requested for the development and support staffs
- PC workstations will be used at the manager's desk, the Customer Service desks and the visitor areas

Networking and Cabling

Wherever there are machines that need to 'talk' to each other, there's networking required. Here is a look at what is being proposed.

- Operations centers — there will be an Ethernet LAN that connects each of the operations center workstations and PC's with each other and with the server. Category V unshielded copper will be installed in each service center for this purpose.
- Operations center to Corporate — there is already T1 service between the operations centers and the corporate offices. Part of the existing bandwidth will be used for communication between the server in each operations center and the corporate server. A packet filtering router will be used on the corporate front-end so that it can act as a web server without the con-

cern that people outside the company will use it as a "launch-pad" for unwanted activity on other company systems.
- Corporate — The workstations will be on an Ethernet LAN with the server. Network hardware will be used to concentrate each work group. The connection between the server and the mainframe will be via SNA LU6.2 over a direct connection.

Software

The customer will be using third-party or custom-developed application software, but there might be systems software needed as well. The recommendations can't be validated until Phase 1 begins because there was no request for proposal (RFP) and thus not enough information to go on, but Daniel picked up enough information to put 'place-holder' recommendations into the proposal, to hold a place both functionally and with regards to budget.

Application Software

- Employee Information Network — Intranet
- Service/Product offerings — World-Wide Web

These applications will all be client-server, in the traditional sense, HTML-based (Internet/intranet), or a mixture, and homegrown. Many decisions will need to be made during the evaluation study as to tools, and the decisions won't be easy since this market is in its infancy and "standards" change rapidly.

System Software and Tools

- Network Management
- System Management
- Operations Management
- Development Platform
- Network Security
- Code Management
- Trouble Ticketing
- Code Deployment

- Backup
- Performance Monitoring

2.3 DRAFT IMPLEMENTATION VISION

At this point there will only be a vision of the implementation as its logistics will be laid out during the project. Using the WBS and experience will provide a framework for creating a vision of the implementation.

Infrastructure services (beginning in section 3.1.1.1) should be linked closely with the application design and the implementation planning. The reasons for this will be discussed later, but for now, infrastructure can and should be a proactive consideration when changing technology. Although the best designed application environment will have little concern of its supporting technology, it can be designed to make efficient use of certain aspects of its supporting infrastructure; hence, the infrastructure taking input and providing output.

In Phase 2 the infrastructure requirements will be defined as will the goals of the deployment. Phase 3 will see implementation of any centralized infrastructure requirements, the design of an equipment staging environment, the planning of the deployment including the site infrastructure requirements, the staging of the equipment and the deployment. There will be many test phases throughout this period as well. Using this vision we can now record it on a relative timeline.

2.4 DRAFT TIME LINE

In creating the draft time line Daniel wants to get a feel for the likely duration of events, and the staffing requirements. He's not out to impress someone with how quickly Phase 1 can be completed, so he's not going to compress tasks at this point. His starting strategy will be to connect each task with a finish-to-start relationship, thus providing him with a worst-case scenario, that no two tasks can be accomplished in parallel; worst-case assuming that the tasks are scoped properly and finish on time, which is not a small assumption by any means. Obviously, if the scope is wrong or the estimates are all short, then the term "worst-case" can take on totally new dimensions.

If he were to compress everything at this point by having overlapping tasks, tasks occurring in parallel, then there'd be no buffer zone should anything slip. If the time line is acceptable without having the tasks in parallel, time can be made up if the project runs late by overlapping some tasks (one begins before the prior one finishes), but if the overlapping, or collapsing, has already been factored into the plan, there might be no way to make up lost time just by reorganizing the tasks unless they can be overlapped even more than they were. Besides, he's trying to create a realistic draft, and the unfortunate reality is that projects don't usually finish early unless the scope is reduced, so the timeline will be more accurate with a relative worst-case scenario.

2.5 ASSESSING RISK

There are entire books devoted to the subject of assessing risk, and they would be well worth the read. The ability to determine risk is required for a number of reasons, primarily to price the project properly and to make the go/no-go call in terms of proceeding.

Four parties here are potentially at risk. As the project manager it's your duty to assess what this risk is. What you do with that assessment will depend on the workings of your organization, but at the least you need to know what you're facing. The four parties to consider follow in no particular order.

Your Company

Here you need to look at the factors that could result in the project, particularly a fixed-price project, not being completed in time, which would result in your company footing the bill for the additional work needed to reach completion. You also need to assess the likelihood that the project can be completed within time and budget, as failing to do that would not enhance your company's relationship with the client or your career. What issues related to planning can prevent a successful delivery? Too many, but here is a representative sample.

- Resource scheduling conflicts.
- Critical path items assigned to uniquely-skilled resources who become unavailable.
- A critical path based on unproved technology.
- A lack of available budget to address infrastructure needs.
- Client internal politics, or external (take-over[1]).

Perhaps you will also want to look at the risk of the possibility of leveraging additional business with the client if your pricing is going to take that into consideration. An example of an adjustment based on the risk is key client resources being available only 50 percent of the time; you'll probably want to adjust the duration of the associated tasks, or account for the probability in the form of a risk adjustment to the final proposal price.

Some customers will understand your building dollars for risk into the project, some won't. The latter will ask if in adding dollars for risk you're feeling less than confident about your team's ability to deliver. The fact is that in adding risk dollars, you're doing so to cover the items that are out of your direct control and the consequences of those items making the project late. If the client is willing to accept all the risk by paying time and materials for the costs associated with time overruns, then there's no need to build in risk, but most likely it will be a fixed-price contract (thus in a time overrun your company is paying the cost of their staff while the profit shrinks and then becomes loss) and potentially penalty money to the client. In that case, if complete control of the project belongs to your company, there's little need for risk dollars, but if there are resources necessary for the completion of the project that are out of your control, the risk is all yours.

Have the roles and deliverables been defined clearly? Scan them one more time to make certain that any subjective or ambiguous terms are either replaced or defined. For example, make certain that assurances of any

---

1. As unlikely as it may seem. This happened to me. After a presales period, solution development, design, and software development we finally reached the pilot stage. Then the corporation lost a hostile take-over, and the project was out the door.

delivery define what will be delivered, when, how, and to whom. Following is an example.

✗ The development team will provide the necessary documentation

✔ The development team will deliver user documentation (see Attachment X for content specifics) in Microsoft Word® 7.0 format to MCT's technical writer one week prior to the start of acceptance testing

Below is a list of additional items which deserve consideration.

- Are the number of man-hours and calendar days available to complete the project sufficient?
- How complex is the management in terms of team members, third-parties and physical sites?
- How many different organizations in your company and in the client's company must work together?
- Is education sufficiently represented to leave the users acceptably knowledgeable?
- Is this project dependent on other projects?
- Is this project dependent on the existence of documentation?
- Does the client's management team and user group understand the project and any demand on them?
- Does the project embody the client's IT/IS strategy, or is it an anomaly?
- Are there policy or organizational changes or overrides needed to make the project successful?
- How complex is the scope?
- How complex is the distributed processing?
- How much turnover is expected based on history?
- Is this new technology?

The answer to the last bullet is "yes" in our context, and with new technology there is always additional risk. There is risk in the technology itself, and there is also risk in the process of deploying it if it is new to the client, even if is not new in the industry.

The Client

The client's success can be affected by many of the same items mentioned above, but also, of course, by their thought that went into what is needed to truly deliver the solution. If this is new technology, as in our context, and the client has not truly fathomed the application development or infrastructure requirements, what can happen? They stand a chance of the solution being late or the solution not being deliverable at all, and depending on the business drivers that drove the project, these might be synonymous. The client is particularly at risk in a time and materials engagement. If the solution is late for whatever reason, the client stands a risk of having to pull the plug due to lack of funding.

Of course, I'm assuming that you and your company are of upstanding character and morals. If so, it's your responsibility to work with the client to minimize the risk to you and them. Depending on the amount of risk, the importance of the project, and how deep everyone's pockets are, there could be justification for the planning of risk mitigation to be a paid endeavor for you, a subproject.

The other risk to the client is with the infrastructure needed for ongoing use of the technology. They don't know what they don't know, and if you don't help them plan for the infrastructure necessary for deployment and maintenance, they stand the risk of the bottom falling out of a mission-critical system.

The End-User

A revolutionary idea perhaps, but if we go back to the discussion of success at the beginning of the book, you will understand that the project can be completed as contracted with the end-user not considering it a success. This can happen, and does happen frequently as a result of the solution not having been properly paired well with the business case to begin with. Should this happen, your company, the client, and the end-user are all losers. Perhaps the most significant function of the project manager at the onset is to determine whether the successful completion of the project will truly spell success.

You

Yes, you! Following are some examples from experience of how you might not be successful despite the other parties being so.

- If the project will put you in the position of stressing several working relationships in order to 'bring it in'.
- If you're sold at forty hours per week on a fixed-price project and the project, like most, will require sixty hours per week. Although the additional time will only cost you, you will have the choice of not being very profitable on paper or understating your hours to be profitable but giving the appearance that the job is easy to do.
- If you're in a multi-entity company and the project will not be bringing in much revenue for your entity.

If you identify the possibility of these or similar issues prior to the project, you might be able to solicit 'waivers' from your company on the profit margin or your next performance revue. Whether you feel that they will be of value when it's time for you to be reviewed is another consideration.

Having determined the associated risk, you need to make the following determinations, and in our case these questions might need to be revisited at the end of Phase 1 and Phase 2:

- Do you proceed?
- Does the client's solution request need to be reworked with them?
- Does the scope, design, or pricing of your solution need to be modified?

If you decide to proceed, there is one thing you can do to eliminate potential risk from the onset: define the roles and deliverables well. Try to remove subjective or ambiguous terms, and remove any unnecessary adjectives, especially superlatives. Also be careful when using words or phrases that provide an implicit guarantee unless that is your intention.

✗ The contractor will provide a quick solution to the problem

✔ The contractor will respond to the issue as per the attached Service Level Agreement, and work to provide a timely solution to the problem

When dealing with client satisfaction throughout the project, it is helpful to have a model that you can refer back to should roles or deliverables become an item of contention.

One final thought. If you're bidding for the business I wouldn't necessarily raise a flag if the client's solution requires rework — address it in a conspicuous place in the body of the proposal as an item that needs to be addressed and indicate that, as with any change, the pricing might be affected.

2.6 SCOPE

A number of consulting services will be required to support each phase, but again, the scope of the Phase 2 and 3 services will need to be ascertained during the preceding phase. At this point, Daniel will introduce the subphases of the WBS as a tool for defining the flow of needed services, and to provide supporting documentation and enlightenment for the customer when read.

Generally, the description of services within the proposal should convey their value to the customer and contain active (will manage) instead of passive (will be managed) language. It's important to pay attention to the choice of verb with regards to definition as well. For example, 'facilitate' is not a synonym for any verb associated with 'doing.' The customer doesn't care about the items you will do which are for your benefit, overhead, or convenience. Drop anything of that nature from this discussion, such as 'readying the workplace,' unless the customer's requirements cause such an item and the associated cost to be necessary. For example, if the customer requires a specific software development platform then the cost of setup, software licenses, etc. should be accounted for.

The project manager will manage the delivery of all activity throughout the project to ensure delivery is ontime, to scope, and within budget. The services to be provided during Phase 1 of the project consist of the following, which might be altered at any time through a change order process to accommodate project requirements:

- Assimilate the client organization's structure and define the project's cross-functional representation requirements.
- Communicate the project's goals and status to all interested (and authorized) parties via a constantly maturing Approach Document, in a timely, regular and concise fashion.
- Interview and (host the meeting to) select internal candidates from which the project team will be assembled.
- Assemble and motivate the project team via a project kick off meeting.
- Develop and incorporate the software development plan into the overall project plan.
- Document the Development, Testing and "Gold Master" platform requirements and facilitate the ordering and implementation of the same.
- Determine and document the customer requirements and the associated implementation costs of those requirements and their alternatives for developing, documenting, executing and reviewing the following Phase 2 subphases:

- Define the configuration-related infrastructure

  1.System and network capacity planning
  2.Backup and recovery
  3.High-availability

- Develop and implement the Alpha configuration
- Alpha test
- Assess the Alpha test results and resulting configuration changes
- Develop the nonconfiguration-related infrastructure

  1.Help desk.
  2.System management.
  3.Network management.
  4.Push/pull software proliferation.
  5.Security.
  6.Disaster Recovery.

7.Operations.

and the Phase 3 services:

- Develop and implement the Beta configuration.
- Perform the beta test.
- Perform the pilot test.
- Perform the user acceptance test.
- Develop and deliver the user education.
- Develop and deliver IS/IT education.
- Provide deployment team support.
- Provide deployment period user support.
- Facilitate ongoing user support.
- Provide equipment staging and deployment.
- Document site staging requirements and facilitate .implementation
- Handoff the production environment.

There also needs to be a discussion of the project management services and other oversight services that will be provided, above and beyond managing the delivery of the services mentioned above. A common misconception is believing that project management and its value is understood. Everyone seems to have their own thoughts as to what comprises project management, and very often the image is incomplete. Everyone also has an impression of the value added by project management.

It never ceases to amaze me that a customer can be betting their career on a multi-million dollar project, and that they want to know if they really need project management. Well, yes, unless you want to leave the success of the project to luck (or unless you have unlimited resources and no hard dates to meet). Equally incredible is the number of people who, having been sold on the value of project management, proceed to ask if they can have it less than five days per week. Sure, what day of the week do you not want me to respond to issues?

You can generally gauge how expansive your description of deliverables needs to be by the client's reaction to paying for project management, although I would provide a full list regardless. If the client feels that they don't need project management, or that they don't need it full-time (these scenarios will be discussed later in the chapter), the client probably does not understand its benefits.

In other words, don't skimp on describing the function of the project manager, and make certain that the wording is such that it's clear that the project manager's deliverables are limited to what is listed. The purpose of providing the description is to ensure that you and the client have the same expectation of what you will deliver.

The best place to begin might be with the obvious. The project manager needs to develop the project plan, staff it, and manage the delivery of the project so that it is completed on time and within budget. Now there might be more than one project plan, as is the case in this scenario — one for each phase since the object of the first two phases is partially to gather the information necessary to plan the next phase — but even then the first project plan needs to come first. There are, however, responsibilities that, if applicable, are not as obvious. The project manager may

- develop a strategy for the delivery of the solution
- manage the vendor (third-party) contracts and agreements
- ensure clear roles and responsibilities
- obtain commitment of all involved resources
- integrate and communicate all plans, contracts, proposals and deliverables
- establish and manage client expectations
- conduct status meetings
- gain client acceptance on all deliverables and overall satisfaction
- keep project documentation
- apply quality improvement processes where applicable
- manage and obtain resolution of issues

2.7 ASSUMPTIONS

Beyond enumerating the services that will be provided, it is essential that the proposal sets expectations as accurately as possible. This document will become the contract, or portion thereof; whenever a conflict in expectation arises one party or the other will eventually point to the contract if no other resolution is forthcoming. However, contractual conflicts are not the only reason to document assumptions.

The mood of a project is much like global weather. Clouds and weather fronts seem to meander around the planet almost randomly, which is much the way the mood of a project can be. It's uncanny how it can change from day to day. Outside factors, such as a person's home life or job pressures, can affect their daily mood, and thus potentially affect their outlook on any given day. One way to avoid having a negative outlook boomerang into your lap (and to establish credibility and the beginnings of a good working relationship from the start) is to make sure you understand what the client is expecting from you and your team, and marry that to what you can provide. It's worth mentioning the old adage

$$assume = ass + u + me.$$

This is your opportunity to define the activities and deliverables in advance, and the scope of each, and not have to later explain under-the-gun why the client is not getting what they expect. I recommend against trying to 'slip anything by'; in reviewing the proposal you should draw the client's attention to each bullet and make certain they understand it.

Why? If during the project the client says that they want a formal daily status report, and you point to 'fine print' in the proposal that says you will only provide a weekly status report, it might get you off the hook contractually, but you'll have blown your rapport. You should do your best to ensure that nothing comes as a surprise to the client. Account for all normal activities, deliverables, and issues, and spell out how the abnormal ones will be managed in terms of the change management process, and the availability you will need to the client's personnel in such cases. If expectations are unreasonable given the budget or time frame, now is the time to either rework the expectations or the limiting factors.

People regularly proceed through their lives using assumptions. They assume that when they open their front door in the morning no one will be standing there with a gun. They assume that when they start their car it won't explode, and that when they back out of their driveway the road will be there, and that when their traffic light is green, the opposing light is red. These assumptions are logical, and when proven correct each day become almost subconscious (I still give a peripheral-vision glance at the intersections to make sure no one is about to run the light). I could just proceed through the green light, assuming that I'll be okay because I have the right-of-way, but what if I'm wrong? In the project management world, assumptions are potentially 'deadly,' even if they are logical.

Minor assumptions gone wrong can bring a major implementation to a halt. Imagine if you will that you're rolling out 1,000 systems. The first 100 arrive at their destinations and the next 100 are on the truck. At the destinations, which are 'identical environments,' you discover that the available space for the system at the pilot site was four inches wider than the other sites, and that without that four inches the systems won't fit. Wake up the bugler; time for taps.

That example also indicates that nailing down assumptions is not a one-time event. It needs to happen throughout the course of the project. Here we will examine some assumptions that are best addressed prior to the start of the project.

An Expectation Worksheet can be used to meet with the client and note their feedback on expectations, thus potentially avoiding an additional round of contract negotiations.

Conduct

It's important to understand how the people you bring in are expected to act. Naturally they will be expected to act professionally, but 'professionally' is somewhat a subjective idea. While gathering data, take a look at how the client's employees act. Do they look over cubicle walls to have discussions? Must they defer to management in meetings? A copy of the client's employee policy document, or the applicable pages, can be helpful. You need to ascertain whether consultants have conduct requirements beyond those of employees. It's always best to err conservatively. Don't take relaxed conduct on the part of the employees to mean that consultants should act the same way, but do take restricted conduct to mean that.

Listing what might seem obvious points can be useful in getting the client to think about what should be listed but isn't. An example is that your people will be ontime to meetings.

Dress is an important point. What is the dress code? Is it suit and tie, jacket and tie, shirt and tie, business casual, just plain casual? Many companies that do business with a client with a casual dress code feel uncomfortable about it because they feel consultants should look the part. The truth is that if you want the consultants to fit in with the client and be able to develop relationships, they should 'look the client.' If the client's dress code is casual, I would suggest putting a limit (internally, not in the proposal) on what is acceptable. You don't want, for example, clothes with holes or T-shirts with any form of message (thus avoiding playing censor day-to-day).

Credibility and Competence

The naturally client expects any consultant brought in to be credible and competent, but to what degree? You might need to expand on this within the focus area of each consultant. For example, the capacity planning consultant might not be a leader in their field and will provide some transfer of knowledge to the client's personnel. Note the use of the word 'some,' it's important to qualify this type of deliverable now as it's much harder to do it after the fact. And who will cover the cost of the knowledge transfer?

Hours and Presence

What are the working hours? Do your people have to take lunch? Is there a specific time that they must take lunch and how long do they get? Projects can get behind at times, and, more importantly, client members of the project team who have other responsibilities may end up doing project work at night and on weekends at times. Are your people expected to work nights and weekends? And if so, are they to do this even if the project is running ontime? Are there tasks that you will have to do outside normal business hours? If you and your people are not expecting to be on site from 8:00 am Monday through 5:00 pm Friday (due to travel), be certain to note that.

Very often work can be done remotely. If you are using resources part-time you can get more availability from them (and less travel expense for the client) if they can do some work remotely, such as developing documentation. Is this acceptable? How is time to be recorded, approved, and tracked?

Meetings and Responsiveness

What meetings are required by the client? Who will run them and set the agenda? Is there a management status meeting in addition to the project status meeting? How often are the meetings and where are they located? Can a maximum length be assigned? You don't want to find out that the management status meeting lasts a half-day (even though the portion addressing your project is only fifteen minutes) weekly, at a remote site. Is anyone from your team other than you expected to attend? What are the client's expectations as to your availability (lead-time) for meetings? What are your expectations as to the availability of the client? If it's determined that conflict will be arbitrated by someone who's calendar is always filled two weeks out, you've got an issue.

What is the client expecting from you and your team as to access and responsiveness? If your people are assigned to the project part-time and typically have a full calendar, this needs to be well defined.

Issue Resolution and Change Management

Who will be the arbitrator in the event that you and your client counterpart(s) have issues that are deadlocked? What will be the process? Is there a project steering committee (if not, you might be continually hamstrung by politics)? What if the client has issues with you or your work? Does the client understand that issues with your staff are to be brought to you before being brought anywhere else? What constitutes a change and what will the change management process be?

Reporting

How often are status reports due? What format will they take ('format' in the sense of appearance and physical form)? Who should the audience be? Is there more than one status report required (i.e. one for management and one for the project team)? What other reports are required? What tool(s) will be used to develop the report (and what tool(s) will thus be required to read it)? Make the client aware that you will be providing status reports back to your company as well. Does the client want to see the updated project plans? And with what detail?

Is that an important consideration? Perhaps not. Then again, if four months into the project things start falling behind and the customer asks to see variance data, that might be the best time for you to consider that you haven't been tracking variance in the project plan — it's a little late to try recreating it.

Security

Will there be an issue of status being provided back to your company? If so, it needs to be addressed in a nondisclosure agreement along with any other concerns about client information. If your people will be doing work remotely they will have data with them. Is that an issue, and is having documents on a laptop? Will the remote people be able to dial in? Will the people on site be able to dial out? Will there be logistical problems in entering and leaving the building with equipment (laptops, etc.)? How will access to the site be provided (badges, etc.) and what hours will that access be available? On one project we could not work late unless we had a 'chaperone,' and this became an issue as we were asked to do many tasks after hours.

Deliverables

What form will the deliverables take (will they be expected in hardcopy and electronic formats)? Are you expected to provide bound copies? In color? To how many recipients? Is someone on the client's staff to approve a draft of each deliverable before it's finalized?

You should have a clause that absolves you of absorbing any cost should there be change necessary due to the client not providing the needed resources on time.

Outside Influences

How are vacation, training, illness, personal commitments, and company obligations (the consultant's, not the client's) to be handled? Here comes the nightmare, right? You have a member of your team with a nonrefundable vacation planned at a critical time in the project. If your company has holidays that the client does not observe, how will this be handled? How will your project schedule be affected by the client's resources' schedules?

Work Environment

Will each of your people have a dedicated cubicle and a phone? Will they have a LAN or WAN port? Will there be locking file cabinets or a locking 'war room' (it's a pain to have to take everything home every day because there's nowhere to lock it up)? Who will be providing the desktop computer equipment such as the one for the tech writer? What tools need to be on it and who will provide them? Where will the office supplies come from? Will there be a dedicated conference room available or will your team meetings need to be off site? Is there somewhere to make calls from that is private (cubicles are not private)? Can you dial long distance? Will you have a secretary available, and what load is she already carrying (what will her turnaround time be)?

Budget

Is there one, and how big is it? Hopefully you have some idea or you might be developing a million-dollar proposal to find an awaiting budget of fifty thousand! But beyond the cost of your services, is there budget for the expenses to the customer that will arise with regards to equipment, software, and infrastructure? In the client-server world there are specialized development products and testing products (which will vary based on the data and application architecture selected). These products increase in their requirement, cost and complexity if object technology is being used. It might be less expensive to code and support object technology, but not to design, develop, and test it. So who will be paying for the products needed to create and test the infrastructure (especially those not required once the environment is in production), and is there a budget for them? Will some development people need to be brought in (this is more of a Phase 2 issue in Daniel's case), and is there a budget for their rates? Might it be more fiscally feasible to use offshore labor? Are there cultural, political, or security barriers to that possibility? And what about the development environment? Who will pay for the pieces and accompanying software licenses necessary for it? Whoever will own the software tools following the project should purchase them, because transferring licenses can be complicated at best.

Expenses

You will probably be charging the client for your team's travel expenses. Will that be per diem or actual, and invoiced how often? Will you charge for their travel time? Will your people who live remotely be flying home each weekend? Some clients object to this, and if yours does you want to know that quickly as it might affect the availability of your intended resources.

If the client is paying for the travel you should state your policy as to expenses, lodging, and car rental. Things that you might take for granted, like a mid-sized car or a private hotel room, might be contrary to the client's expectations. Does the client have standards that will require your restricting your team members' choice of hotel, meals, and rental car? Does your company allow you to do that? Does the client require original receipts (if your team members are being reimbursed by your company, it might require the originals too!)?

Sign-offs

Judging when the discussion ends and the project begins is not too difficult in most instances (it can be in terms of deciding when to cut over from "free" to "paid"), but when is the project over? If it is a time and materials project, it's over when the time or money runs out. If it's a milestone, or deliverables-based, project, is it over at the end-date or when the last deliverable is delivered? Neither. It's over when there's a mutual agreement, and to reach that point there needs to be a sign-off at the end of each milestone on some deliverable, and a final sign-off at the end of the project.

Why does there need to be a sign-off after each milestone? Well, let's say you're at the project's end and you hit this scenario:

Customer: "Project end? What about the Widget document?"
You: "Widget document? We delivered that last month."
Customer: "Yes, but it's completely unacceptable."

So now what do you do? If you want to keep the customer, you work until the customer is satisfied. And you're doing that work on your company's nickel. What if the customer doesn't seem to get to the point where the deliverable is acceptable? Sounds like time for an arbitrator. Depending on the environment, you may want to state the maximum time beyond your understanding of project-end that can pass before arbitration is called for.

2.8 PRICING

Each company has a different method for arriving at pricing, but there are some things to be considered.

If you are going to bid a fixed-price project, have you accounted for the risk you've determined? You should assign risk to the bottom line. Why is that? Look at Table 2-1.

Charges For Code Development

Requirements Study	$15,250
High-Level Design	$8,500
Low-Level Design	$23,200
Construction/Unit Testing	$64,500
System Testing	$12,000
	$123,450
Risk	$12,345

Table 2-1 Charges for Code Development

You might ask why we don't assign risk to each phase, so that if one of the phases is removed the risk is as well. To some extent that makes sense, but in most of the engagements I've seen, if my completing my portion depends on the completion of another portion, and someone else not under my control is doing the other portion, the risk has gone up, not down. If you will have the ability to re-price when, say, the system testing piece is pulled out, then you can pull out its risk and add back in whatever risk is appropriate. If you will not be able to re-price then you will at least have the original risk included. On the other hand, although clients understand that there are risks to be considered, they don't like seeing it added as a line item.

Each person's travel will need to be accounted for both in terms of actual expense (or per diem) and travel time unless the engagement has been set up for travel to be invoiced separately. Are there other expenses to be incurred? For example, is there equipment, software, software licenses, or other items that are needed specifically for this project?

You need to state what will trigger the invoicing of the client, and this can affect the project greatly. It's worth taking a look at the more common methods of billing.

Periodic

If the project is being billed as time and materials instead of fixed-price, you will simply invoice for the time and materials for the prior month. With a fixed-price project of, for example, $120,000 and an anticipated duration of six months, you would invoice $20,000 at the end of the first month (price divided by duration).

Modified Periodic

If you need good faith money up front because of risk or cash flow or the need to order equipment, you can invoice a lump amount up front and then periodically as the project progresses. For example, if the project is expected to be one year in duration, will cost the client $150,000, will be invoiced quarterly and you require $30,000 up front, following the first invoice you would send out quarterly invoices of $30,000.

Milestone/Deliverable Billing

Upon the sign-off of each deliverable (and that might be simply a document stating that a milestone has been reached), an invoice will be cut. The determination of how much each milestone should be worth needs to account for the effort in reaching it as well as any cash flow for up-front purchasing that needs to occur for the next milestone. Typically under this method a percentage is required at the time of the order, such as 20 percent.

So why would you care about the billing method? Well, because you'll be tracking effort and cost, and you're gonna have a helluva time matching the resources and effort and their cost to the revenue if the billing scheme doesn't reflect those costs. Let's look at two examples.

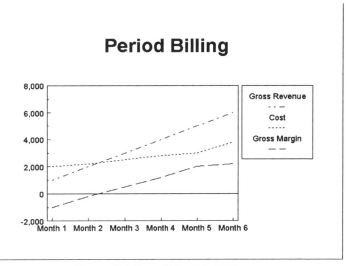

Figure 2-1 Equal Monthly Billings

Figure 2-1 shows what can happen with equal monthly billings. The effort doesn't occur in equal monthly amounts (less hours at project start-up for instance), so at times during the project the accumulated cost exceeds the accumulated revenue. Is that a big deal as long as revenue wins in the end? Well that depends on

Milestone Billing

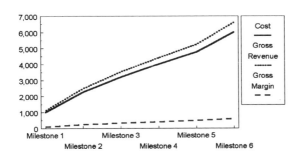

Figure 2-2 Milestone Billing

- Are the funds available to lay out in advance of the revenue?

Is there any risk of the project ending while in a negative cash flow position?

Figure 2-2 shows milestone billing. Assuming that the estimate of effort necessary to reach each milestone has been accurate then the amount being billed at each milestone is in excess of the cost of reaching that point.

2.9 REVIEW

Since I can't take the time to cover proposal generation thoroughly, I thought I should at least provide information regarding the review of the document. There are a number of things to look for to be certain that you have a quality document.

- Has it been proofread and the spelling checked?
- Have the deliverables been defined well?
- Has what is in-scope and out-of-scope been defined well?
- Have the deliverable formats been defined?
- Have all steps in reaching the deliverables been considered in the timeline and pricing?
- Have the tasks been well-defined?
- Does the timeline provide time for the administrative tasks, i.e. status, change management, individual team-member meetings?
- Has the pricing been worked out to minimize risk and provide the needed cash flow?
- Has the proposal been reviewed by the team members?

This last bullet more than the others is a must. You should never ask someone to deliver against a scope and time line into which they have not had input. If certain team members have not been identified yet, run it past someone who does the same type of work and has a large body of experience. Actually, if you have the time and the luxury of the same expertise available in additional resources, you might have them review it too. Occasionally a fresh view can lead to insightful comments.

2.10 Delivering the Proposal

If this is a bidding process you might have to drop off several versions of the proposal and leave it at that. If not, this is the time to go over the proposal with the client. You don't want them to misread something, feel something was omitted or incorrectly inserted, or suffer 'sticker shock' and be left to stew on it. Phone ahead and ask for an appropriate amount of time with them to be able to review the proposal cover to cover.

Review the general scope with them and then the price. If you make it past the price, you should then review the detailed scope and assumptions item by item. Don't just read from the proposal, explain the rationale for including the item (in case it's not evident) and ensure that the client feels comfortable with the material.

2.11 THE CONTRACT

Well, you've finished the proposal. Your company will be moving on to contract negotiations at this point. That's a whole different subject, but there is one aspect of contracts worth consideration here.

Very often the contract signed with the client that will cover a project such as we're discussing will contain two items you should review and pay particular attention to: the client's project management delivery requirements, and specifications as to liquidated damages should something go wrong.

Regarding the latter, I'll just say that you need to make certain that your exposure is limited, and hopefully limited to an amount that you can live with (not in excess of your profit would be nice — not in excess of the project revenue would hopefully be the worst).

As to the former, I'm bringing it up because far too often I've seen the contract having been developed from boilerplate, or cut and paste from earlier contracts. The results are requirements that are completely irrelevant.

An example would be a contract for you to provide support for a client's application. They find a bug — they call you — pure maintenance and bug fixes, no enhancements. This is a completely reactive environment, yet the contract states that you must provide a detailed project plan, and that any changes to the plan need to be approved by the client's project manager. Well, I'd burst the bubble by pointing out that there is no detailed task planning to be done for activities that are short-lived and reactive in nature. I'd be told at that point to not worry about it, that the text was just standard stuff that got included in all their contractor agreements. Sorry, but the first dumb mistake to be made (and typically the last to be realized, because it's typically on the forefront just before the contract is voided) is to sign a contract making promises that you have no intention of keeping. If the client, or your sales force or management, won't relent, I'd make certain a dated document of concerns is created and archived by you, or that you run away.

Another example of reviewing the proposal is a definition of terms. Using the software support scenario again, what is classed as a bug as opposed to an enhancement? To some, a bug is when the application works in a way inconsistent with the detailed design. Okay, what if there's no design document? What if the customer's business changes somewhat and the code needs to change as a result in order for them to continue business, like the addition of a product line? They might consider that a bug. Pivotal terms need to be agreed to in writing before the contract is executed.

If the contract is signed, you should move on to the next chapter, which deals with project initiation.

Chapter 3

Congratulations! You sold the client on the engagement. Now you need to get the project rolling. "So, where's the client-server stuff?" you might be asking. Keep in mind that much of the planning and execution necessary to roll out new technology transcends that technology itself, but as we move more and more into the implementation, the issues relating specifically to client-server and Internet technology will arise, some beginning here.

This chapter covers the activities associated with launching a project: the internal kickoff, the project team interviews, the client kickoff, the project marketing, and the start of the feedback process.

3.1 THE INTERNAL KICKOFF

With any project in which reaching the ultimate deliverable requires the exploring of uncharted territory, it's vital that the team members have a clear understanding of their role and responsibility.

That understanding is necessary in every case; you don't want people tripping over each other or duplicating effort, but in a project involving new technology the need for clarity is enhanced.

With the new technology comes the challenges of identifying the infrastructure needs and mapping them as much as possible to the existing client infrastructure. The fact is that the new technology can have implementation or support requirements that do not map to the client environment, or that map in a way that is not readily evident.

It should come as no surprise that I have an analogy for this. Picture if you will two computer back planes, such as the back of a PC where the connectors are. On one are a number of connectors of different shapes, sizes, and configurations, and on the other connectors that are all identical (and unlabeled) — the uniform connectors being the client's IT organization (a known entity — to them) and the other being the support requirements of the new technology.

Your team needs to determine how to cable one side to the other. So not only do they have to determine how to make the connections to the back plane with dissimilar connectors, but where to connect to on the back plane with identical connectors. As important as this is; who will be making the determination with regards to each connection? You don't want five different people going to the same client contact at different times with the same questions — it won't help establish the credibility of your team.

Let's take a look at the agenda that Daniel has set for his kickoff meeting. Naturally, there are many ways to successfully hold such a meeting — this is just one that works.

MCT Kickoff Meeting

9:00-9:15	Welcome and Introductions
9:15-9:30	Background
9:30-10:30	Roles
	Break
10:45-11:00	Deliverables
11:30-12:00	Administrative
	Lunch
1:00-4:00	RACI[1] diagram/Time Line

After welcoming the team members and going around the table with introductions, Daniel proceeded to provide them with his take on the project as background. We've already seen that information, so I won't spend any more time on it.

---

1.   Responsible - Accountable - Consulted - Informed, see section 3.1.4

3.1.1 Project Roles

The next item on the agenda was Roles, and it was here that Daniel provided his view on what the role of the team was, and the role of each individual. He then asked for feedback. This exercise served to give the team a clear understanding of their direction and to raise awareness of the co-dependency team members had on information (which would help in the later agenda items). So first let's review what Daniel provided as his vision of the roles.

> You are going to be the bearers of success to MCT, make no mistake about it. The success of their company rests on the successful deployment of their new application, and the success of that deployment relies on the product being sound, the implementation being sound, and the infrastructure to support the product and its users being sound.
>
> MCT is venturing into the client-server world for the first time. They are betting their future on applications designed around a new technology. They have a very large and active IT organization, but that organization, responsible for providing the supporting infrastructure, is steeped in mainframe technology, as was the development staff who are developing the application.
>
> For all of MCT, from the president down to the customer service people, this project represents a paradigm shift. The shift is severe. You all know enough about it to understand the level of complexity in making this shift. We're not only charged with enabling the implementation, but in providing direction to the software development effort so that it results in a product supportable in this new environment, and an infrastructure to provide that support. This paradigm shift stands to rock MCT's foundation, and our job is to make certain that they don't stumble when the paradigm shifts.

Daniel gave the team a few moments for his message to sink in, and then took a few questions. He felt that the answers would come out in the discussion on individual roles, so he wrote the questions on the flipchart and deferred discussion for the time being.

3.1.1.1 High-availability

Claudia Culbiens is the high-availability specialist. High-availability is, in the context we're using, the use of software and/or hardware, sometimes redundant or additive to the system configuration, to ensure the desire amount of system availability. Let's face it, if you're used to a mainframe system then you're used to seeing that symbol on the bottom of your screen indicating the system is down. In some environments it might be acceptable for the system to be down during working hours, but not in others.

Claudia's first job will be to map out the anticipated hardware and network topology and identify all the potential points of failure. For example, if there is a single network link between the client site and the server site, then this is a potential single point of failure. Having identified the points of failure, Claudia must then weigh their significance. Why? Because removing points of failure can be very expensive, so Claudia must understand the significance and the requirements.

Requirements, with regards to high-availability, translate into the user's definition of how often the system must be available. If the user requirement is normal business hours, five days per week at eight hours per day (5x8), then the expectation should not be too difficult to meet. If, however, the user requirement is 7x24, the cost can be extraordinary.

To weigh the requirements, there needs to be a business impact analysis. Claudia will determine if one has been done, and if not will do one. This analysis will also be important for disaster recovery and backup and recovery, so it will be somewhat of a team effort. The impact analysis focuses on each function of the software the client is to use, such as entering an order, billing, and so on, as well as the dollar impact on the company if that function were to become unavailable.

Weighing the impact and requirements will enable Claudia to develop a recommendation with alternatives. If, for example, the requirement is 7x24, which will cost $1 million to attain (no logical piece of the configuration ever being down), but the impact of being available 7x20 instead of 7x24 is only $50,000 and the high-availability cost is only $150,000, the recommendation will probably not be for 7x24. If, however, the company would lose $250,000 per hour if the system were unavailable, the recommendation could be different.

One other study that Claudia needs to do is assessing the historic availability of the network and other systems from which the application will depend on data or to which the application will provide data. If the network has been available 7x18 historically, it might prove difficult to provide 7x20 access to the application.

Having developed a recommendation and alternatives, Claudia would then put together a hardware and software configuration to support it. The configuration, when combined with the recommendations of the other team members, would be tested. In order to test high-availability there needs to be more than one system available (so that you can make the first fail and, hopefully, the second kick-in) and, depending on the applications running on the systems, a fair amount of environment configuration. Some high-availability solutions work with pure hardware, some, such as MC ServiceGuard, protect units of code as well. Whatever Claudia develops as a configuration will need to be scripted so that it can be pre-configured during staging.

3.1.1.2 Backup and Recovery

Marguerita Bass has a task even more complex than determining how to keep the environment available: defining how the environment, or portions thereof, will be recovered in the event of loss or corruption of data.

One of the complexities of data recovery is determining how various components of data interact. Recovering one dataset to a particular point in time can render another worthless unless it is recovered to the same point in time as well. In the client-server world, the complexity can be even greater because a single dataset might be distributed across several systems and sites, so not only might the data being recovered impact other data, but if the system needs to come off-line during the recovery, more than one site might be impacted.

Aside from determining the method of recovering the data, there is the issue of knowing what to recover. If a database gets clobbered and has to be restored, defining the data to recover is fairly straightforward. However, if a dataset has been updated by several applications, and one of them has been providing bad data (usually due to a coding or operator error), then the solution might be to back-out the bad transactions. Determining what those transactions are is a function of good logging planning during application design, and the Backup/Recovery person needs to provide that input.

Having determined what data to restore and how to restore it, we're hoping the data will be there to restore. The Backup/Recovery person needs to ensure that, based on the needs arising from the impact analysis data, backup methodology is satisfactory to enabling the recovery needs.

3.1.1.3 Disaster Recovery

Disaster recovery is one of the least understood of IT requirements, and Marguerita Bass will have to deal with it as well. Many companies look at Disaster Recovery as 'insurance' that they're either not willing to pay, or are willing to have 'minimal coverage' only.

Should a disaster strike, not having a Disaster Recovery Plan can leave the company out of business permanently. Many people within a company as well as those outside of it don't understand how little it would take for the company to be put out of business. Even some of the largest companies in the world can fall victim if unable to take orders or deliver product over as little a period as three days.

MCT might have a DR plan, but that is unsure, and certainly the introduction of a client-server environment can complicate the recovery from a disaster: a single system waiting on the sidelines might no longer be sufficient.

Marguerita can leverage again off of the business impact analysis. This will give an indication of the length of time a function within the company can be down, and the associated cost. This will help determine the disaster recovery need and thus the associated scope.

Potentially, the possibility of needing to continue business in a minimal environment might contribute to some of the application design considerations. Normally there isn't the luxury of developing the DR plan concurrent to the development of the mission-critical application. MCT may have thought of this, but I wouldn't count on it.

3.1.1.4 Network and System Management

A distributed application can encompass production systems at multiple sites, and providing operations staff at each site can be cost prohibitive. There needs to be an attempt made to centralize the monitoring of and management of the environment. The NSM person is responsible for this empowering.

Assuming we find a way to manage the environment from one location, how is that site going to know what has to be done day to day? How will the support staff know what is wrong when something goes wrong?

Pam Jogger is charged with determining the network and system management solution. This solution will be comprised of software and hardware that allows for the monitoring and managing of the client-server enterprise as centrally as is possible and practical. If the client is already using some form of system or network management software that can be leveraged, Pam needs to determine the logistics for doing that.

A primary consideration for her is the client-server application being developed. There are many points along its daily path of data and code transfers where something can go wrong. Pam needs to work with the developers to make sure that the application will effectively communicate with the NSM solution. Only some of the information the solution needs to monitor is 'pull' information, where the NSM software can go and look for it. Most of the activity monitoring needs to be in a 'push' fashion, where the application architecture is providing the information based on various events taking place.

3.1.1.5 Capacity Planning

Mike Thewuss will be leading the capacity planning effort. He will need to work closely with the software developers so that he can develop a complete understanding of the software architecture and the transaction architecture. As each application is defined, it will be modeled so that any performance issues can be uncovered, and to the extent that they stem from the application design, remedied while the application is still being developed. Mike will also be hunting down transaction volume estimates as well as 'typical' user characteristics.

The data that Mike collects will be used to determine the optimal hardware configuration for the client and server platforms. Another factor in that consideration will be other requirements such as transaction throughput (portal-to-portal user response time) and the excess capacity needed on each system for growth and high-availability fail-over. If the system is 90 percent saturated out of the box, it would not be long before it needs to be upgraded, and if it had to pick up the processing load for a failed system there could be trouble.

3.1.1.6 Networking

Lindsay Coffee will be focusing on networking as well as the network capacity. Using much of the same data as Mike, as well as data volume and flow models, Lindsay will estimate the peak and normal data volume that the network will need to handle. Lindsay will then need to design the operations center network as well as the client-server network topology.

3.1.1.7 Education

David Wolfen will be responsible for education planning. David will first need to determine the content of what needs to be learned, and then work within MCT to develop a method for educating the audience. There are MCT users spread out over a large geography who need to learn to use the new application. There are also remote support people who need to learn to support the new equipment. David will work closely with Joules to develop 'Help Desk' personnel for MCT.

3.1.1.8 Technical Lead

Joules will be Daniel's technical lead, and thus his right arm. Does a project manager need a background in the technicalities of the tasks being managed? Opinions vary greatly; mine is 'yes, somewhat.' You could probably squeak by with a strong technical lead, but there are three areas where you will have issues.

The first is in developing the time line. If you don't understand each task, you will be depending completely on others with regards to determining the task effort and dependency to other tasks. Second, should issues arise (and they will) during the project, you will again need to be under constant advisement as to resolving them, which will pull your technical people off what they are doing. Sure, the president depends on his advisers, his cabinet so to speak, to resolve issues, but that is an expectation of the way he does his job, and this activity is going on behind closed doors out of the eye of the client. Lastly, if you're always deferring questions from others at meetings regarding the time line and issues to your technical person, you will soon lose credibility and people will go straight to your technical person instead of wasting time asking their questions twice.

The background doesn't need to be deep, just an understanding. Daniel will depend on Joules to keep him abreast of the ramifications of daily events as they translate to affecting the course of the project. Joules will need to be a 'Jack of all trades,' and a master of most.

3.1.1.9 Logistics Coordinator

Amber Darling works in the support area of Hewlett-Packard, and will assist Daniel in developing the implementation logistics. There will be staging issues for the equipment, installation issues for both the systems and their enabling infrastructure (such as cabling) at the operations centers, and Amber will help Daniel to plan through these issues. Amber will spend a good deal of his time infiltrating the IT organization, since the success of most of the staging and implementation issues will depend on their assistance. Amber will also design a support plan to meet MCT's needs.

Daniel will also depend on the people who have an ongoing relationship with MCT, like Megan Cobb the sales rep, to assist him in expanding his contacts within the company. Perhaps she can also assist in getting the ear of people higher up the 'food chain.'

3.1.1.10 Process

Al Ferreman is a SEPC (Software Engineering Process Consultant) at Hewlett-Packard in the Telecom Software Solutions Program. This group specializes in software development and maintenance, and Al is their Open Architecture expert, specializing in intranets.

It will be Al's job to head up the team that develops the software solution for MCT.

3.1.2 Deliverables

Following is a generic summary of each document deliverable, and how Daniel views each. He mentions that the presentation version of each deliverable (as opposed to works in progress) will be produced by him from the team members' drafts, thus ensuring a consistent appearance and form. The electronic version of each will then be put out on a 'share' (an electronic filing cabinet from which other people can view the files) and left as perpetually maturing, or 'living,' documents.

- Approach Document — The ultimate deliverable of each person is fairly well understood by the client, but not the route to get to that deliverable. Producing a document that details the data that will be used, as well as the thought process or method that will lead from having that data to generating the requirements will help to avoid trouble from invalid assumptions later.
- Needs Document — Again, avoiding issues related to assumptions, this document will lay out in summary the understanding of the need that is driving the deliverable.
- Requirements Document — A detailed accounting of the user and architectural and organizational (IT) requirements that are driving the definition of the solution. Following this information is a definition of the recommended solution as well as alternatives to the recommendation if appropriate.
- Test Plan — Many of the areas of focus will need to be tested, such as high-availability, staging, etc. A plan that details what will be tested, how it will be tested, for what purpose it will be tested, and what result will be acceptable will be published, thus validating in advance all testing and testing results.

- Production Plan — The hand-off of, for example, the NSM concept, scripts and procedures to the organization that will use them in production is not necessarily as straight forward as saying, "Here, you take it." The method for accomplishing this hand-off will be documented. The production plan will also contain the earlier documents so that there is one repository for all the activities that lead to the production environment.
- Screen Presentation — A computer-based presentation that can be 'thrown' onto a screen via an overhead projector will be developed for the purpose of being able to quickly deliver an awareness of this team's activity and objectives to people not closely related to the project's daily activities — a necessary PR function.

On the software development side, there will be several additional documents beyond the approach and needs documents. Most of these documents are part of the normal software development cycle.

- Architecture Definition Document — Lays out the software architecture that will exist in the delivered solution, as well as the underlying layers of architecture necessary to support the applications.
- High-Level Design (Functional) Document — Describes the business rules and high-level functionality behind each screen or window, report, and batch program.
- Low-Level Design (Detailed) Document — Provides a control-by-control description of each item on each screen or window, a line-by-line description of each report, and a layout for each.
- Unit Test Document — A plan for testing the functionality of each application component. The testing will depend on the intended functionality in the low-level design.
- System Test/Acceptance Test Plan — Sometimes these are separate documents, but often the act of inputting meaningful and typical data and following its course and effect throughout the application differs between the two only in the Acceptance test having an end-user representative present.

3.1.3 Project Administration

A subject that most people like to blow off, but a necessary evil. Daniel hands out a small document containing the information shown below.

- Recording of Time — If the client is paying time and materials, they probably have some form of time recording and time sheet that they want used. Also, Daniel explains how the time is to be recorded internally. Why record the time internally as well? Because whether the project is time and materials or fixed-price, Daniel will have no way to track whether tasks are being completed using the effort estimated for each unless he knows how much effort is being expended.

- Expenses — Daniel has laid out what expenses will be covered, and what the expectations are as to what is a 'normal' dollar value for each, such as a car rental rate. He has also listed a number of hotels in the area, asking that an attempt be made to use them first, thus providing a budgetable rate. He has also covered the fact that he will be approving all expense reports before passing them on to the person who normally approves them.

- Phone numbers — Each team member's phone number is listed, as well as their beeper number if applicable.

- Communications — Daniel has laid out what levels in MCT's organization the team should feel free to communicate with without going through him. The directors and higher are off limits, as Daniel wants to ensure a consistent message going to them and not be blindsided by them finding out something of which Daniel is not yet aware. Also, Daniel wants to insulate his team from being contacted directly by those people, and you can't have it both ways — if communication is acceptable in one direction it will be hard to prevent it in the other. Daniel also lays out when he expects to have team meetings (and that if a person is not on site that he will set up a bridge line for them to phone into) and when he expects to have a status report each week (Monday, lunch time, so that any resource whose home location is the west coast has time to get it in).

- Access — Daniel lays out the hours of operation of MCT and what the access of the team to the facilities will be. Unfortunately, if the team wants to work after hours, a MCT 'chaperone' will be required. For the development team, Daniel notes the details of the connection requirements needed to MCT (the development will be done remotely).
- Equipment — Daniel lists the equipment that the team will have available to them, and provides a form for them to request and justify anything beyond that list.
- Personal — Daniel has them complete a form providing personal information such as address, birthday, and so on; the information he needs to request security passes, e-mail, and voice mail for them at MCT.
- Calendar — Daniel asks for a calendar from each person showing any vacation, training, or other commitment time that they have scheduled.

3.1.4 RACI Chart / Time-Line

The morning session was the easy part. Now the team is going to give an exhausting concentrated effort to add detail to the high-level time line that was created for the proposal, the idea being to develop a comfortable going-in position.

One of the most difficult things to do when beginning a project is to develop a realistic time line. You'll remember that the time line, or Gantt chart, is broken down into the individual tasks that, as a whole, define the project. The reason it's difficult to develop this chart is because of the amount of detail that needs to be associated with each task in order to make the time line realistic.

There are a number of decisions that need to be made to accurately capture a task. The first global question is how much detail do you want to include? Keep in mind that you will need to update the status of each task, so it probably doesn't make sense to identify tasks with a duration of less than a half day (unless it's critical — like "Launch Missiles"), otherwise trying to stay on top of the status of each task will drive you insane.

The other consideration is that if your performance, and that of team members, is going to be based on the timeliness of each task, the statistic will probably not be flattering if the tasks reflect minutiae. After all, you have a much better chance of being successful if given a day to accomplish something than being given eight one-hour units to accomplish the eight subtasks. For example, if the task is to drive downtown and pick up a certified copy of your birth certificate in one day you will probably be successful. If, however, that task is broken down into twenty minutes to drive to the county office, five minutes to park and get inside, etc., many of those subtasks might run late. The final consideration is this: At what point do I not care anymore if the pieces are occurring on-time so long as the whole is, and will I be able to ascertain that the whole is proceeding on time or not without managing the pieces?

Let's take a look at the questions that need to be answered in order to develop the Gantt chart.

- What tasks, if any, need to start or end before this task can begin?
- How long will this task take to complete?
- Are there points at which this task relies on other events in order to proceed?
- Whose effort is required, and what is their availability?
- Does the completion of this task result in a deliverable?
- Does a subsequent task depend on this task's beginning or ending?

The answers to these questions will determine how the task is represented on the Gantt chart. Let's take a closer look at each of the questions and how the time line is affected, and then we'll look at an example.

What tasks, if any, need to commence or end before this task can begin or end?

There is the possibility that a given task doesn't need to have anything happen before it can begin. This is the case with the first task in a project; it has no predecessors. Usually a task won't begin until 'something' else first happens. If that 'something' is another task finishing, then the two tasks have a finish-to-start relationship. That is, the second task will not begin until the first task ends.

But what if the first task doesn't necessarily need to finish, if it simply needs to be in progress, at a certain point, before the subsequent task can begin? This is then a start-to-start relationship; that is the second task cannot begin until the first task has begun.

The relationship is not always that straightforward though. Often the subsequent task won't begin the moment the first task begins or ends; there's a lag. This lag is recorded on a project plan as, well, lag-time. For example, if the second task can't begin until two days after the first task ends then the relationship is finish-to-start with two days lag. If the second task can begin three days before the first task ends, then the relationship is finish-to-finish with negative three days lag. And if the second task can begin one day after the first task begins, the relationship is start-to-start with one day of lag.

Determining the type of relationship isn't that difficult — but deciding precisely which tasks form the relationship can be. The easiest way to understand this is to pick any normal event, like grocery shopping for a party, and lay out each task involved in the process, and how the tasks relate to each other. You might come up with something like Table 3-1.

Task No.	Task	Dependent on task	Dependency
1	Create shopping list		
2	Get shopping cart	1	finish-to-start
3	Select food	2	finish-to-start
4	Put food in cart	3	finish-to-start
5	Pay for food	4	finish-to-start

Table 3-1 Party Tasks

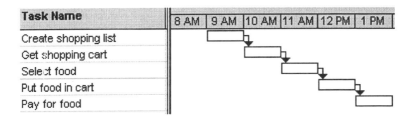

Figure 3-1 Party Gantt A

Figure 3-1 shows the tasks in Table 3-1 in time line form. At first glance it seems sensible enough, but there are some adjustments that can be made, adjustments that refine the dependencies. They will also serve to shorten the overall duration, something that is always welcome, especially when the project is running late.

Do you really need to have a shopping list in order to get the shopping cart? Sure, it's a logical progression, but getting the cart is not dependent on your having a shopping list. Selecting the food (at least with me) is dependent on having begun the shopping list, but I can begin that without having the cart. Assuming I'll have more than an armful of food to gather, I know I'll be limited to needing the cart ten minutes or so into selecting the food. Certainly, putting the food in the cart is dependent on having begun to select it, but I don't need to have finished selecting it, the two tasks almost run parallel to each other. Now, I'm going to get a bit picayune with the last task, but we can select food while we're paying for other things in the cart, because of that last minute stuff hanging from the racks by the register, and in that case you also haven't finished putting things in the cart, but you cannot finish paying for the food until you've finished selecting it. The modified version is seen in Table 3-2.

Task No.	Task	Dependent on task	Dependency
1	Create shopping list		
2	Get shopping cart		
3	Select food	1	start-to-start plus 5 minutes
		2	finish-to-finish - 15 minutes
4	Put food in cart	3	start-to-start + 1 minute
5	Pay for food	3	finish-to-finish
		4	start-to-start

Table 3-2 Party Tasks with Dependancies

So what we have here is that you can get the shopping cart without consideration of the shopping list. You can begin selecting food soon after you start the shopping list, but can't finish selecting food until you have the shopping cart ('cause you can't carry it all in your arms). You can put the food in the cart as soon as you start collecting it and finish getting the cart. You can finish paying for the food as soon as you've finished selecting it — and because we know you can't carry it all, we know that if you're not ready to pay for it if you haven't begun putting it in the cart yet, but you don't need to finish putting it in the cart. This is reflected in the time line in Figure 3-2.

Obviously, in the scheme of things the technicalities of grocery shopping is a 'who cares,' but keep in mind that planning a deployment is a bit more complex, and so then are the tasks and dependencies. You need to do your best to make certain that they're accurate, or you'll find later that a task is not beginning or not ending due to something that was not listed as a dependency; "Everybody knows that you have to wait for the stuff to be bagged and then carried to the car" — that five-minute "gotcha" can turn into a day or two in a real project, and then everything subsequent to that task, including those that needed to be scheduled in advance (like having your cable TV service installed), slips!

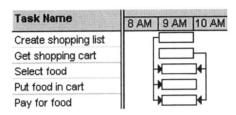

Figure 3-2 Party Gantt B

Feed the dependency back to your team; "So what you're saying is that as soon as this first task has completed ...". Do it for every task. It might seem tedious (and is), but it's the best way to assure accuracy. Giving the team members a plan to read won't cut it; they're not used to looking at a plan and seeing dependencies in their mind any more than you would be able to look at a house blueprint and quickly realize the bathroom door can't open out.

One last consideration with dependencies is group items. Let's expand the shopping example to account for doing something else afterwards in Table 3-3.

We've added a new group of tasks for making dinner. You'll also notice in Figure 3-3 that we now have summary-level tasks; that is, 'Gro-

Task No.	Task	Dependent on task	Dependency
1	Grocery Shopping		
2	Create shopping list		
3	Get shopping cart		
4	Select food	2	start-to-start plus 5 minutes
		3	finish-to-finish - 15 minutes
5	Put food in cart	4	start-to-start + 1 minute
6	Pay for food	4	finish-to-finish
		5	start-to-start
7	Make Dinner		
8	Unpack groceries	6	finish-to-start + 20 minutes
9	Rinse vegetables	8	finish-to-start
10	Cook	9	finish-to-start

Table 3-3 Party Gantt with Modified Dependancies

cery Shopping' and 'Make Dinner' are group headers, with a number of tasks grouped under them. There are two reasons for doing this. One is so that when looking at a Gantt chart you can see the status of the task group easily, especially when you 'roll up' all the subordinate tasks (have only the summary tasks displayed on the screen). The bar representing the summary task will begin with the earliest start date of the first subordinate task, and end with the latest end date of the last subordinate task (first and last with regards to date, not the order in which they appear).

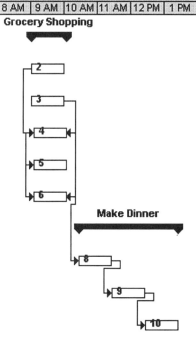

Figure 3-3 Party Gantt C

The other reason is so that dependencies can be managed more easi-ly. You'll notice that we won't start 'Unpack Groceries' until twenty min-utes after we've paid for them, allowing for the trip home, and so on. However, what if we later need to add 'Pack Groceries in Car' as the last task under 'Grocery Shopping'? We would then need to change the de-pendency so that 'Unpacking Groceries' won't happen until a number of minutes after 'Packing Groceries in Car,' otherwise packing the car would be superfluous because nothing would be dependent on it. Likewise, if we were to add 'Unpack the Car,' we'd have to change the dependencies as well. In using summary tasks, we can eliminate some of the modifications that would envelope us later. Table 3-4 shows, by way of the dependencies, how to do this, and Figure 3-4 establishes the time line.

We've changed two things in Figure 3-4. The summary task 'Make Dinner' is now dependent on the summary task 'Grocery Shopping' ending before it can begin. This means that no matter how many tasks we add to 'Grocery Shopping,' 'Make Dinner' will not begin until the summary task has completed, which means all tasks in that group need to complete. Likewise, we've removed the dependency of 'Unpack Groceries' on 'Pay for Food,' because 'Unpack Groceries' can begin as soon as the group 'Make Dinner' can begin.

How long will this task take to complete?

You might notice that the task bars are of identical length in the preceding figures. The reason for this is that we haven't yet assigned a duration to each task; they're all set at a default of one hour. We'll need to add some realism to them as soon as we discuss some of the finer points of duration.

Task No.	Task	Dependent on task	Dependency
1	Grocery Shopping		
1a	Create shopping list		
1b	Get shopping cart		
1c	Select food	1a	start-to-start plus 5 minutes
		1b	finish-to-finish - 15 minutes
1d	Put food in cart	1c	start-to-start + 1 minute
1e	Pay for food	1c	finish-to-finish
		1d	start-to-start
2	Make Dinner	1	finish-to-start + 20 minutes
2a	Unpack groceries		
2b	Rinse vegetables	2a	finish-to-start
2c	Cook	2a	finish-to-start

Table 3-4 Party Tasks with Dinner Added

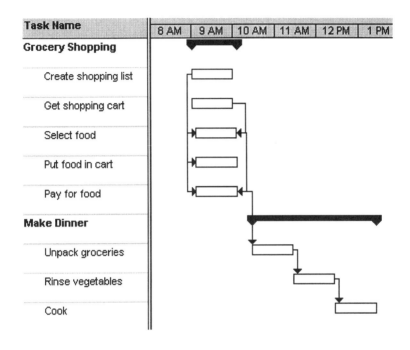

Figure 3-4 Party Gantt D

First, there are two types of duration, elapsed and effort. You experience this on a regular basis in terms of "hours" versus "man-hours." Hopefully, this explanation will make the concept simple: Elapsed duration, measured in hours, will remain constant no matter how many people you add to the task, an example being making a two-minute hard-boiled egg. Effort duration, measured in man-hours, will change as a result of the resources brought to bear on it, such as painting a house. Therefore, you need to ascertain what type of effort the task requires. A task can not require both! If you feel that it does (painting a house, one hundred man-hours plus twenty-four hours drying time), then you need to split the conflicting events into multiple tasks.

Next: judging the actual duration. The best person to ask is someone who has done that type of work before. It also helps to know the work habits of the person who will be doing the work. If the person who will be doing the work has never done it before, I take their opinion and multiply it by .25. I then take the opinion of the person who has done that type of work before and multiply it by .75. I then add the two together. If the person doing the work is the only one available for the estimate, and they've never done that type of work before, I multiply their estimate by 1.5. You will also want to take note of any reputation the person might have for overestimating or underestimating their estimates. If they typically overestimate, I'd leave the estimate alone unless there is some reason to feel that they'll be motivated to complete the work in a more reasonable time. If they typically underestimate, multiply it by whatever factor seems reasonable. What we're doing here is adding realism into the estimate, not padding. We'll discuss more realism later, as well as some examples of what we just covered.

Now that you have a effort estimate for the task, you need to account for additional factors: the number of people assigned to the task, their productive time, and their availability.

In the context of these considerations we're talking about effort duration. It makes no sense to assign someone to a task that is of an elapsed duration, because by definition that person can't do anything about getting the task done (the 'doing' should be one task, the waiting (elapsed time) should be another). So if we're talking about effort, the number of people assigned to the effort will affect the duration but not the effort. That is, if the effort required is five man-hours, and you put two people on the task, the effort will still be five man-hours, but the duration of the task could very well be two and one-half hours.

Optimally, if the task requires two man-hours, then assigning two people to it will reduce it to one man-hour, but that is never the case. First of all, there is overhead in having a number of people, two or more, work together. Also, they don't necessarily produce identical effort. Here also the final factors come into play: productive time and availability. If your resource gets a cup of coffee four times during the workday, and talks to people on the way to and from the coffee pot, they'll have less productivity than someone who works heads down. In addition, the resource might have other responsibilities and can only devote a percentage of their time to this project. So how do you derive a duration from these factors? Here, have a formula[1].

Duration=W/(N*(1-NP)*(A*.75))

where:W = workload
N = number of people
NP = nonproductive time (percentage)
A = available time (percentage)

so in the case of one person working on a task, where that person states that they're available 50percent of the time, and we're going to assume that 30percent of the day is nonproductive, we see the following for a task that is estimated as requiring one man-day of effort:

Duration=1/(1*(1-.3)*(.5*.75))

which results in a duration of 3.8 man-days. Duration is a very important concept — remember, a day is not always a day. In fact, be very careful using 'day' as a measurement with project management software. If a task requires eight man-hours, and you define it as one man-day, you need to understand the definition of a 'work day.' It obviously isn't twenty-four hours in your mind, it's eight, but what if the work day is lengthened to nine hours — if you've defined the task as 'one day,' then it will now require nine hours to complete in the schedule. It's also worth noting that on average you only get six productive hours out of an eight-hour day from a resource. When I set the working hours on the calendar in my projects, I set them from 8:00 a.m to 3:00 p.m. to account for this.

---

1.   Derived. Miller, Dennis. Visual Project Planning & Scheduling. Copyright (1994 The 15th Street Press, Inc. Boca Raton, Florida. p81.

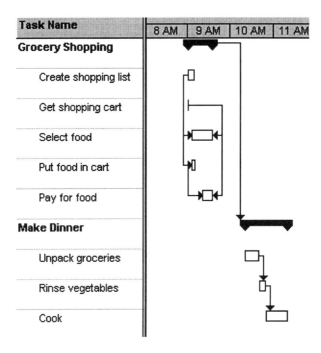

Figure 3-5 Party Gantt E

The shopping/cooking chart modified to account for duration is shown in Figure 3-5.

Are there points at which this task relies on other events in order to proceed?

We've seen various types of dependencies, and you'll notice that they all are some combination of start and/or finish. There is not a dependency type of 'some point-to-some point'. So what do you do if right in the middle of a task something is needed to proceed? Simply set up the dependency so that Task B starts at some point during Task A with a start-to-start dependency and lag time, right?

Well, no, not quite. For example, let's say we're mixing a certain type of epoxy. Chemical A needs to be mixed for twenty minutes, with Chemical B being added to it after the first fifteen minutes of mixing. A dependency could be set up to say that fifteen minutes after the mixing begins (task 1), Chemical B should be added (task 2). What that does is make certain Chemical B is added, and not until fifteen minutes has passed. What it doesn't do is create a dependency that task 1 can not end until task 2 has; as far as task 1 is concerned, it occurs for twenty minutes and then ends, no matter the status of task 2. Well, can we set an additional dependency of task 2 finish-to-finish with task 1 so that task 1 can't end until task 2 does?

It might make this circumstance easier to deal with, but would complicate project plans unacceptably if two tasks could have multiple dependencies; therefore, it's not done. The solution, though somewhat more work, is to break the stirring up into two tasks (task 1 and task 3), with task 1 having a finish-to-start relationship with task 2, and task 2 having a finish-to-start relationship with task 3.

- Does the completion of this task result in a deliverable?
- Does a subsequent task depend on this task's beginning or ending?
- Whose effort is required, and what is their availability?

At this point, we've haven't identified the client team, so tasks requiring client resources will have those resources entered as a generic 'Client.' Once the actual resources are entered, some tasks will start moving to the right on the time line due to the resource's unavailability.

The way we deal with availability in a plan is by using resource calendars. I'd strongly advise against project planning software that doesn't support resource calendars. The reason becomes apparent when you try to have the software handle an instance of someone being on vacation.

If the software only supports a master calendar that controls all resources (with regards to workdays, hours of operation, holidays, etc.), then having someone become unavailable for a particular period of time (instead of a percentage of time over the entire length of the project, like 75 percent available) isn't possible unless you set an absolute start date subsequent to the vacation for the task. Then, however, if earlier tasks finish sooner than expected, if any of that resource's tasks could occur prior to the vacation, they won't show up on the time line that way because the start date will still have an absolute setting.

With resource calendars you can simply change the vacation days on that resource's calendar to nonworking days and then any tasks that would fall during that period will be moved automatically.

Moving on to another subject, consideration needs to be given to who the appropriate resources are. In some cases the decision is a 'no-brainer,' but with others it might make sense for more than one person to work on the task. In our current context of infrastructure development and deployment planning, the focus of our group, there are investigations where the questionee has answers needed by more than one person. If access to the questionee is limited, it could be worthwhile to put the questioners together so that only one interview session needs to be scheduled. Also, many points of data will be required by more than one person.

For example, a data flow model will be required for the capacity planning, network capacity planning, high-availability, and backup/re-covery considerations. There might be a 75 percent overlap of data need on the subject, and then information specific to each focus above that, so each of those resources might want to be present for the data gathering. Typically, there is limited access to the client's resources, and they are almost always the holders of the needed information. Sometimes the resources are hostile (not the shooting you with a blowgun type of hostile, but the hostile witness kind). You should totally avoid sending them more than one person with the same questions. There is a method for doing this, and Daniel discusses this with his team.

The optimal way to gather data is to put the people who need the data together as a group and send them for it. The next best way is to have the group draw up a list of questions and send whoever has the opening on their calendar that matches the client's. The reason the second method is not as satisfactory as the first is that the answers to questions will typically lead to a tangential line of further questions that were not on the list. If the networking person is doing the questioning and one of the answers would normally lead to a tangential line of questions on recovery, the network person will probably miss that need and opportunity completely; it's not their specialty. Therefore the second method typically will require a scrutinizing of the answers by the interested parties, followed by more questioning. It would be prudent to arrange the follow-up session in advance as well, because calendars fill up quickly and you don't want to have to wait for a long period of time to gather the data. Another method is the tag-team approach. The interviews are scheduled during a morning or afternoon or over a period of a few days. Each team member getting a shot at the data holder. After one interview, the questions and answers are reviewed by the next interviewer. Questions that have already been answered will not be asked again, but the answer might be mentioned as a segue into a tangential line of questioning.

For example, if the high-availability person is told that availability will be restrained by the network availability, when the network person does the questioning later on they might say, "You mentioned earlier that the network might restrain availability, can you tell me which portion(s) of the network tend to problematic?"

Daniel's intent in covering this material is to have the team understand their co-dependency on much of the data, so that they begin working as a team in obtaining it, and so the act of obtaining it can be accounted for on the project plan with the appropriate resources identified. That's all well and good, but how does Daniel go about determining who the resources are and what data is required?

One of the tools used in planning is a RACI (Responsible, Accountable, Consulted, Informed) chart (see Figure 3-6). The look of the chart can vary, but basically it's a spreadsheet with the input to and output of tasks down one side, and the resources, team, and client across the top. In each intersecting cell one of the letters (RACI) might be placed to indicate whether that resource has any connection to the data item. The legend for the entries is as follows:

(R)esponsible (A)ccountable (C)onsulted (I)nformed

Item	Cap Plan	High Avail	Bac/Rec	NSM	DRP	Ops Plan	App Dev	IT	Support	User Req
Logical Data Model	I	I					R			
Physical Data Model	I	I	I				R			
App Architecture	I	I		I			R			
Data Distrib. Model	I	I	I	I			R			
Data Flows	I	I		I			R			
Service Level Agreements	I	I		I					R	
SLAs - batch jobs	I	I		I					R	
SLAs - response times	I	I		I					R	
SLAs - volumes	I	I		I					R	
Legacy apps & availability	I	I	I	I				C		
Legacy recovery	I	I	I	I			R			
Network availability	I			I				C		
H.A. requirements	I	R	C	I	I	I		I	I	
Bac/Rec requirements	I		R	I	I	I		I	I	
Ops Planning requirements	I	C	C		I	R				
NSM requirements		I	I	R	I	I	I	I		
CapPlan requirements	R	I					I			
Business Impact issues	I	I		I	I	I	I		C	
Hardware Configuration	R	R	R	I				I		
Logging Requirements			R	I			I	I	C	
Transaction backout			R				I	I	I	
Environment config req's		C	C	C		C		I		
Legacy function map		I			I					C
NSM event detection	I		I	R	I	I				

Figure 3-6 RACI Diagram

- Responsible — The resource is responsible for the item, such as creating a report, defining requirements, etc. This would be the person(s) entered on the project plan as owning the task.
- Accountable — Not the person doing the work, but accountable for it or its results. This would typically be a management type who needs to buy in to the assumptions that the item will be based on, the item itself, or both.
- Consulted — Someone who has information that will allow this item to be begun or completed; the people who will be interviewed for data.
- Informed — A benefactor of the task, someone who needs the data (sometimes unbeknownst to them). The Responsible

party in a task will typically be listed as a Consulted party on the line where the task is used as input.

Creating the RACI chart will cause the team to consider the following:

- What data is needed in order to produce recommendations for the next phase?
- Where will the data come from?
- Who needs the data?
- Who will gather the data?
- Who will the data impact?

The development of these questions and their answers for each data item will become the next layer of the project plan, and allow Daniel to identify availability requirements of the client's resources, as well as formulating dependencies between each task; an order of data development with, hopefully, natural progressions toward defining the requirements for each focus.

The RACI chart will also provide an outline from which the team can start formulating their questions for the interviews. You don't want a scenario where they walk into the interviews and shoot from the hip. There's a chance they might be good at it, but more of a chance that it will be a waste of time, particularly for the interviewee, and might be the last chance to meet with that person.

The project manager should review the question list. There could be questions that reveal themselves as emanating from an out-of-scope basis, or you might see a logical follow-up that could stem from the answer that isn't accounted for. You might also notice that questions needed to be asked aren't present. True, you aren't a Subject Matter Expert (SME), but you probably have your arms around the ultimate intent of the project more so than the team at this point, so you might see an absence of detail (in the way of questions), the answers to which would lead to the big picture. Make sure you posture your interest in the questions that way with the team, otherwise they might assume that your faith in their competency is less than sterling.

Let's take a look at a RACI chart for the team, and then we'll work on promoting it to a Gantt chart.

As you can see in the RACI chart in Figure 3-6, the Accountable personnel haven't been entered. At a high-enough level the management is accountable for everything going on, but they haven't exposure to the details and thus are not the best resources for evaluating the data.

Moving from the RACI chart to the Gantt chart is a matter of identifying tasks versus data. Tasks involve some expenditure of effort, obtaining data usually does not, but can still be a task. Receiving a document from someone can be a task, even if only fifteen minutes in duration. It might seem that it's not worth including an item such as that in the plan, but there is the possibility that the data item, or lack of it, will become a stumbling block.

It's easier, and more graphic, for the offending task to be identified as the data item on the plan not having been received than as the subsequent task not having been completed. This is another example of where summary tasks come in handy. You can create a summary task for, let's say, a document that needs to be created. The obtaining of the data to be used in the document, the internalizing of that data, the development, production, review and editing of the document can all be tasks under the summary umbrella. That way it will be easier to visualize the overall status of the document, and to see which task, if any, is preventing the preparation of the document from moving forward.

Now we'll turn the RACI chart into a Gantt chart. This will give us a preliminary view of dependencies and the time required for the investigation – a check against the time that's been budgeted.

The screen-shot in Figure 3-7 is from Microsoft Project®. You can see a number of summary task items indicated by the long rectangles pointing down at each end. They show the beginning and end of the tasks contained within them based on their duration, dependencies, and resources. You'll notice that the ID numbers of each of these summary tasks is several more than the one before it. This indicates that there are a number of subordinate tasks (and perhaps lower-level summary tasks)

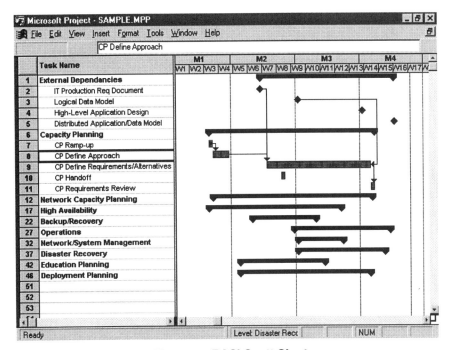

Figure 3-7 RACI Gantt Chart

that are not shown. For purposes of discussion, two of these summary tasks have been 'exploded.'

The first task shown is entitled 'External Dependencies' and is comprised of data items, represented as tasks, resulting from the RACI chart. Lumping together the data items that are required by, but not produced by the project team is one way of easing the dependency list and management of that part of the project.

If you were to look at any of those items in detail, you would see information similar to that for the first detailed task (second overall task) shown.

TIP ☞   When deciding how to group tasks
within a plan, put them where you'll
easily find them later

This task is assigned to the client's Operations group. They are the one from whom the document, one that shows what is required for a new application to be taken into production, will be obtained. The duration type is 'Fixed' because we know that the document exists and handing it over should not have to be an effort-driven event. The duration is zero days because this item is defined as a milestone, an event that marks a notable point of the project being reached. The fact that the task is a milestone is also shown on the Gantt chart by its being a diamond instead of a task bar. Some of these external documents are not linked to subsequent tasks at this point, as can be seen by an absence of dependency lines leading from the milestones, but will be once the plan is finished or will be removed as being unnecessary items.

The Capacity Planning activity is also exploded. You can see that each subordinate task's title begins with CP. This is a little trick to make life easier when printing reports. Often, reports printed from Project Management software list tasks that have something in common other than the summary task to which they belong, such as the resource assigned, the start date, the fact that they're running late, and so on. If the tasks were not labeled with CP, it might be more difficult to identify what task is actually being referenced because, for example, the High-availability resource also has a 'Ramp up' task, so seeing 'Ramp up' on a report might leave you scratching your head as to which of eight similar tasks was being referenced.

If we look at one of the Capacity Planning tasks in detail we can get a better idea of the dependencies that are shown by the arrows leading to it on the Gantt chart.

The 'CP Define Requirements' task created in Figure 3-8 is shown in Figure 3-9 being dependent on three other tasks. Task 2, which we discussed earlier, must finish prior to this task beginning, as must Task 8.

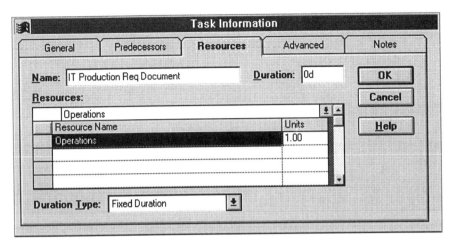

Figure 3-8 Project Task

This means that those two pieces of documentation are needed for work on this task to commence. The third dependency is a finish-to-finish dependency with lag time. What it means, in effect, is that no matter how far along this task gets, there are five man-days of work that will have to occur before it can end, and those five days of work can not begin until receipt of the Logical Data Model; hence, this task can not finish until five days after receiving that documentation.

Hopefully you have a good idea about the content and benefits of the internal kickoff meeting now. Let's leave Daniel and the team to finish their meeting (and don't forget the team dinner), and we'll catch up with them at the client site for the project team interviews.

3.2 THE PROJECT TEAM INTERVIEWS

There are a number of reasons why client personnel would want to be part of a project such as this, but there are also a number of reasons why they would not want to be part of a project such as this. You can't have (and don't want to have) everyone on the team. If you're lucky enough to have the client let you select the team members, you'll want to have some method of determining who will give you the best chance of succeeding, and hopefully they're among the ones who would want to be on the team. Here is some insight, beginning with a list of motivating or demotivating factors for potential team members.

The following list presents some of the factors that would lead people to seek inclusion as a project team member, or to avoid such inclusion. There are two additional columns, one that indicates the rationale as being a 'plus,' the other indicating the rationale is a '-.' You'll notice that both columns have entries in every case. This is because staffing the project with that person based on each of the rationale could be a benefit or detriment, it depends.

Mostly, the deciding factor is a combination of the person's skill as compared to the project requirements, and the politics they bring to the table. Using an example from the table, a resource might not want to join the project because the project represents new technology, being a part of the project (in this person's position) would require that they 'cross the technology' bridge to the other side. They might not be comfortable with the technology's future as a whole, or the technology's future in the company, or with their ability to make the change. They might feel that they'd be moving from a senior position (twenty years as a systems programmer on mainframes) to a relatively junior position on new technology.

The first thing I would do is make a short list of possibilities, definite yes' and definite no's, but if almost any rationale could swing either way, how do you make the list? Well, a good place to begin is knowing what type of resources you'll need. Following is a list of typical resource requirements on this type of project; you'll need people with a thorough understanding of the following areas (DS signifies Deployment Site (operations centers, in the context of this book) and SS signifies Server Site):

- Facilities (DS, SS)
- Site networking (DS, SS)

- Site IT (DS, SS)
- Site business operations (DS)
- Site security policies(DS, SS)
- IT staff education (SS, DS if applicable)
- User education (DS)
- Purchasing
- Application development
- Application testing

Rationale for (not) being part of the project	+	-
To impress manager or another manager	+	-
Feels project will bring recognition	+	-
Wants to retool to new technology	+	-
Doesn't want to retool to new technology	+	-
Something different/challenging/exciting	+	-
Job depends on it	+	-
Asked by manager - no clear project benefit	+	-
Job function ties directly to project	+	-
Unknown reason for wanting to be included	+	-
Unknown reason for not wanting to be included	+	-

Table 3-5 Resource Rationale

We'll discuss later why these and other people will be important to the project, for now just ride along with me. If there is only one resource available to you in one of these categories, such as purchasing, they become a 'definite.' If a Site IT person is already versed in the new technology, all other considerations (reputation for delivering on commitments, ability to work with others, etc.) being equal, they would go on the list too. An appointee of senior management is, naturally, a 'definite,' but keep a close eye on them, because there is a chance that their other qualities would have put them on the 'definitely not' list.

So speaking of 'definitely nots', what puts someone on that list? Someone who is overly negative might be someone you want to miss. They might know what they're doing, but you don't want them bringing down the morale of the team.

On the flip side, someone who is overly positive might not be a good idea either, they can be overly anxious to get on the project but not have much to offer. Someone with a longstanding reputation of not coming through on commitments is probably someone you don't want to use if you have another choice. There is the chance that keeping a tight rein on them will help assure delivery, but that's something that will take time that you will probably need for other matters. The middle road, 'possibility', takes in just about everyone else, but there are other considerations, such as politics.

Politics can play a very important role in who can benefit the project, and who can hurt it. Certainly, resources from departments that have much to gain will be motivated to have the project succeed, and will therefore do their utmost to be an asset. But hurt it? Yup. There's always the possibility that someone will accidentally do harm to the project, but I'm referring to premeditated damage — sabotage. If you're reticent to believe that someone would be provided to the project and actually sabotage it, I have a bridge for sale.

What could cause a person or persons to want to sabotage a project? The possibilities are too numerous to cover in depth, but I'll give you a few examples.

Client-server technology is, by its nature, not centralized, whereas mainframe technology typically is. Very often mainframe technology has been in place for many years within a company, and the organization that owns it has developed a power base. A client-server enterprise is a large technology base in itself. Sometimes the new technology ends up being managed by a separate IT organization, and the manager that owned the mainframe technology, which represented all of the technology, now manages the 'legacy technology'; a diluting of the power base that can leave that senior manager with not just part of an organization, but what might be looked at as the less important portion. Sometimes it happens just that quickly, and just that black-and-white. Sometimes there is a long, nasty power struggle. In either event, there are occasions where the 'legacy' manager feels that the way back to the top is to damage the credibility of the new manager. What better way to do that then to assure the project meant to justify the new technology fails? And what better way to do that, assuming the premise of the project is good to begin with, than to stack the deck against it?

It might sound like a plot out of 'Dynasty', but television writers didn't invent politics. These things happen. I've seen it happen, but more often I've simply seen the old manager welcome the project with less than open arms, and could see that his staff did what staff do – they looked out for their boss.

If you're not adept at reading politics, and you're an external consultant, use your sales representative to help you read them. Figure out who stands to lose, or might feel that they stand to lose, if the project is successful, then look carefully at any of their staff presented as team members.

For most people the new technology will be a paradigm shift. Many will have no background in this technology. For people like operators and programmers, this will mean a retooling, especially if, like in many cases, application development on the mainframe will cease. For example, a MVS COBOL programmer in most cases will not find a large call for COBOL programming on the new technology. Switching from MVS and COBOL to UNIX and C++ is not a minor move. If the person is not educated correctly, they could end up 'writing C++ programs in COBOL', that is, using COBOL-style logic to write the applications.

Not everyone will make that transition, and not everyone might need to if development will continue on the legacy equipment. However, who will make the change? Who will sign up for, in effect, learning to speak another language like a native? Is it that difficult? Let's take an analogy.

When someone begins to learn Japanese, they naturally have to learn another alphabet (for those of you who know Japanese, I'm referring to Hiragana). Assuming they've done that, they then begin to learn words. Having learned words and how to conjugate some verbs, many people then head for the dictionary and try to write someone a letter. The problem is, there is no direct word-for-word translation possible. The sentence structure is completely different. Where we say "I'll go to the store with you in a moment", how would that be said in Japanese (using English words)? Firstly, the Japanese put their sentence particles in order of importance to the sentence, so they would say "in a moment with you to the store I will go." Yet the Japanese have no future tense, so it becomes "in a moment with you to the store I go." Oh yes, the Japanese typically avoid the use of pronouns; they are implied. So now we have "in a moment to the store go." Ah, and if you directly translate the phrase 'in a moment,' it has no similarity to anything meaning 'soon,' so we need to say, "soon to the store go." Lastly, they might not use the verb 'go' when speaking of going to a store, after all, we have 'set' verb-noun pairs, such as 'slop the pig.'

So now this person understands these rules – but how do they do translating on the fly, throwing sentences with the correct structure and words out one after another? There's as much similarity between CO-BOL and C++ as there is between Japanese and English, except of course the alphabet is the same. So yes, it's a very long and steep learning curve, and that's just language and syntactical differences without any thought of the mindset change moving from procedure-based code to objects.

Who will make that change? Is there a profile of the likely candidate? Perhaps, but I've never seen one, nor can I deduce one, from the people I've seen take either side of the challenge. It might seem that age is a likely factor, that someone who's been coding in COBOL for twenty years would be unlikely to make the change. Not always. I've seen people five years from retirement take the plunge. Sure, as a percentage it's likely that an older age group would have less 'converts,' but you don't know which part of the percentage you're dealing with. Simply put, someone who is excited by new technology, new opportunities, and perhaps the chance to get out of a rut, will be a likely candidate, and a good candidate as long as they have the talent and it can be of use to you in the time frame you have.

The next question is who will be allowed to make the change coincidental with your project? Why is that a consideration? Because the client has an existing environment that needs to be maintained. That maintenance will continue throughout your project and beyond. The hard fact is that many of the people who would be ideal candidates for the initial 'jump' will be held back because they are critical to the success of the current environment, people like system programmers and networking gurus. They might be allowed to 'get their feet wet,' but will probably not be available to you to the extent that you'll need the warm body. You also need to consider that many of that type of resource might be needed by you in their current role, to support your efforts to connect to and coexist with the current environment. If they were to 'jump ship,' would the person filling in for them be able to provide you with the expertise you need? I'm not referring to their not having the technical knowledge, but would their expertise be that great that they could give you the bandwidth you need and still meet their normal commitments?

What I've alluded to is that you might need to avoid taking on some people in order to protect the project's success. That could of course cause hard feelings. The best of both worlds in that case would be if there were a second person who could fill in for the first in the current environment, and that the person making the jump could spare some bandwidth in their ex-expertise to fill in the extra bandwidth that their replacement needs but doesn't have.

This need to keep the current environment running could also result in the client only offering up 'second-string' candidates, either out of necessity or because it seems the safest thing to do. Of course, they run the risk of irreparably de-motivating the staff left behind. They might be the 'big *kahunas*' on the old environment, but if they feel that the future is with the new environment and have been passed over, they might consider their career options to be anywhere but on a sinking ship.

As to the selection in general, my best advice is to proceed like you're hiring the person to work for you, but assume that you can't go look for other candidates beyond the ones you are given. After finishing this book you'll have a better idea of each person's role, and thus how much they'll mean to you. There are a lot of people out there not fit for their jobs, and I have to assume that in most cases their manager didn't hire them with that knowledge, so if you do end up with a few people who don't represent the best choice, you're human.

Now what about the organizations represented? Again, we have to look at politics. What I'm about to say is typical, but by no means the rule, so please don't write to me to tell me that your organization is different – I believe you!

I've seen many projects where the impetus behind the project is activity by the application development group, and as a result, they end up being the initial staff as well as the selectors of the initial project team. I've also seen that the application development organization and IT don't always share a wonderful relationship, and as a result very often the team is lacking in IT resources, although they are often fundamental to the deployment being logistically successful. If you find this to be the case, you need to gather your list of staffing requirements (in terms of functional responsibility) and lobby where the two organization charts come together. Don't try to do it without them, and don't feel that you can wait until after the project begins – everyone has an ego, and you don't want to try to win over a department whose collective ego has been bruised.

3.3 SETTING UP SHOP

Moving a project team into its new environment can be a perplexing event. Hopefully, the negotiation on assumptions that took place up front has paid off, but don't leave it to chance. Visit the site alone a week in advance and see if they're ready for you (same goes for your own site if you will have some folks working out of your office):

- Does each person have a work area ready for use?
- Are there keys for the desk and filing cabinets? (typically there are not, but you should be able to have someone order a key by giving them the numbers off the lock)

- Have the phones which will be used been added to the extension list?
- Are there forms to be completed before voice mail and e-mail can be set up for each person?
- Is there a form that needs to be completed to obtain a security badge or card?
- Does the work area have a company phone book?
- Are the required number of workstations present, are they loaded with the correct software, and are they configured to provide access to the network?
- Is there an area from which confidential phone calls can be made?
- Is there a conference area you can use which will actually be available?
- Can the phones dial out? Dial long distance?
- Is there a modem line available (to dial into your company's network)?
- Is there dial-in access to the network from outside (if you will be doing any work back at your office)
- Are there sufficient electrical strips?
- How do you send and receive mail?
- Can the customer receive Internet mail with attachments?
- Is there access to the Internet? Is it through a firewall?
- Can your team be given a mail bin?
- Where can you make limited and bulk copies?
- Is there background documentation you can have waiting for your team?
- Do you have administrative support?

These might seem like trivial things in the overall scheme of things, but you can waste several days, even weeks, if you wait to discover that these items have not been accounted for.

My main objective is to always make it easy for client resources to contact me. I want to become part of their organization, and I can't do that if they have to call my office to leave a message even though I'm located on the same floor as them, or if they can't copy me on an e-mail message. Expecting everyone to go out of their way to include you in communications is not feasible.

If an e-mail or voice-mail message is being sent to multiple recipients, you might be included if they can just add you to the list, but if they need to fax you a message because you're not on e-mail (or because you or they don't have Internet e-mail access) or they have to send an additional voice-mail because it needs to be left in your box back at your office, you'll find that you're not being included. Similarly, if you have a mail slot or bin that they can drop a copy in, you might find yourself being added to distribution lists.

Access to their network is also important if you're expected to provide things like status reports electronically. If you don't have access to the network, and to the software they use to create messages, you're going to be doing extra work at a point where you don't have extra time. Do not depend on the import/export features of the word processor software (Word, WordPerfect, AmiPro⁽). I can practically guarantee you that if you create a formatted message or document in one of these because it's the software you have, and export to the client's software (or have the client import the document), the results will not be satisfactory. The same holds true very often when going from one spreadsheet to another. One reason is that they don't seem to put a lot of effort into the import/export filters, and the second is that the filters always seem to be for the previous version of the 'other' software, not the version you're using.

One approach that does seem to work with documents is to save the document as .RTF (Rich Text Format). The latest versions of each of the big three seem to handle importing/exporting that well, but be warned, RTF files are usually twice as large as the original, and as you'll want to keep the original file as well (for subsequent editing) you'll be using 3 Mb for a 1 Mb document. Also, RTF isn't the format to use for embedded illustrations or objects.

3.4 CLIENT KICKOFF

Well, the project is ready to officially begin, so it's time to roll out the carpet and start the band playing! All right, that might be a push, but only just.

The main reason for having a kickoff meeting is to instill in the participants a feeling of belonging. Luckily, the desire to belong is human nature, so long as the group doesn't represent something distasteful to the individual (and sometimes despite that). Because of that, the challenge is lessened; use the meeting to build on the participants' natural impulses.

The other reason for having a kickoff, of course, is to disseminate reason behind the project, the direction it will take, and to get everyone working off the same page, because it's easier to do it right the first time than trying to fix it later.

So where do we start? How do we put together a kickoff meeting? The first consideration you must give is a location. Are all the players located in the same geography? If not, they need to be flown in or attend via a video link. Make sure that this is feasible. Everyone who will be on the project team should be in attendance, either physically or technologically. Once the number of participants is determined, a conference room large enough to hold everyone has to be arranged, and a date set. Asking everyone to select a good date is logistically unfeasible, so only ask the senior participants to do it. That brings us to the next consideration, the senior participants.

Of utmost importance is a call to arms. The clear, concise message in the call must be the driving business need for the project, and thus the impact of the project's success or failure upon the business. The most appropriate person to make this speech is the person ultimately responsible for the project, typically the CIO. One proviso here is that this person should also be a 'solid-line' manager to all the people in the room, so that they take the message with more than a grain of salt. If not, then it would be appropriate to have the person where the lines of the organization chart come together provide a quick 'this project means a lot to me' message and then hand off to the responsible manager and leave. The remainder of the meeting will require the participants feeling they can offer up their comfort or discomfort, and the latter will not be unveiled if they feel intimidated. You can't expect people to wave their hand in the air to signify their lack of buy-in or lack of understanding with the 'head honcho' in the audience, the equivalent of saying, "Hi boss, yes, over here, me, I think it's a dumb idea."

In the cast of MCT, the initial message should come from Joan Thewad, with the major delivery coming from Daphne Hutago. The idea is that the staff needs to be motivated and have a clear understanding that their cooperation has been committed to by their ultimate manager. There should be no gray areas with regards to the marching orders.

People respond well to pageantry and fanfare. If you can't arrange for a brigade of mounted Highlanders and a drum & bugle corps, at least make it festive with balloons, badges, and food! This project is a positive event, and if its importance was not evident to the team at the start of the meeting, it should be before you get to the business part of the meeting thirty minutes to an hour later.

While the presentations are taking place you have a job to do, and that is to watch the body language of the attendees. You may not be an expert at it, but if you see arms folded across the chest, smirks, hard stares, and so on, then you may very well be looking at someone who has a problem with the person presenting, or that is skeptical about the need for or potential success of the project. Store this information away for now.

So now it's your turn. What are you going to do? Again, this meeting should be upbeat, so now is not the time to bog it down. Save the real work for another day. This would be a great time to introduce yourself and give some short background information. If the project team is small enough for everyone to introduce themselves then do so, otherwise I'd avoid introducing your team, as you don't want the rest of the project team to feel like you're setting your people off as being more important.

After the introductions it's time to lay out the big picture, and a picture it should be. I would use either a PC with a screen projection device or a 35mm presentation, this is too big an event to be flipping transparencies.

For a group of people to start forming into a team they need some form of shared vision. The first step in developing that vision is to have a mission statement and objectives. The group received a description of the business issue, now solicit the development of a mission statement and objectives. With those in hand, a little rewording will lead you to the scope. Show the scope of the project. Don't assume that everyone knows what it is, or that those that think they do actually have a clear understanding. Try to instill not only a sense of what the project scope is, but what the scope means in terms of logistics, at a high level. This will get the people who know how the business runs thinking about the obstacles that will need to be overcome in order to be successful.

Next, you should present a time-line. Now let's keep in mind that at this point we're starting Phase 1, the investigation, so the time line is going to be vague at best, but most likely we know when Phase 1 should end, and when Phase 3 needs to. The other dates can be filled in between as a best guess, and be honest about it being a best guess at this point, indicating that the initial effort will be to replace the guess with a detailed plan.

I like to enlist participation early, and there's a convenient method to do that at this point. We have a need to begin a project newsletter. If the client platform was already rolled out to the users, the newsletter could be in an electronic format, but for now it will need to be hardcopy, and it will need a name. Most people enjoy positive recognition, and an easy way to provide it is by having a contest to pick the name of the newsletter. Give them a week and then you and your client counterpart pick a winner. Omit your team from the contest to avoid the embarrassment of one of them winning. You should also sign up a 'reporter' or two so that you don't have to provide all the content for the newsletter. You can decide the publishing frequency (weekly, biweekly, etc.) based on what makes sense in your circumstances. The 'Big Three' of word processing software all provide newsletter templates that you can use.

The last thing to cover in your kickoff meeting is the project organization and the next meetings that need to take place. Once this is done you can turn everyone loose to mingle, chat, and eat. You had a great meeting.

Next, we'll be moving through Phase 1, investigating the issues facing deployment, taking a closer look at what the application development team needs to develop, and the effect the development and the infrastructure have on each other.

Chapter 4

Investigation. That's what Phase 1 is all about. We need to publish an approach, investigate the requirements, begin the software development cycle, and produce recommendations that will lead us to the deployment phase.

4.1 THE APPROACH DOCUMENT

The approach document is one of those rare encounters in a project, yet much of the headache and rework of a development project (software, hardware, procedural, infrastructure, and so on) could be avoided were this document to be part of the methodology employed.

Simply put, the approach document describes for the reader the approach to the development of the solution; not how the solution will actually be developed, but how the data needed to define the solution will be gathered. If you consider the statement of the need as Point A, and the solution as Point B, the approach defines the path to be taken from one to the other.

The idea is to publish the approach document so that the intended path from Point A to Point B can be scrutinized by the people who have more insight than you (or those that have perhaps less insight than you but whose acceptance will be required) before you do the work. That way if there's a flaw in your assumptions or in the data upon which you'll proceed, corrections can be made early on, while time and money are still on your side.

A failed project is never fun, but the worst reason to have one is because what was delivered doesn't match what was required. When that happens, all the struggle to plan and execute properly, to manage tasks and resources, to ensure that all the pieces fit together, all of that is for naught because the original premise was incorrect. Receiving feedback isn't a guarantee that that won't happen, but the absence of feedback makes it virtually inevitable. The approach document is a feedback mechanism. It doesn't provide feedback, but it implicitly solicits it. You'll probably find that the client will be caught off guard when presented with this document. Being told in advance what the solution will be based on and where that information will come from will certainly be a surprise, and as such will draw the readers' attention, and attentive readers will quickly ascertain whether the approach matches their mindset.

The role of the project manager during the generation of the approach documents is firstly to facilitate the availability of the informational resources necessary for the project team to determine their approach. The resources can be people, internal to the client or external, or documentation. Some resources might not be client employees. They could be contractors or vendors of the client. It could save you an inordinate amount of time if you have the client 'pave the way' for you with a conversation so that cooperation is forthcoming, especially if the resource is a political opponent of the project or a contractor that is a competitor.

You as project manager also need to keep your team members focused on the task at hand. The approach document is meant to represent a certain level of abstraction, otherwise you would just be documenting the progression of the project until it is completed. Just as code development offers the enticement of creeping elegance, so does the development of an approach document offer its writer the lure of drilling down and getting lost in the details. You want the effort to be like a Steven Segal plot — get in, apprise the situation, strike quickly, and get out. Of course, in this situation, you're hoping for the 'get out' to be getting out of the approach and proceeding.

Your role also is to plan and facilitate the investigation, and assure the quality of the deliverables in terms of direction and content. You will also want to assure the deliverables have a consistent format and flow. If you have six approach documents coming out of the team (or one with six chapters), you want each to read like the next, like encyclopedia volumes.

This is a period for your team to get their feet wet, to test the waters. Since the purpose of the document is to validate that their approach is on-course, you don't want the document development itself to go off-course. Daily reviews of progress are very important. If your team member is having trouble getting time from resources, or simply isn't assertive enough to obtain the time, you want to resolve this quickly as well as make determinations of any potential issues with resources or team members now instead of later.

Let's take each section and look more closely at the intention. You can assume in this discussion that each of the separate approach discussions can be in their own document or be chapters of one overall document.

1. Description of the subject

What is this document and what is its purpose? What are you expecting from the reviewer? (answer: A validation of the approach) What is the issue to be addressed by the topic being approached? How does the topic fit into the larger picture?

2. Anticipated data requirements

What type(s) of data will be required? What is the anticipated duration of the acquisition (with the explicit assumption that the source(s) will be readily available)?

3. Anticipated data source(s)

From where, and if known, whom will the data be collected? How much of their time will you need? What has led you to believe they hold the data you need (so that the correct person can be provided should this person not be)?

4. Data evaluation methodology

What are you going to do with the data? Assume that the reader knows very little about the topic. Assume that there will be a change of project sponsor during the course of the project and that this will serve as documentation. How are you going to quantify, sort, categorize, and manipulate the data you've collected? To what end? Picture yourself going to the accountant. You drop off your W2 form and a box of receipts (the data), and eventually receive a tax return as a result. How did the accountant go from the data to the recommendation (the particular tax form(s) and deduction(s) being the recommendation)? If you're not familiar with accounting and tax returns then you probably don't know. You might think that you don't care, but if millions of dollars are riding on the result, as well as your future, you ought to.

The client might not understand precisely what your team will be doing in generating the requirements to meet the business need — but they ought to. If the methods you use, and the assumptions you make, to take the raw data and generate requirements and recommendations are inaccurate, the project, the client, and you will in all probability fail, and fail miserably. So you need to make certain that there is a clear description of what within the collected data will be meaningful to you, why it is meaningful, and how you will massage it from one side of the equal sign to the other.

TIP ☞   Read Douglas Adams' Hitchhiker's
              Guide to the Galaxy, then under-
              stand the Approach Document's
              function is to 'CYA' when the an-
              swer really turns out to be 43 and
              you don't have a towel to put over
              your head.

5. Mapping data to requirements

How will you determine the requirements from the data? Sometimes data points in an obvious way to an answer that can be incorrect. If I have six ounces of one solution and six ounces of another, how large of a container do I need in order to combine them? Well, depending on the density of each solution or their chemical reaction, I might need a container that is smaller than twelve ounces (try water and alcohol). The reader may draw some conclusion from what they read, or perhaps retain the preconception they had prior to reading. If you feel that conclusion might be incorrect, here is your chance to steer. Don't count on being able to do it later; you might win the battle, but you also might never do business in that market again.

6. Defining the recommendation

If given the opportunity, how many of us would vote away the IRS, or even Income Tax entirely? Our tendency to give strong consideration to eliminating something that displeases us, if given the chance, without consideration of the long-term effects is probably one reason why our forefathers decided upon representative Republic and not a popular vote Democracy.

TIP ☞   Sometimes the recommendation needs to be contrary to the popular opinion; sometimes contrary to the perceived requirement.

If the requirement will implicitly define, in a de-facto manner, the recommendation without the need for other considerations, state that.

If there are numerous considerations that can seemingly show the recommendation to contradict the requirements, state that! Don't wait to justify it until you make the recommendation and everyone scratches their heads. Prepare them now. If there is a penciled-in recommendation that will either be reinforced or invalidated by the requirements, state that as well. That recommendation might fit well enough to use when the requirements don't say 'nay', but don't offer an apparent choice either.

For example, I have one hundred Brand X PC's sitting in a storeroom. If the requirements turn out to be consistent with the capabilities of the Brand X systems, then it makes sense to use them since we already have them. But to someone without a warehouse full of computers, a review of the requirements might lead them to see Brand Y as the logical choice. Perhaps Brand Y *exceeds* the requirements instead of simply being *consistent* with them.

It's important to present the existence of a *de facto* recommendation early in the document, namely, that in lieu of any requirements to the contrary, the Brand X PC's will be used. Psychologically, it's better to present this before the analysis of the requirements than as a defensive postscript to them.

TIP ☞   For your conclusions to be shared and embraced, you should present your approach in an order that reflects your thought pro-cess.

7. Developing the prototype solution

As we'll see later, an inordinate amount of confusion arises around a prototype due to differing expectations. Unfortunately, the fact that there was confusion typically doesn't surface until the prototype is being reviewed, to the shouts of "Is that all it does?" and "Hey — it's only a mock-up."

The approach document should clearly define what is in-scope and what is not in-scope for the prototype. Not at a detailed level (since the detail of what the prototype will look like is yet to be defined), but functionally. What will the prototype touch, and what won't it touch? Will it touch live data? Will it make any network connections? Will it do any edit checking?

It's best to make as many of those determinations as early on as possible so that you can set expectations, so that you can get your team in lock-step so that they're all delivering the same message to those who ask, and also so yours can be set if your idea of a prototype will not be satisfactory.

8. Developing the deployment plan

A critical piece in the whole process. You will probably find that the sponsors of the project have little idea about the complexity of deployment since they've not had a mass deployment of new technology. Spell out where you will look for deployment issues, who (functionally or specifically) you will need to communicate with (often there can be political rifts between the user community and IT — give a 'heads-up' that you'll need to work outside of IT), and how far you're willing to plan for contingencies (the lower the budget, the more things you'll have to assume will go right).

9. Testing

What is the testing philosophy going to be with regards to alpha, beta, parallel, etc. If this determination has not yet been made, what data will allow it to be made? How will you approach going live with respect to the testing (that is what will get you over the hurdles)?

10. Implementation

You'd think that once the testing is complete all you need to do is throw the switch like they do in the movies (did you ever notice that when people type on their keyboard in the movies they never need the spacebar?). You and I know it's not that simple, but don't count on everyone else knowing it. There will be issues of code freeze, data transfer, possibly network address changes. How will these issues be uncovered and what will be the approach to accounting for them? You can't throw the switch if you have your hands over your eyes.

Naturally, in the development of the approach document many things are going to occur in parallel since the team members will be working on their approaches in parallel, but unless you want to read multiple pages simultaneously, we'll have to do things serially, and since we'll be doing them serially, it will be easier to divide the investigation into each focus.

4.1.1 High Availability

Description of the Subject

High availability is when something is available a percentage of time higher than the average. With regards to computers, it is the use of software, hardware, or procedures so that the Service Level Agreement of system availability can be met.

Providing high availability can be as simple as installing a UPS (Uninterruptible Power Supply) so that a power failure won't "crash" the system, or as complex as having two of each system component with automatic switchover in case the primary system goes down.

Each method provides a different level of coverage than the other. What determines the level of protection is often the available budget. What should determine the level is the business need coupled with the budget.

Anticipated data requirements

The data requirements to determine high-availability needs and recommendations are varied. The first consideration is the business issues. What are the needs for availability? The determination shouldn't come from one source, but from a collecting of each function of each application and the associated requirements.

In addition to understanding the need, there is also a requirement to evaluate what about the physical environment will contribute to or detract from fulfilling the need. What will the topology of the network be? What will the system architecture be? And what is the historic availability of the network, each legacy application needed by the application architecture and each system needed to support those applications?

Anticipated data source(s)

The business issues, the requirement of availability, needs to be determined by the owners of the data. The accounting department is probably the best source for relating the need for access to the accounting systems. The worst case scenario needs to be accounted for. Again, using accounting as an example, access requirements during year-end closing are probably different than those during a normal week. Take a functional map of each application and query the application users. In addition to the availability of each function, the cost to the company of that function not being available will also be needed, for example, not being able to take customer orders. What is the cost per hour?

The topology information will come from the IT people, as will, hopefully, the availability statistics. Obtaining those statistics might not be easy. They might not exist, and if they do, their owners might not want to share them. They are extremely important, though, as we'll see.

Data evaluation methodology

Evaluating the data which leads to a recommendation on high availability is a long and winding road (forgive me, Paul, it fit). Here is just one example of how to evaluate the data. The idea is to take everything you gathered and create a map. The map needs to have locations. Start with each function and data source being a location on one side of the map.

After the processes have been inserted, the systems which run those processes need to be identified and added. If more than one system is needed for a process, make sure that fact is accounted for.

The network connecting the client processes to the servers needs to be inserted; the systems being available is of little consolation if the connections between them are not. As you might imagine, with processes being run in many sites and multiple routes across the network from user to system, the diagram can become very complicated, but then I never meant to imply that this would be easy, though it is well worth the analysis time if a lack of availability could cost the company its life.

Finally, with all components identified, the identified processes need to include IT processes such as back-ups and scheduled downtime. Along with the processes needs to be the hours of the day that each needs to be available on normal work days, and cyclical events like month-end processing.

To this point the data gathering and analysis could all be done by the project manager — useful if the high-availability resource itself has availability issues; do the groundwork as much as possible before bringing the resource in.

When presenting data, it is important to identify its source, whether it was obtained by you or derived (and if so, how and from what), and identify any assumptions made and the level of confidence (a percentage) in the assumptions and data.

For example, a piece of data that is the result of a study or is documented, like net profit for the prior year, will have a confidence level of 99 percent, a SWAG (scientific wild-ass guess) a level of 25 percent, and a WAG (unscientific) might have a confidence level of 10 percent.

The SWAG might be perfectly acceptable — it might involve a minor piece of data, or the potential result based on all possible outcomes may have variances so small that the impact is trivial. On the other hand, a 10 percent confidence level might be unacceptable for a go-ahead decision (like launching the D-Day invasion), but could stay as a place-holder until better data is available. Whatever the importance assigned to the confidence level of a piece of data, making it visible is important so the client can decide to proceed anyway (and assume the risk), get better data, or change data requirement. Keep in mind also that if a piece of data with a low confidence level will be used to derive other data, and if the value of the derived data is impacted severely as a result, then the confidence level of the derived data should be no higher than the original piece. Here's an example.

I just finished taking an exam. I have a 10 percent confidence level that I'll receive an 'A.' In estimating my confidence level of receiving an 'A' for the term I need to assess the impact of that grade. If I have an 'A' average thus far and the exam counts little, then my confidence level is high despite the low confidence level on that particular grade because it will have little impact. However if I currently have a 'B' average and the exam counts for 25 percent of my grade, then my overall confidence level will be low. Derived data confidence levels should be published and explained.

Mapping data to requirements

It's now time to move from the diagram to a table to analyze the data. This is the really difficult part, and this is when the high-availability specialist needs to be onboard for the complex analysis. We could continue with a diagram, but having spent a great deal of time trying to arrange all the data into a picture, we'd still be left with something not easily internalized. A table allows us to prioritize the presentation of the data instead of being force-fed all of it so that we can scan it as needed. The human method of assimilating data seems to work well with columnar data. For example, think of how we go about finding a phone number in the phone book.

1. We scan the last names until we find the one we want

    Smiley
    Smiley
    Smiston
    Smith

2. Then the first names

    | Smith | Bill |
    | Smith | Charles |
    | Smith | David |
    | Smith | Frank |

3. Then the addresses

    | Smith | Frank | 123 Kharis St. |
    | Smith | Frank | 456 Maple Rd. |
    | Smith | Frank | 7890 Imhotep Way |

4. And finally the phone number.

So we'll use the same method to somewhat ease the assimilation of the process data. We need to evaluate the relative merit of each process' requirement, but in the end keeping a logical process available will mean keeping one or more physical systems available, so we'll order the table by system, and then by the time the processes running on that system need to be available. Chart one cyclical period (typically one week or month) and year-end to summarize the availability data.

The chart should capture the time that the system is in use. Use four-hour increments, or modify as needed. The graph acts as an accumulation summary for all the processes running on that machine; at a glance you can see the apparent availability requirement for the system.

A similar chart ordered by process will be valuable as well. One chart will make visible the demand for a particular system, the other the requirements in keeping a process available.

Defining the recommendation

Once the data has been safely integrated into a table we can take a breath – but a quick one. The lion's share of the analysis necessary to develop a recommendation should fall to the high-availability expert, but the project manager can certainly bring to the table the ability to focus (and continually refocus) the recommendation addressing the business issue(s) in the most effective manner.

The means to assure high availability vary in scope and price, and the selection of one over the other will depend on the cost of the solution compared to the cost of 'being down' and the associated risk. For example, if the system needs to be available twenty-four hours per day, seven days per week (known as 24x7) and the cost of being down is $1000 per hour, then there might be justification for redundant systems, but if the application requires four different systems and two separate networks be up with the same assurance, and the risk is $100 per hour, there might not be the justification, another less costly solution could be recommended.

We'll look more at the specifics of the possible solutions later when we discuss actual requirements, but in general they include making the infrastructure or pieces of it more robust or providing a means with which to transfer control or processing to another environment should the first become nonviable.

The recommendation will also contain alternatives. The recommendation might make perfect sense based on the data which was analyzed, but the data or its relative business importance can be changed by the client, especially the assumptions. Identifying alternatives, including the changes to the data that would make the alternative a recommendation, can save going back to the drawing board. This way if the client says, "I'm not prepared to spend the extra money just to avoid that particular risk," you'll already have the alternative(s) ready.

Developing the prototype solution

I'll repeat this more than once I'm certain, but what is your definition of prototype? You may not agree with mine, but I provide it so that you can understand my frame of reference.

> Pro•to•type — a model that provides sufficient functionality and resemblance to the envisioned final product to gauge whether it will fulfill a need.

So a prototype can be simply a mock-up so long as the end-user can determine its applicability without adding a higher level of current functionality.

Therefore, what needs to be described is the intended scope for the prototype. What will the prototype include, what will it achieve, and what resources will it require? If there is a large technology hole between the proof of concept and the final solution (because the hole is costly to fill and shouldn't be necessary to get buy-in), then perhaps a pilot will be necessary.

Developing the deployment plan

How will the deployment plan be developed? That is, we're not concerned, at this point, with what the content of the plan will be. The deployment plan is covered in the final two sections, but where does the information that is needed to develop the plan come from, and how will that data be used? This portion of the approach might be skeletal at first until details can be added as the project proceeds, but certainly any specific data necessary to ascertain how best to deploy the hardware, software, and procedures necessary for the high-availability solution needs to be accounted for here.

Testing

How will the solution tie in with the testing to be done. That is, if there is to be a beta, in-house pilot and external pilot, which may not be decided until later), to what degree will the high-availability solution be integrated into each of those tests, and how is that decision being made?

Implementation

What information will determine whether there are any issues associated specifically with moving the solution into production? An example would be if data mirroring were part of the solution and the 'mirrors' needed initial loading.

4.1.2 Networking

Description of the subject

If there's one certainty with client-server computing, it's that there is networking involved, usually a lot of networking. The clients are networked with the server (their being able to communicate boosts productivity tremendously), the server may be networked with other servers, and often there will be a mainframe in the picture with yet another level of network connectivity.

The bottom line of the networking engagement is to ensure that there is an adequate network with which to enable the environment. A topology will need to be documented, with those items in the topology that require change from the current environment being accounted for as well as a method to ensure the bandwidth will be satisfactory.

Anticipated data requirements

There are a number of things we need to know in order to evaluate the network requirements.

- Which systems will talk? Connectivity
- Why will they be talking? Availability
- What language do they speak? Protocol
- What will they be saying and how often? Traffic

Anticipated data source(s)

The complexities of networking are immense. The solution is often simply elegant, but the data points requiring consideration are almost without end. The keepers of the data often don't realize that they have it, and often don't want to share it when they realize they do. Obtaining the data points, even discovering the owners, can be a large exercise in politics,

In terms of the current topology, you can typically look to IT. The type of data being passed, the quantity and frequency, will probably be split between application development and the users: count on them having the knowledge necessary to provide the data, but don't count on the data to be already documented and waiting for you.

Data evaluation methodology

One method of evaluating the data is to segregate it by the OSI layer (see the Introduction); look at the data that will help define the physical requirements (what cable and network components do we need and where should they go?) working up to protocols. This will not be a trivial task, as networks can be very complex to design, and the design can be viewed as a summary of the data. Also, adding elements to an existing network can be more complicated than starting from scratch to avoid 'breaking' what's already in place.

The next consideration is redundancy. If there is only one way to get from point A to point B, and that line goes down, what are the business consequences? The cost of the network being down is data that needs to be analyzed. Once this evaluation is underway, it will also be the time to evaluate network bandwidth.

Everyone seems to have their own method of evaluating network bandwidth, but one thing all methods have in common is that they look at network needs from the aspect we wish our roads departments would: traffic patterns and peak volume. Most of the volume data will be discarded in favor of that reflecting peak periods of activity. There's no sense designing a road to handle 1000 cars per hour when there will be 7500 cars using the road between 8 and 9am. Likewise, with a network. If the average traffic is twenty packets of 256 bytes each minute, designing the network to handle that load will not earn us many kudos if the traffic is one hundred packets per minute first thing in the morning.

Mapping data to requirements

Developing the physical requirements after the complex analysis is actually not as daunting a task as you might think. Network requirements need to map to network hardware in the same way that appliances map to power. If I have a 220 volt clothes dryer, I know a 110 volt circuit won't do. And if the dryer draws 16 amps of power, I know I need a 20 amp breaker (since breakers don't come in 16 amp). It's much the same with network hardware. Once I realize the bandwidth I need to accommodate at peak periods, I map that requirement to network hardware that provides at least that bandwidth. The pieces of hardware need to be accounted for — routers, hubs, bridges, and concentrators. These and the services need to be looked at with a eye toward redundancy and alternate routing.

The data gathered that shows the cost of the network being down needs to be compared to the cost of assuring the network stays up, keeping in mind that the network is no more stable than its most unstable link.

Protocol is an entirely different bag. If you're lucky, the network will be something vanilla that ties in to the existing network fairly easily, but if not, protocol conversion, embedding and wrapping, and bridges are items that can add logarithmic complexity to the recommendation.

Defining the recommendation

The recommendation for networking is typically a larger document than the others. There are graphics that need to be presented to add weight to the recommendation, such as (in this case) the network map for representative offices, or a typical office if they are all the same, the store-to-corporate connection(s), and software and hardware that will accommodate the monitoring of the network and its performance.

Alternatives will need to be mentioned, including network hardware, which allows for growth and for greater or lesser redundancy.

Developing the prototype solution

Careful consideration needs to be given to the feasibility of the level of networking involved in a prototype. Certainly the minimal connectivity necessary to display functionality must be present. However, including all the networking can be quite impractical. For example, if the offices have no network connection to the corporate office at present, creating that capability for one prototype could be very expensive — think of the cost of prototyping an aircraft carrier for a company that has never made one; after setting up the infrastructure to create the prototype a fleet of them is smooth sailing. An extreme example, but if the network requirements represent completely new wiring or protocols, selective prototyping will need to be done. We'll cover this in more detail further on, but keep in mind that what needs to be presented in prototype as opposed to being accepted as achievable because it's in general use in the industry (like a parallel port on a PC) can be an emotional issue for some; logic and reason do not always win.

Developing the deployment plan

The deployment planning in its entirety will often be driven by tasks in the network focus, and this is often due entirely to reality; lead-time in obtaining the phone lines or satellite links, and most of the deployment work needing to be contracted out to third-parties. You will find that a deployment planned with an elegantly staggered implementation can be defeated by the inability to stagger the installation of the network connections in the same fashion.

Testing

The testing of the network will accomplish a number of things. First, HP OpenView® will be used to do a "discovery" of the network to show that all "discoverable" pieces are found, then each SNMP-addressable network device will be pinged to prove that it has been configured correctly and is on-line. Testing will be done to make sure that appropriate packets are routed and/or bridged as planned. Finally, a stress test of the network will be performed by simulating a level of load to be decided later.

Implementation

Like any part of a project that centers around physical installation and third parties, the network deployment will require a close look at delivery lead times (especially in the just-in-time environment, where stock is built to order), configuration and testing, and the related dependencies. This is true for both wiring and the network hardware components. These concerns will be covered more fully in chapters 7 and 9.

4.1.3 Platform Architecture and Capacity Planning

Description of the Subject

As we have seen, there are many facets to a client-server deployment, but when it comes down to it the day-to-day visibility is on the systems, the clients and the servers.

Selecting the systems can be a complicated process. If you, as the project manager, are lucky, the client will have already selected the system vendor(s), and will have done the job properly. It's a toss-up as to which of the other two possibilities is next best:

- the vendor was chosen but has no systems which meet the bill
- the vendor has not been chosen, and the finalists will all be competing for the honor

The latter was my experience at a large retail client. Three vendors competed through the proof-of-concept to compete for the honor of being the systems provider. It was a stroke of genius, actually. The CIO at the time had the time and the resources to have three vendors simultaneously attempt to prove their respective concepts. Among other benefits, this enabled the customer to get past the doubt as to where the potential vendors' marketing hype ended and the new technology's delivery potential truly began; better to find out then before having awarded the contract and moved down the road to a point of no return. The only drawback to me was that there were planning and data gathering activities that needed to be occurring during this period but could not, because the vendor's project manager could not become active until the vendor was selected due, in part, to the strain three project teams gathering data and doing planning in parallel would put on the one set of client resources.

The systems have to meet many requirements, some straightforward and others quite obtuse. The approach will be to determine what data will provide the requirements which have to be met, and how to make the requirements determination.

Anticipated Data Requirements

Requirements need to be generated for five different system configurations.

- Office server
- Office clients
- Corporate/Web server
- Development server
- Development clients

Each of these systems will probably have different requirements, which will most likely result in a different configuration being recommended for each, although there is the possibility that the differences in each set of requirements will not be mutually exclusive and a common configuration will handle each need.

To determine what data needs to be analyzed, we could work backwards somewhat from what category of requirements the systems must meet. Let's take a look at a table (Table 4-2) that facilitates the gathering of the data.

It's worth taking a look at each row in the table to explain the signicance of each requirement. Let's do, using the client as an example.

- TPS — Transactions Per Second. Many machines are advertised with a MIPS (Millions of Instructions per Second) rating. Well, great. How many MIPS is each user generating? I don't know either. Most software is transaction-based, and quantifying the users' transaction rate is more feasible than MIPS.
- Web Hits — Every time a user clicks on a URL (Universal Resource Locator) such as http://www.myurl.com to go to a web page, there is a resulting 'hit,' or access, on the server, and subsequent 'hits' for each item linked to that web page, such as graphics. Servers are being rated for the number of 'hits' they can field per day. A good example of this is the type of transactions we see occurring when 'browsers,' applications used to view web pages, are used with the Internet or intranets. Here are some examples you would see in using a browser.
- No network activity — The browser is being used to display local files, as is often the case when web pages are being tested before being uploaded to the web site.
- Low network activity — The user is displaying a web page, reading it, then moving on to another page.
- Medium network activity — The user is 'surfing' from link to link or accessing pages with large linked graphics.
- High network activity — The user is downloading files while viewing pages, using pages with high server interaction items

such as Java scripts, audio or motion, or doing both simultaneously.

- MFLOPS — Millions of Floating point Operations per Second. If the application relies on graphics (CAD/CAM/CAE), then this rating could be important.
- Max Connections — How many users will the system support? Will the users be connected directly, via LAN, virtual connection? The limitations of the system will need to be known.
- Max Memory — Each user on the system will be running one or more pieces of software. How much memory does the system use for itself, for a user session, for each instance of the application and associated libraries and data for each user? And then how much memory does the system support?
- Max Disk — Gauging how much disk space a system will need is very difficult and must account for intangibles such as virtual memory, swap space, etc. However, if an estimate can be generated, that estimate can be compared to the disk space supported by the system. Other considerations will need to be given when we look at the backup/disaster recovery concerns. Hand in hand with the disk capacity is the disk.
- Networking Capability — Each system will be communicating with at least one other system, perhaps many. How will they communicate? If it has been decided that the clients will talk to the servers via TCP/IP, then it makes sense to look at a server that supports a TCP/IP connection.
- Networking Connections — How many connections does the system support? If the system needs to speak TCP/IP to its clients, and SNA® to a mainframe, and only supports one network card — wrong system.
- Operating System — There are specific operating systems that the client will support.
- Software — If there is software strategic to the client's operation, that software needs to be able to run on the systems being considered. The operating system will be the first hurdle ("What? They don't have a MVS™ version of WordPerfect?"). The system itself might be next ("Yes, we have a version that runs on UNIX®, but only on the HP-UX® flavor of UNIX"). And as we'll discuss later, the version of the software that runs on the system can be a showstopper. The tools

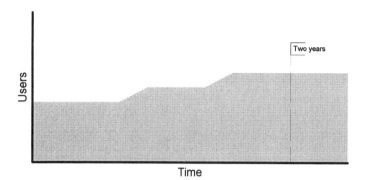

Figure 4-1 User Growth

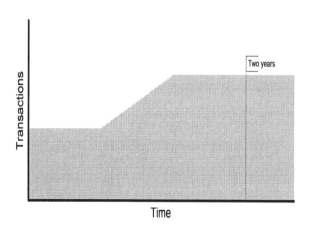

Figure 4-2 Customer Transaction

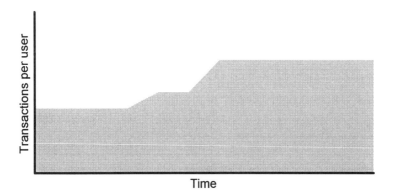

Figure 4-3 Transaction Growth

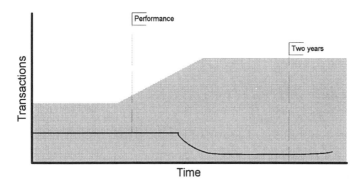

Figure 4-4 Performance Impact

being used to develop the software have to be considered, especially if portions will remain with the run-time code.

- Dimensions — yes, dimensions. I would imagine it could be quite embarrassing to ship two-hundred systems out to two-hundred stores that are all two feet wider than the physical opening available.
- Environmental — No, I'm not asking if the system is recyclable, but what operating environment does it need in order to function. Can you plug it into a wall and shove it under the desk, or does it need a cooled room with conditioned three-phase power?
- Growth Percentage — okay, the system will handle the memory, disk, network connection, and user requirements. Will it still handle them when you add fifty users six months from now? The amount of capacity used the day the system is delivered should leave an acceptable margin for growth.
- Upgradability — When the system runs of steam, can you slap a new processor in or is the next step up a watercooled roomfull of metal?
- Technology — Technology considerations can be very important, especially on the client side where the technology changes monthly and the software always seems to push the envelope.

Defining requirements for all the above aspects is the goal, so first we have to gather the data the will allow us to map requirements. Hang on, this is going to be a bumpy ride!

Anticipated data source(s)

TPS — It might seem that it would be easy to gather the transaction processing requirements. Each application has certain transactions that can be performed — all we need to know is the maximum we can expect from a given person, right? Wrong. Let's take a look at the complexities.

First, has the design of each application, whether a new application or one being redesigned to be client-server, sufficiently progressed to where its transaction architecture is available? Well, since we haven't begun the software development cycle yet, the answer is 'no.' In order to grasp the transaction volume, someone has to know what defines a transaction within that application.

For example, adding a customer can be one, two, or maybe three transactions depending on the screen layout and what information is passed between the server and client systems during the process. The architecture of the transaction will therefore also determine how many one person can complete per second (although, typically, user transactions should be measured per minute since the user takes at least that long to complete a transaction).

The interesting thing is that during the construction of a user transaction, such as adding a customer, there can be one or several application transactions taking place too. For example, while adding a customer, the user might first ask the customer for their phone number. Having entered it, the application might poll the customer database to see if there is already a record. Having entered the customer's zip code, the client might ask the server to supply the town and state.

Second, not only do we need to know how the application behaves in terms of segregating the transmission of data by the "screenfull," but we need to understand the relationship between the client and server. Here are some of the possibilities with regards to user transactions.

- No client data is persistent (resident and the primary source of its content), all data comes from lookup requests sent to the server (heavy transaction traffic)
- Some client data is persistent. Typically a storeforward scenario is used. An amount of space is set aside in a data structure on the client, such as an order database, intended to be a volatile subset of a server order database. If the application needs order #1, and it is not present in the client database (DB), then the client architecture requests the data from the server. Eventually the client DB is full, so the next record brought in overwrites another record in a FIFO-like (First-In First-Out) arrangement. The bottom line is that the data on the client can be refurbished at any time by the server, but having it there reduces transaction hits against the server.
- All client data is persistent. Perhaps it makes more sense for certain data structures to be resident on the client instead of

the server. This would greatly reduce the hits against the server (assuming the data is needed regularly), but would complicate the recovery strategy.

So, many facets of the application architecture will be required to analyze TPS, such as user and application transaction rates based around modeled use cases, and that information will come from the application design group. The big question: Will the architecture be available at the time you need it? If the application development is at all coincidental with the rest of the project, a likelihood, then chances are good if you were brought in early enough to do the job properly that this and other data will not be available early on. This will require the "placeholder" approach mentioned earlier in this chapter, to go from SWAG to hard data.

Now let's look at the other side of the coin — application transactions. We just considered whether the application architecture that describes the user transactions will be available, and that, of course, assumes an application is being developed. Even if we have an existing application and understand the user transactions, that doesn't necessarily mean that we understand the transaction load in its entirety. Applications can manage transactions in a number of ways, and these transactions aren't necessarily launched by a conscious user effort.

MFLOPS — This is perhaps one of the easier pieces of data to collect. Presumably the application that takes advantage of MFLOPS will be a purchased design tool and not something that is homegrown. This means that the behavior of the application should be available, since it is not under construction, and that, based on what elements are being designed, the instruction load on the client and, if applicable, the server will be available or derivable. The answers will come from the users in terms of their activity, and the software company as to how the users' activity translates to load. It's a safe bet that any data of that type needed from a software vendor will be more forthcoming if your customer is a strategic client of the software vendor as opposed to having bought a few copies off the shelf.

It should also be noted that while this data is being analyzed to determine the type of system required, the findings will also be important to the network considerations. The three examples of data persistence shown above translate directly to the load put on available network bandwidth.

Maximum Connections — The system needs to handle the peak load of connections, but is that simply the number of users? Not necessarily. Depending again on the architecture of what the users will be running, it's conceivable that a user sitting at an X-terminal with several windows up has several physical and even more logical connections going between their client and other systems. So once again information is needed from the user base as to their work habits, or intended work habits, and the application group as to how those work habits will translate into system load. Also, once again, this information might not be available from the start.

Maximum Memory — I hate to seem redundant, but you need to know what the users will be running and how that translates to memory requirements. For example, I have 8 Mb of memory on my PC. Sounds okay, but not if my environment calls for me to be running Windows 95® and four major applications, like Microsoft Word and Lotus® 1-2-3®. So how many processes will each user have running? That's a tough question. How many screens will they have up, and how many processes does that translate to? One screen, depending on what it's doing, can actually have several processes running. A multi-threaded environment like Windows NT® makes this an even greater likelihood. So again, we're back to the users to find out what they typically do, and the software vendors or in-house developers to find out what that means. And keep in mind that there is overhead when it comes to memory, not all of it is usable by the user, just as not all of your income is usable by you — the government gets theirs first.

Maximum Disk — This is one of the most difficult things to quantify. We'll assume that the data structures don't exist yet. Perhaps there are a few DB2 databases sitting out on a mainframe or two that are going to be converted to, or more probably be a steward for, a relational database or two on the data server(s) and/or clients. So, can't you just look at how much data is being used on the mainframe and assume the same amount of data on the server. Nope.

One thing that is a certainty is that relational databases are a strange beast. You move to relational because it gives you the ability to establish relationships between data items dynamically and not be constrained by the typical master-detail hierarchy. There are two items that are not reasons for going to relational databases: system overhead and disk space; you won't find either to be less with relational databases than with hierarchical or network databases. You might find that this data needs to be derived and fine-tuned as you progress; it's not something that is typically concentrated on until someone runs out of it. The location of the data and the associated strategy as well as the considerations regarding high availability; you might be using disk mirroring or some other such strategy that will affect the required disk space.

Local storage for the users is also tough to gauge. Some organizations don't want the users to have any local storage, and have the configuration contain a 'diskless' PC or workstation. Others want the users to keep as much of their volatile environment local as possible and put 1 Gb disks in each workstation. You'll probably have no shortage of opinions on the subject, but knowing how much is enough is a different matter. Luckily, you will only need to analyze the data and provide a recommendation based on the data.

Networking Capability — Many off-the-shelf PCs have no inherent network capability other than what is possible using the fax/modem that most come with.

There are a surprising number of ways to communicate with just a modem, such as serial (a normal dial-up connection), PPP (a dial-up LAN-type connection), and X.25 (a dial-up WAN-type connection), but if the networking requirement calls for a LAN connection (nondial-up) or an SNA connection, it's time to make sure that the PC can handle that. Nine out of ten times the environment into which the PC is being introduced will be one of two industry standards, but that tenth time the requirement might not be so straightforward. Even when the environment will be standard, the card being added to the PC may not.

Okay, you find out, for example, that the LAN card will work in the PC, but

- will the LAN card work with the other add-on peripherals?
- will the port for the LAN connection on the card be accessible when the other (such as the modem) peripherals are in use?
- will the drivers that control the card conflict with other drivers?
- will the version of LAN card and its drivers work with all the software?

The last point is the most difficult to determine beforehand. (See the following section on software.)

Networking Connections — If we determine that the user needs to have a LAN card and an SNA card, do we have a problem? Will the PC physically support both cards being installed and active, and logically support both communication protocols and stacks?

Operating System — There aren't that many around, but enough to cause a predicament if the PC comes loaded with the wrong one (this can be remedied in the integration process discussed in Chapter 9). The choices are pretty much Windows, Windows NT Workstation®, and Windows 95 at this point for a PC client.

Software — Version conflict is a continual headache, especially when there are numerous versions of a standard (an oxymoron I know, but a prevalent one — try passing around a TIFF file from application to application). Good luck! There's a wide spectrum of responses that you'll receive from software vendors when asking them about compatibility between their product and another (perhaps a competitor's?) product.

Although seemingly impossible to resolve, the approach will be to try. There will also be the logistical 'Catch-22' nightmare testing subsequent versions for release to the user.

There can be nothing more frustrating than having a project go down the tubes because, for example, the word processor everyone in the corporation uses won't import the spreadsheet data that was the bottom-line output of the entire project.

Up to this point the software being discussed can be considered stable in terms of standards. For example, using Lotus 1-2-3 for spreadsheet development is, in the absence of unusual considerations, a safe bet. PC software, UNIX software, and mainframe software have been around for some time; making a selection from available packages, assuming each meets the functional requirements, should not be an event that comes back to bite you in the posterior. Ah, but what about new technology? What about the Internet and intranets?

The Internet and intranet are evolving at a rate too fast to measure. The major software players at this point — Microsoft, Sun Microsystems and Netscape are all jockeying for position by trying to leverage their idea of the future into a position of being the standard. Netscape and Microsoft do it by continually adding extensions usable only by their browser to the one existing standard, HTML, and releasing them to the Internet user-base who greedily snatch them up to make their web pages more attractive. Microsoft has their own extensions built into their Internet Explorer. The two companies have moved beyond simply battling over who will own the browser and are attempting to own the desktop environment as well. Sun and Microsoft are also battling it out in terms of adding application functionality to web pages, Sun having a headstart with their Java product, and Microsoft coming from behind with ActiveX and VBScript while supporting Java as well. Software companies that specialize in add-ons to products like these also need to decide whose camp to park themselves in, unless they're in the enviable position of being able to develop for both.

So, with all that in mind, if you're going to develop an intranet, develop a presence on the Internet, whose software do you go with? If there are only two leaders, and you have the resources, you can develop for both and bet that one will emerge as the standard or that the differences between the two will narrow until a standard is born. There are many thoughts on the correct approach to take, and some people are quite adamant about their position, but I'll tell you now that in any event it's a gamble. How many people went with Macintosh or OS/2? Each has their place, especially the Mac in the publishing/graphics world, but in the rest

of the commercial world where access to software solutions is everything
...At this point we don't have to make a selection. We'll just indicate that
a decision will need to be made, and hope that by the time we get to that
point there will be requirements that make the decision easier in the short-
term (there's always the chance that the selected software, despite the requirements pointing us that way, will turn out to be the loser).

Dimensions — So, let's say we've got 249 systems being integrated
to be deployed to 249 offices, and we are in the process of installing the
first of them at the beta site. We roll it in and, lo and behold, it's three
inches bigger than the opening available for it. I imagine the feeling of the
project manager at this point would be quite similar to showing up at a
costume party dressed as a tap-dancing marshmallow only to find that it
isn't a costume party. We'll need to get the weight and dimensions (physical and what's needed for 'breathing room') for each piece of equipment
to make certain we will have no issues with transport, storage, or installation.

This could be a hassle at this point in the game, because the decision
on hardware might not be made until much later. We could end up requesting the specifications on numerous models of systems from various
vendors (assuming more than one vendor is in the running). The dimensions of the available opening for installation will come from the facilities
management group; in our context that will be Office Operations.

Environmental — In our scenario we'll be installing servers into a
service center environment, which will typically mean into a closet or
work area in the back of the building. If the server requires air-condition-
ing, we will have issues. We need to know what the requirements for each
piece of hardware is regarding temperature, humidity, and power. This information will come from each vendor and can be a hassle to obtain just
as the dimensions. The thing to consider is that if the equipment does
have environmental needs, and if its having environmental needs doesn't
eliminate it from consideration, there could be a need further on to consider the high-water environmental needs of the systems under consideration and plan around them; in other words, the lead time on adding

environmental factors to the intended location might require the work to be done before the final system selection.

Growth Percentage — If we order systems that will handle our transaction and connectivity needs, are we in good shape? Not necessarily. If we have 250 users, and the server handles 255 users, we'll probably outgrow the system in a few months. We need to determine

- what percentage of transaction/connectivity growth will be seen in the company over that period.
- how much room for growth is desired on the hardware (in elapsed time — such as two years before an upgrade is needed, and then only a board upgrade).
- how do the growth projects tie into the system capacity; that is what does the system's performance knee look like? Can we add fifty more users, or only two?
- what upgrade path and logistics need to be accounted for with the hardware in mind. Is it a board upgrade or a box swap? Does the new box have the same footprint and environmental requirements?

The growth projections should be available through IT, but more likely will have to come from the end-user arena. This is a major area of concern for most companies, as it affects their capital expenditure budgeting and the ROI on the initial purchase. We'll want to generate the following four graphs for this evaluation:

- Projected user change — How many users will be added? Will the accounting department be adding twenty people next year?
- Projected causative transaction volume increase — How many transactions will be added to each user's workload due to an increase in business or application changes? Will each ac-

counts payable clerk need to process 150 transactions per day instead of eighty?

- Projected resultant transaction volume increase — What will the transaction volume be once we've figured in the projected number of users and their respective transaction load?
- Projected resultant transaction versus system performance — Every system has what's called a performance knee, which is the point on a graph of transactions v.s. performance where the system can't handle any more transactions and the performance drops off, thus causing a "knee" in the graph. How does the projected transaction load map against the system's capabilities?

The reason we'll be looking at incoming and outgoing transaction volumes is reflective of the difference between them, as can be seen in Figures 4-1, 4-2, 4-3 and 4-4.

Data evaluation methodology

The evaluation of the data is a matter of plotting it out on the graphs. The Y-axis will be volume, and the X-axis will be time. The resulting line will show a projection for growth.

Mapping data to requirements

Once we've gathered the data we need to do something with it. In this case, that 'something' will be looking at the transaction volume projections through the window of investment return. For example, if the customer wants the hardware to handle the volume throughout a two year period from the data of purchase, the worst-case load during that time will show whether the requirement will be met.

The worst-case load will not always be at the end of this time period. Reorganization, resturcturing, and other factors can cause a spike elsewhere along the way, but typically you won't be privy to the strategic decisions that would have that affect, so growth "up and to the right" is typically a safe assumption.

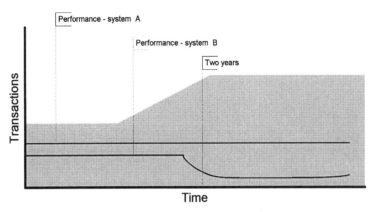

Figure 4-5 System Performance

Defining the recommendation

There might be more than one recommendation here. If the results mapped like they do in Figure 4-5.
Potential recommendations are:

- purchase solution A, it provides for growth beyond the window of concern.
- purchase solution B, it provides for growth to a point almost at the window of concern, and costs much less.
- purchase solution B, and at a certain point prior to reaching its limits (say 80% capacity) purchase an upgrade.

Again, it's all right to have more than one recommendation. If you have enough data available to squeak by a single recommendation, do so, and then present the other options as alternatives.

Developing the prototype solution

Well, you won't get very far mocking up the platform. To do a prototype you'll have to use real hardware, but how much? Of course the answer is "it depends." The best case would be that a single small server could act as a client and a server and a net server for the sake of minimizing the cost of the prototype.

Developing the deployment plan

The deployment plan would seem to fit in well with the discussion of staging later on in the book. It does, but at this point it isn't certain that the client will go with the concept of staging so we need to give it some consideration. Besides, most of the considerations will need to be addressed whether we stage or not. However, for the sake of organization and avoidance of redundancy, we'll save this text, as well as the Approach sections of Testing and Implementation, and the Approach Document for Implementation Support and Ongoing Support for the chapter on Staging.

4.1.4 Backup, Recovery and Disaster Recovery

Description of the subject

You can't get much simpler than a standard backup – pop in a tape and let 'er rip. Ah, but let's add some complexity.

- Multiple systems.
- Multiple tiers.
- Multiple locations.
- No local operations personnel (outside the corporate site).
- Twenty-four hour user operation.
- Databases that can not be backed up while online.

Okay. I think you're starting to get the picture. Rather than being a straightforward-who-cares topic, the need for safely storing data to provide a recovery path in instances of disaster can in and of itself be a direct driver of some of the hardware and software choice made.

So what about data recovery? Again, it would seem straightforward. Put the same tape(s) in the tape drive(s) and go! Well, what if portions of the data is stored in numerous systems? What if we have the following scenario:

- office A and Office B enter data until midnight;
- the data from Offices A and B is rolled up to a corporate database server as it's entered;
- the data from the corporate database server is backed up at 4am when it is backed up, and;
- the data from the corporate database server is continuously drawn into corporate mainframe systems.

With that foundation in place, let's picture the corporate database server going down at 10 a.m. and the database becoming corrupted. Well . . . even if it were logistically possible, would we want to take the entire corporation back to the previous midnight? Perhaps we can take the database back to then and do a transaction roll-forward to 10 a.m.?

Nope. Because the data that was in place at midnight has been used by the mainframe applications ever since.

Luckily I don't have to provide the answers because this is a book on project management and not data recovery, but you can see the problem.

Now onto disaster recovery. Recovering from a disaster is easier than properly planning for the recovery, but to plan you need to know what to plan for. Plan for a disaster! Sure, but what type?

- The computer room gets flooded
- A tornado takes out one of the sales offices
- A chemical spill prevents entry to the corporate IT site
- Terrorists take over the long-distance switching office

The planning of quickly implementing new hardware, loading data, transferring phone operations, and so on. can get quite complex and quite expensive. Some of the disaster scenarios are quite farfetched. However, it's not up to you to decide.

Many businesses would have to close their doors for good if they were unable to manufacture or take orders for a number of days — so what risk is acceptable to them? What percentage of risk of a magnitude of disaster would be small enough that they'd be able to walk away from it happening and the company going under with a clear conscience?

Luckily, when implementing new technology there is typically old technology, and often a disaster plan to go along with it. In those cases, planning for recovering the incremental environment may just be a matter of appending the existing plan, but it may be much more if this is the first time the technology spans multiple sites.

Anticipated data requirements

In order to develop a process for backing up data, we need to know what the data is, where it is kept, and when we can have it. If the various groups that decide these things haven't reached that point yet, we might actually have input into the components of the decision such as the data model instead of simply recording it.

The physical data model will be needed for us to know what needs to be backed up and where it will be located. We'll also need to know the backup and activity schedules of any systems out of our control that might be hosting this data, any systems out of our control that depend on this data, and the activity schedules of all systems that will be under our control.

For data recovery the logical data models will need to be studied, or in the case of being proactive, developed with an eye towards recovery, the dependence upon transactions by each application, and how the data in these transactions might be otherwise populated into database tables.

For disaster recovery the network layout, office layout, and hardware configuration(s) will be needed.

Anticipated data source(s)

For the most part, the system and backup schedules will come from operations, the hours of activity for the new systems will come from the user community, and the logical and physical data models will come from the development team. The network and hardware configurations will come from the current team, and again, with the ability to be proactive, can be driven somewhat by the recovery needs.

Data evaluation methodology

Perhaps an oversimplification, but the evaluation will consist of working backwards from various recovery-need scenarios to what position, based on varying recovery strategies, we would be in to smoothly affect the recovery. A determination must be made as to what if anything stands in the way of that, and which parameters we have control over, such as the hardware configuration, logical data model, and so on.

Mapping data to requirements

Once the issues are identified, as well as the parameters that can be modified to address them, they need to be translated into requirements such as additional network, software, and hardware components. You might infer from this that the solution will be simple, but that isn't necessarily the case — depending on the requirement and the issues the incremental cost of the solution can be very high.

The worst-case load will not always be at the end of this time period. Reorganization, restructuring, and other factors can cause a spike elsewhere along the way, but typically you won't be privy to the strategic decisions that would have that affect, so growth "up and to the right" is typically a safe assumption.

Defining the recommendation

The recommendation will be in two parts, backup and recovery, and disaster recovery. The backup and recovery portion will perhaps turn out to be a combination of additional hardware components for mirroring data, and consulting services to develop scripts to aid data recovery.

The disaster recovery recommendation will depend on what level of disaster will be planned for. The solution can vary from off-site storage to a hot-site (a site that has hardware and networking ready to mirror the predisaster site) with many possibilities in between. There might be more than one recommendation if there is a large difference in the price tag between the top two contenders or if the level of disaster for which to plan has not been clearly defined.

Developing the prototype solution

Prototyping a recovery, either data or disaster, is almost an oxymoron. Prototyping is the demonstration of a specific capability with external influences stubbed off. The recovery of data requires a large number of external influences because removing those influences will result in proving nothing except you can mock up a data recovery simulation.

If we're looking at planning for a disaster that would render the current computer room or building unusable, then it won't be possible to have a prototype because of the cost and complexity of recreating the environment. This activity is more appropriate for an annual disaster recovery simulation. The other factor, of course, is that in the stage of the project where a prototype is done there will be no code or data to recover. We could extend the project to an additional phase to account for prototyping the infrastructure solutions following the completion of the code, but that shouldn't be necessary unless the infrastructure solutions themselves need to be proved conceptually.

Keep in mind that no prototype doesn't mean no testing, it simply means that we'll proceed through the planning stage to implementation with the understanding that the solutions' designs are acceptable.

Developing the deployment plan

The complexity of deployment will depend on the physical design of the solutions. If the backup and recovery solution design is primarily software-focused, then the deployment requirements are minimal. On the other side of the spectrum, if the solution is primarily hardware, such as network and storage hardware for mirroring or backup devices on each workstation, then the deployment will require more planning.

Testing

A test plan for the backup process is needed. The complexity of the plan will depend on the complexity of the backup architecture and the window of opportunity. Following are two examples of backup scenarios, one that is simplistic and one that is fairly complex.

Developing a test plan for the first scenario should be trivial, but a plan that tests the second scenario will be complex. Certainly it needs to be tested, but one of the key decisions will need to be that considering the complexity of putting the components into place to allow for testing (such as the databases) does the testing need to occur on the critical path, or can you just test the backup architecture, the software and moving the data across network legs from the hardware, and wait until the application is in place to test the data?

Testing recovery processes, data or disaster, is not necessarily a given, but ought to be. As mentioned before, there probably can't be a test until the application is available and the data is in place, although in some cases the data will be centralized so testing recovery might just be a matter of ensuring the recovered data matched the prerecovery data — "might" because depending on the transaction model, you might not want the recovered data to exactly match the original data.

For example, let's say that we have a screen for adding new customers. Adding the customer is done in two steps.

1. Entering the customer's name and social security number causes a validation that the customer does not already exist in the database.
2. The remaining customer information is entered to complete the user's contribution to creating the record. Once entered, the following substeps occur:

    *   The customer index is reserved in the database
    *   The customer master record is added
    *   The customer address record is added
    *   The customer credit record is added

There you have it, a complete Add Customer transaction, but what if the system goes down midway through the processing? So now we have the customer index and master record, but not the address and credit records.

Perhaps the application is not set up to add a customer address record or credit record from a user screen, there is only meant to be one of each and they are created when the customer is added. Maybe we can't delete the customer because part of the deletion process is to delete these records that should exist but don't. So at this point we either need to have the database put into a state where the customer doesn't exist at all (so it can be added again), or a dummy entry needs to be created for the address and credit records so that they can be modified (the nonmodifiable fields in those records, if any, setup with the proper data).

That example was simplified by the data residing in lone location. What if the existing portions of the failed transaction were on different machines in different locations? Database transactions can be designed so that incomplete transactions can be backed out by the system, but the point is that, in these cases, testing the recovery and validating the test results becomes more difficult. Disaster recovery testing can be tremendously more complex and expensive than data recovery testing (consider that data recovery testing can be a subset of the disaster recovery).

Recovery testing truly needs to occur, but does it need to occur serially, in-line? Probably not. Sure, the project manager and developers and many other people would be more comfortable if it did, but typically the time will not be available. So part of the testing approach needs to be a recommendation of when the testing occurs, and what the risk is of extracting it from the critical path of the project.

Implementation

Implementing the backup solution will often be a mostly software consideration, but again, depending on the complexity of the solution, it can become quite involved — tape units, optical jukeboxes, additional network nodes, and so on. Being prepared to perform backups will be a critical path item: The fact that the backup implementation is necessary denotes that production use of the applications should not proceed without the backup solution in place, so careful consideration should be given to the lead time on implementing this solution; it would be an irony, and costly, if the solution designed to insure business continuation of the production system were to prevent its use due to delayed implementation.

The implementation of data recovery and disaster recovery should be minor when compared to the deployment and testing. Most of the considerations in the absence of the need for recovery are process considerations — this should all be fairly transparent and unobtrusive. There still could be some considerations though, perhaps the initial synchronization of systems and/or databases.

4.1.5 Education

Description of the subject

There are two facets of education to consider: education of the customer's computer staff, and the education of the user community. Ah, so what's a little user training? Trouble. The actual training is a breeze, it's the logistics that are often a nightmare.

Anticipated data requirements

The computer staff education will typically encompass the following topics:

- Development platform
- Development tool set
- Development processes used
- Application architecture
- Data architecture
- Operations requirements
- Troubleshooting (application specifics)
- Data recovery

If the list looks vaguely familiar, it's because these items are many of the project components that are being developed, the thought being that the ownership and knowledge of the components might eventually need to be turned over to the customer's staff for ongoing maintenance and support.

The education of the computer staff will naturally center around the use of the applications.

Anticipated data source(s)

Aside from the data reflected by the above topics which will come from what the team develops, we'll need to identify the following data items:

- What are the target audiences?
- What facilities are required and are available?
- What is their availability (time and location)?
- What are the training materials requirements?

The last two are the most important from the standpoint of impact. It takes three days to develop one day's training. The problem is that the information needed to develop user training — training on the applications — is typically unavailable until the applications are nearly complete.

So let's say that the user training will be three days and there are thirty users to train. Will all thirty be convened in one venue? Can all thirty be taken off-line for three days simultaneously? Let's take a look at the potential impact.

In the two figures here we look at the scenario just presented. In Figure 4-6 we'll look at the best-case: the training materials can be completed during application system testing, and the thirty users will be:

- in one location;
- in a location with facilities that will accommodate training them in one session, or;
- able to come off-line.

In Figure 4-7 we look at a case that's not very good. I won't say worst case, because the worst case is full chaos.

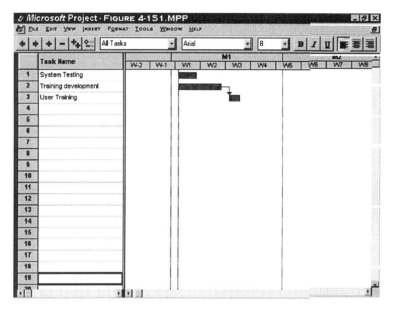

Figure 4-6 Training Scenario 1

- The thirty users are split evenly in three locations.
- We only have one trainer available.
- The training materials will be developed following application changes resulting from testing.
- The user can not all be off-line at once (business goes on).

As you can see from the illustrations, the impact on the project can be considerable.

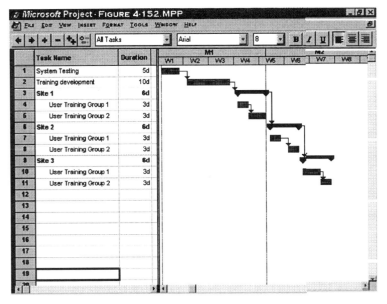

Figure 4-7 Training Scenario 2

Data evaluation methodology

Evaluation will be focused on what we've discussed;

- Need
- Availability

We'll then look at the options with regards to the number of sessions, number of trainers, number of locations, etc.

Mapping data to requirements

Once we have the above data, we need to look at possible courses of action. One major consideration we haven't mentioned to this point: What will the deployment schedule look like? We don't have a deployment plan at this point, but has the requirement been defined to the point where we know if it will be a phased deployment? Can it be? If we have ten sites to deploy, do they all have to be done simultaneously or can they be phased?

The reason we're asking these questions is so that we can evaluate what to do if we can't train everyone at once. You don't want to phase the training if the deployment won't be phased. Why? Because people don't retain what they've learned unless they can put it to use, so if we train a group and then wait three weeks to install their equipment, the training has gone to waste. It's not the end of the world though, there are options available, such as train-the-trainer, so that if we have a need to train massive amounts of people at one time, and don't have the training staff (or the funds for it) or the facilities, we can still accomplish what we need. These days, computer-based training (CBT) is sometimes an option too.

Defining the recommendation

The recommendation might be difficult to develop as there are many conflicting logistics, but what's needed is for the training to provide what we feel the user will require. We don't want them to end up being trained by the help-desk staff responding to trouble calls. That might not always meet the time-frame or funds available, so, like everything else in life, we might need to make some compromises, but not to the point where the user is unprepared or we need to raise a flag up the flagpole.

Developing the prototype solution

Normally, we'll only prototype the training if it includes technology that isn't represented anywhere else in the project, such as CBT.

Developing the deployment plan

The training portion of the deployment plan will need to be completed well in advance of deployment so that the user base can be scheduled and so that the facilities and equipment can be reserved.

Testing

Education needs to go through user acceptance testing just as the applications do, but normally this would not be done concurrently — we want to make sure the application is clean, in terms of user acceptance, before testing the training, otherwise they won't be concentrating on the training.

Implementation

The training itself should be designed to be as positive as possible. Keep in mind that the users are the barometer of success, and many of them might be coming to training not wanting a new application. If there's room in the budget, try to provide a little decoration to the facilities to make it a little festive — have lunch brought in, etc. If you lose the users during training, you'll have a big hill to climb to win them back.

4.1.6 Operations Planning

We don't really need to publish an approach for operations planning as we did the other topics unless one of the pieces, data acquisition or data analysis, will be accomplished in a manner other than what would be expected, or if the customer hasn't experienced operations planning in the past.

What we want to consider is any active role operations will need to play in, for example, daily batch processing. The requirements of the application as well as checkpoint restart need to be incorporated into the overall operations schedule and procedures.

4.2 LAUNCHING THE SOFTWARE DEVELOPMENT CYCLE

So far in this chapter, we've discussed publishing an approach for the infrastructure that will support the new technology, but we also need to start looking at the applications themselves.

There's a lot of work to be done to get the applications ready, but remember, we're working from a three stage approach. In this stage Daniel's team is not going to do any coding, or any design for that matter. Their activity will be limited to some vitally important preliminary work in which they'll determine:

- the application requirements;
- the development platform;
- the development methodology; and
- the application development plan.

So what are we waiting for? Let's get busy.

4.2.1 Requirements Study

Here's another topic that can be a book on its own, so we won't be describing a full requirements study, but portions of it are worth noting. The information we need can be divided into three "communities" and numerous categories. The "communities" represent a grouping of what should be common requirements, such as: 1) business; 2) user; and 3) IT.

It's important to detail the business requirements first, because when you're noting the desires of the User community and IT, there must not be any significant conflict between them and the business requirements, since the business requirements are driving everything.

So what are the business requirements that drive these applications? There are only two; far reaching but not too difficult to get our arms around. The business needs that launched the project have been worked into the high-level description (at this point) of the solution the team has in mind.

- An Internet solution that solicits, encourages and facilitates residential customers ordering incremental services.
- An intranet solution that disseminates company information while fostering a feeling of employee involvement.

Those, in a nutshell, are the business requirements, aside from the boring stuff that we won't go into, such as how the service pricing needs to tie into the latest tariff data. Now let's move onto the user requirements.

There are two types of users, and three sets of them here:

- Internet application
- the residential customers
- the service order activation people

- Intranet application
- all company employees as the intranet users.

So what are the user requirements? How do we determine them? Well, we talk to the users. Each scenario will warrant a different approach toward a "statistical population," but in this case the two users from each functional part of the company were interviewed, a mail survey was sent to 500 residential customers, and the service activation manager and several supervisors were interviewed. The requirements of all were very similar.

- Ease of use
- Intuitive interface
- PC-based client
- Simplified locating of data

Well, that's pretty straightforward and easy to live with. No surprises there. Now what about the IT requirements? We need to pay careful attention to these to make sure that we can live with them.

- Readily available development components — The concern is that if a software component from some nebulous third-party is used, would the application require major rewriting should that company go out of business.
- Industry-standard hardware platform — Staying with standards ensures that the customer can purchase expansion hardware based on the deal available to them and not be locked into specific hardware. For example, if an application is written using a Microsoft Windows®-based compiler on an Intel-based platform, the customer has a large selection of hardware available to run the applications.
- Transaction recoverable — The IT group doesn't want an application that requires, should processing fail, a large flurry of manual activity to recover the processing.
- Fully commented and documented code — This ties to maintainability. Should the IT group decide to maintain the application or farm out the maintenance to another company, the ability to maintain it will depend on how quickly a bug can be isolated.
- Secure transactions — Customer data. Giving the customer access to order services implies that you'll have a method of verifying that the customer is who they're supposed to be. There won't be a photo ID, so there needs to be way to protect the customer and the company.

4.2.2 Development Platform

We need to take a close look at what hardware and software platform will be used to develop and run the applications. It might seem that this discussion is premature, but let's take a look at some of the things that are affected by the selection.

- The skill sets required of the development team members, which in turn affects the lead time in assembling and cost of assembling the team.
- The development tools and licensing.
- The hardware platforms and their cost.
- The development methodology.
- The development time-line.

There are two development projects to consider: the Internet project and the intranet project. We can start by discussing the hardware considerations for each, but we might as well handle the potentially contentious discussion first, the one that will be revisited with different names in any scenario where the technology is fluid and a single step ahead of the people using it: Netscape or Microsoft?

Software technology never used to be the hotbed of debate that it is today. Back in the mainframe-only days, you developed in COBOL. I suppose PL/1 may have caused debate in some arenas as a contender, but those debates were far and few between. More likely there was disputation over whether DB2® or CICS® should be used. In any event, the basis of the software technology was pretty much set, the decisions were more akin to deciding on the carpet, wallpaper and paint colors for a house. Yet to the homeowner these decisions can be very emotional, and so can software platform decisions to the software developer.

To an application developer, the core development tools are terra firma. Telling the developer that 'other' tools are going to be used can leave them feeling like they're on terra-far-from-firma.

Luckily, we're in a position here where the development is going to be done by a team of designers with contracted help. The designers could care less what tools are used (beyond the ramifications the choices bring to the design), and since the contractor hired will have those tools in their skill set, they won't care either. If the customer's staff were doing the development though, there could be any number of responses to learning the development was being done on PC and UNIX platforms; some would look at it as a great opportunity to make the move to this kind of development, and some would look at it as threatening.

Despite the development team not having the skin in the game to care much one way or the other, the subject of Netscape or Microsoft will elicit opinion from just about everyone. The reasons why they take a side vary. To some, any business is the underdog when compared to Microsoft, and should be favored at any point just on that basis. To others, any business is the underdog when compared to Microsoft and stands no chance in the long run, so why bother wasting time on the competitor's product?

Having considered a comparison between the two products (as they stood at the time of this writing), two things in particular made the decision easier: security and relationship.

Due to security concerns, the Internet applications will not use client-side applets (small add-on applications i.e. Java®, VBScript® or ActiveX®). The security issues revolve around the the user is having executable applet code downloaded from the Internet and executed on the fly. The applet is not supposed to be able to interact with files on the user's system — "not supposed to" being key. There is a minute chance that the applet code can be hacked (or perhaps just have a bug?) so that it does affect the user's system in a nasty way. Small chance, but is it worth it? The Internet site is a revenue-raising PR exercise. How much return on investment would there be after one bad incident?

With that in mind, the recent announcement of Netscape SuiteSpot® and Netscape Communicator® from Netscape Communications, and Hewlett-Packard's embracing of those products in its strategy are enough to swing the pendulum into the Netscape Navigator™ corner.

In this case, since both products are very similar, if the need arose later on to migrate the applications to Internet Explorer®, the Microsoft product, the effort would be minimal. The truth is the decision is not very great in impact, but not all participants might agree (based in part on the emotional part of the equation). Every new technology implementation will have a similar decision to be made, whether or not it revolves around the software, but some could be more volatile still. If we look back to the birth of C++, those who understand the severe difference in the design of a C application and that of an object-oriented application written in C++ can understand the debates that accompanied the decisions to make those early applications object-oriented. Those debates still rage today.

The discussion doesn't always revolve around compilers or enabling software. You might remember the wars that sprang up around relational databases like Sybase, Informix and Oracle when most of the world was still using Network or Hierarchical databases.

We're ready to take a look at the software configuration. It's shown in Figure 4-8. With the pieces identified, a background activity needs to

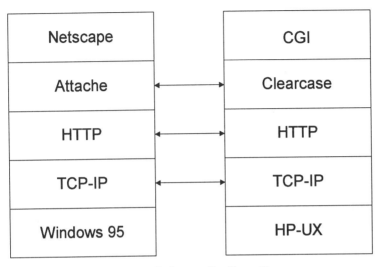

Figure 4-8 Software Configuration

take place where we gather the pricing for each component (software, software license(s), and support) and decide whether they will be built into the project cost, whether we already have them, or whether they will be capitalized as overhead (since they will most likely be used again). The one thing we will probably not do is use customer copies of the tool software for our development. The are too many ramifications in putting customer software on your hardware and using it for a profit-making venture. There are even more to your charging the customer for the software, purchasing it, and turning it over to the customer later on, such as transfer of licenses and discount schedules with the software vendor, etc. The best way to stay out of trouble is to use customer hardware with customer-owned software, or your (or leased) hardware with your own software.

The hardware is going to be fairly straightforward. The applications, being Internet/intranet, will be two-tiered, with each tier being different hardware. We're going to do the client development aiming at a Microsoft Win95® user environment. We'll put a bit more horsepower in the client than the user will have because we'll also have various development tools to contend with. There will be a user client system as well for testing. This system will be configured to identically match the customer's client.

On the server side, we will actually have two servers. One will be acting as the Web server, hosting the Web pages in the same way that they will be hosted by an Internet Service Provider (ISP) once the system is live. The other server will be a development engine, providing, among other things, version control, and will be used for developing the server-side code. Yes, there will be server-side code. Since we won't be using applets, we will use CGI scripts to accomplish that functionality. The servers will both be small UNIX servers.

We've resolved some of the initial development issues, but only among ourselves. We've made decisions on software and hardware technology, but these decisions need to be approved by the customer. After all, the customer will have to live with the application once it's done. Is that an issue? Sometimes, and it could very well be in this instance.

Mid-Central Telephone has no experience with this technology. They do have the hardware, but they aren't using it for client-server technology. Also, the Microsoft-Netscape issue is something the customer has probably been reading about in various journals and magazines. They might already have an opinion on the issue, consciously or subconsciously, and that opinion might be counter to ours. So while there might not necessarily be issues with the customer, a large amount of the discussion revolving around new technology could translate to some long, and perhaps challenging, meetings.

4.2.3 Development Methodology

How are the applications going to be developed? There are numerous development methodologies and, yes, software development methodology is definitely a book of its own subject. We'll cover some of it here because it is a critical piece of the development puzzle.

TIP ☞   If you're going to project manage a
                development project, ask the team
                lead what development methodolo-
                gy the team will be using. If the an-
                swer resembles a blank stare or
                shrug, this would be a good time to
                use some of those remaining vaca-
                tion days.

What if there isn't a methodology? Well, there has to be. Why? Because no methodology is in itself a methodology. Most of the software developed today uses this methodology — the "On the Fly" Methodology,
as seen in Figure 4-9.

You can see that it is the "On-The-Fly" Methodology because the
various phases of development, each as important as the next, design, construction, testing and implementation are all done on the fly if at all.
Thereby, construction might be launched as a result of some level of design, and implementation might be preceded by some level of testing. The
result of this methodology is that you might end up with a usable product,
and if you're very, very lucky, it will be available on time and within budget — but I wouldn't count on it. The odds are in favor of delivering a
product that is buggy, costs far more than it should have, and that is late.

Waterfall Methodology

Okay, so a better methodology is needed. The first candidate that
comes to mind is the most well known: the Waterfall. This methodology
can be seen in Figure 4-10.

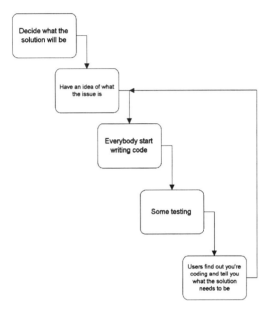

Figure 4-9 On-The-Fly Methodology

What makes the Waterfall the most common methodology is its sim-plicity. You start with a requirements analysis. You then move on to translating the requirements into a high-level design. The high-level de-sign, which describes the functionality goals, is then brought down a notch to a low-level design that accounts for the logistics of the system, the screens, programs and reports, and describes the functionality of each, as well as what the data structures need to contain. With the low-level de-sign complete we begin construction of the application, coding. The cod-ing is followed by testing, which can be take various forms as shown in Figure 4-11, and finally by the implementation.

The problem with the Waterfall Methodology is its simplicity. Each phase is completed before the next phase begins causing the entire cycle

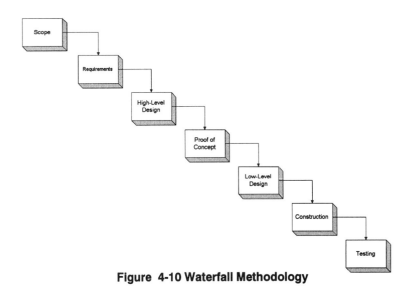

Figure 4-10 Waterfall Methodology

to be a sequence of serial events. It takes the approach of allowing the phases to be independent of each other in timing and personnel, but in this there lies an inherent problem. I contend that if a number of people gather together and have discussions and raise a document that summarizes those discussions, someone later reading that document will have less insight into the summarized situation than those who were present at the time. That delta in insight can make a difference in interpretation, which can translate to a shortfall in execution. I propose that a transfer of insight should be made, by way of a review, before the preceding phase is closed in favor of its successor.

Cascading Waterfall Methodology

Another popular methodology similar to the Waterfall Methodology is the Cascading Waterfall, shown in Figure 4-12.

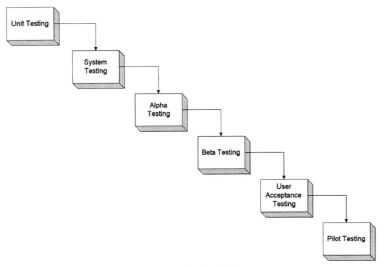

Figure 4-11 Testing Stages

The improvement is that phases are occurring somewhat in parallel now, thus bringing in the end-date. The bad news is that the logistics are more complex because of the subsequent phases beginning while their predecessors are still being completed. One other benefit is that if you base your time-line on the Waterfall but run it based on the cascading model, you stand a good chance of bringing the project in early, but you can always fall back to the Waterfall method if the logistics become too complex.

There is another difference between these methodologies that is not so apparent; resources. If the resources in each phase will be unavailable in the subsequent phase, you really need to have a clean line between phases and a handoff with documentation as well, and the Waterfall methodology is a perfect fit for that. If there will be some or full continuity with personnel, then the handoffs and documentation aren't necessary, so not only is the second, shorter time-framed (because of the overlapping phase

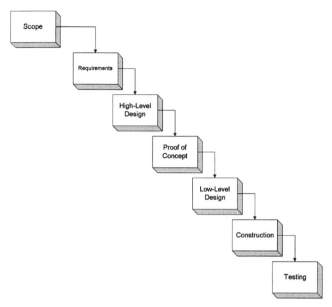

Figure 4-12 Cascading Waterfall Methodology

:s) methodology viable in this case, it removes the increased overhead of ɔre-handoff documentation.

There are drawbacks. One drawback of both preceding methodolo-ɡies is that nothing is delivered until everything is complete. That means hat if the project were to run late, the customer would have nothing to how for their money on the scheduled end-date. There is a way to assure hat this is not the case, and that is to phase delivery, as shown in the three ɾemaining methodologies. Another drawback, and more so for the Water- all methodology, is that should the need for rework of a previous phase ɾises, it could be difficult to achieve because the personnel or infrastruc-ɯre are no longer in place.

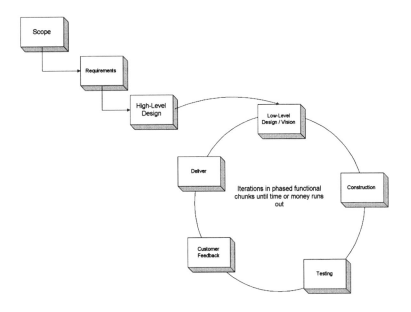

Figure 4-13 Phased Delivery Methodology

Phased Release Methodology

The first of these methodologies is simply called Phased Release, and is shown in Figure 4-13.

As you can see, with phased delivery the customer will certainly be using something come the scheduled end date, but what? Will the pieces we were able to deliver have any meaningful functionality without the remaining pieces? Perhaps, but there's a way to raise that with a higher level of certainty, and that is the next methodology.

One way to internalize the differences (and thus the need) of the preceding methodologies is to see their relative impact upon a project. In Figures 4-14, 4-15 and 4-16 you will find a small project as planned using each of the three methodologies. We're going to have a delay in each at the

Methodology	Plan $	Actual $	Planned Effort	Actual Effort	Planned Duration	Actual Duration
Waterfall	$18,000	$20,000	360h	400h	45d	50d
Cascading W/fall	$18,000	$20,000	360h	400h	34d	39d
Carousel	$18,000	$19,200*	360h	384h*	42d	45d*

* Phased Release methodology breaks the deliverable into phased chunks and develops each chunk until time runs out. In this case the final chunk was partially developed, but had to be canceled due to time running out, thus realizing a waste of 24 hours and $1,200.

Figure 4-17 Methodology Cost

same point, and what we want to pay attention to is the finish date of each. In each example there is a plan and the actual results. Following the presentation of each plan is a summary of the associated costs (Figure 4-17).

One thing to note in the cost comparisons is that the following formula is not always true:

Cost of an individual = individual's effort * rate

Why? Because if you have a contractor sitting at a desk for three days while they wait for someone else's late task to finish, you're paying for them despite the fact that the time can't be attributed to a task on the project plan as 'effort.' There is also an unfair comparison in this example; the Waterfall methodologies are allowed to complete despite being late, while the Phased Release methodology stops at the deadline with the result of wasted effort. It's important to note that if the deadline were indeed hard and fast, that there would be no delivery of a usable system with the Waterfall methodologies, while the Phased Release project would have delivered the first two phases.

Carousel Design Methodology

Also known as the Design to Schedule Methodology, the 'carousel' comes into it because in this methodology the development team divides the deliverable into groups of meaningful functionality sorted by priority, highest to lowest, and then develops, tests, and implements each grouping until the money or time runs out, whichever happens first, like riding the carousel until the music stops and the ride stops (see Figure 4-18).

Depending on the time available, the low-level design might also become part of the cycle instead of all being done up front.

The project plan will provide an estimate of how much functionality will be delivered before the cutoff. This methodology provides the most opportunity for usable functionality of a large system to be delivered. If the deliverable is smaller in quantity of applications or disparate functions, it might better be served by the next and final methodology.

Evolutionary Delivery

Evolutionary delivery takes the approach of a new house. In order to move into a new house, there is minimum functionality that is required, but the aesthetics don't necessarily have to be available. Once you have moved in, you can add to the house (garden, shelves, decoration, etc.) to bring it up to a level commensurate with your taste. The same can be done with an application. A core of complete functionality requirements can be delivered, and then a revolving series of design, construction, and user acceptance can occur until the application has evolved into what the users are most comfortable with (see Figure 4-19).

There is a drawback for this methodology, and that is that tracking variance from the estimate is all but impossible because there is no estimate *per se*, and that is because there is no ultimate detailed design, the design evolves.

The best fit for this methodology is where there is a wide gap between the business requirements for the application and the user requirements (such that the incremental user requirements don't represent base

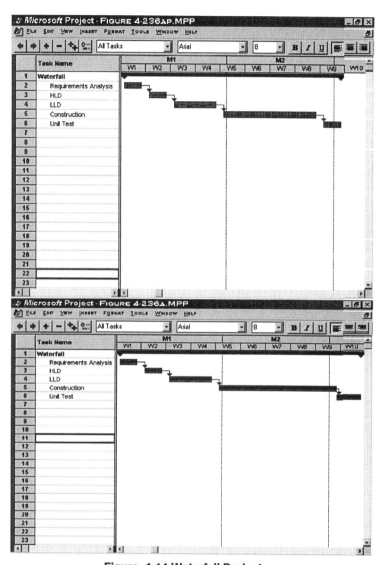

Figure 4-14 Waterfall Project

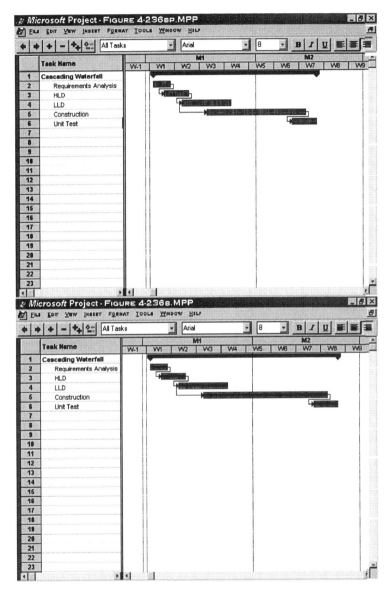

Figure 4-15 Cascading Waterfall

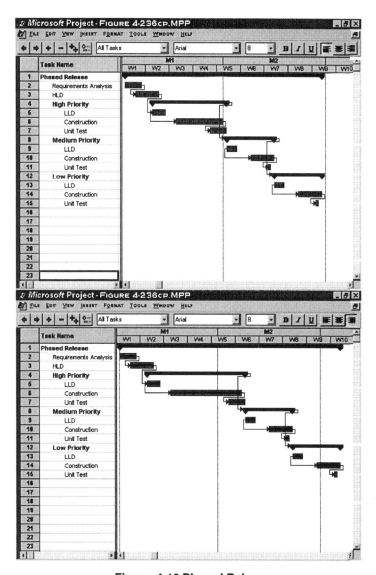

Figure 4-16 Phased Release

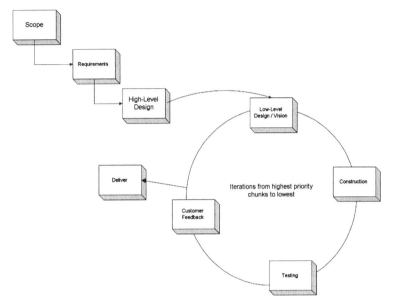

Figure 4-18 Carousel Methodology

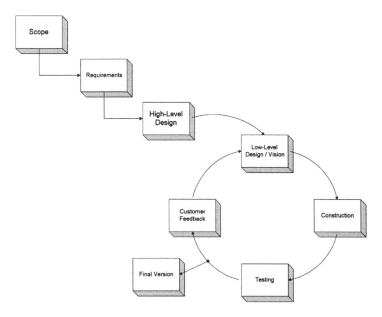

Figure 4-19 Evolutionary Methodology

functionality that should have been in the business requirements but were mistakenly omitted).

Also a good fit, and not necessarily mutually exclusive from the former, is when the resources providing the initial functionality don't necessarily need to be the resources providing the evolutionary functionality, so that a handoff can take place.

Those two considerations both apply in our case study. First, if necessary, a handoff can occur from the team of consultants to internal resources anywhere along the evolutionary path following the initial delivery. Second, a web site need only have one or two pages, a minor development, to be considered initially functional, and this would apply to both the intended Internet site as well as the intranet site. This concept is illustrated in Figure 4-20.

The page shown in the figure would lead you to think that there needs to be several subsequent pages to handle the links, but actually there

Figure 4-20 One-Page Web Site

are two ways around this. One is to have frames as shown in the figure, and feed information to the main text frame instead of traveling to another page. That's kind of cheating though, because the data for that frame will be coming from a separate file which is the same as having a separate page. The other method is to have the link take the reader to another spot on the same page, much like jumping to a specific paragraph.

Now you'll get no claim from me that a one-page web site is the best example of a web site for attracting attention, except for specific examples like personal web pages, but the point is that with the one page you can be up and available for web surfers to find and view, and then improve the site later. This method works with web sites — it won't necessarily work as well (or at all) with other application technology.

Another technology-specific reason makes this the better methodology. Remember that web pages are viewed with web "browsers," applications that, in their simplest form, translate the HTML code they receive from the server into a visual on your screen. For the most part, they are limited to handling text, graphic images, tables, and electronic forms. With the introduction of Java, JavaScript, ActiveX, and VBScript, the browsers become equipped to allow programmatic control (and some dynamic creation) of the text, graphics, table, and form elements. There is much more functionality that can be achieved with web pages though, and to provide this functionality you will need "add-ons" or "plug-ins" (basically the same thing, but each browser vendor uses their own terminology).

Add-ons and plug-ins are available for many different types of functionality, such as providing

- video
- streamed video
- streamed audio
- animation
- 3-D graphics
- virtual-reality

The thing to note is that these add-on and plug-in modules are almost always provided by a company other than the one that provides the browser. The problem that goes hand-in-hand with this is that many of these modules are free or very inexpensive. Why is this a problem? Because if they don't work, you might have a very hard time getting the company that provides it to sit up and take notice when you paid little or nothing for it — and that can play havoc on your construction schedule. That is of course unless you don't care. If the modules are being used to evolve the application, so long as the core functionality is in place and working you won't necessarily lose much if you have to bypass, for example, putting sound on the web page if the sound plug-in doesn't quite work the way you need it to.

There is one more reason that this methodology will work better in our case study, and this is, perhaps, specific to the Internet/intranet technology: the development cycle, on the intranet cycle in particular, will require a larger amount of user input than the normal development cycle. The reason for this is content. Think of the underlying intranet application being like the curators of a museum — once everything underlying the exhibit is ready, we still need the exhibit. That is what the content of a web site translates to. The application will link various sites or pages together, allow input, validate, respond to user requests, but what will be provided to the user, what they've come to see, is the content, and that content, be it policies, forms, etc., will need to come from the customer.

TIP ☞   A project manager working with
               new technology must be open to
               evaluating new methodologies, and
               equally open to re-evaluating old
               methodologies.

Now that we have chosen the development methodology, let's move on to putting together the development plan.

4.2.4 The Development Plan

You might think that with our chosen methodology Daniel's off the hook no matter how little is delivered, after all, it can evolve. Well, that's not really the case. The evolution is from a baseline level of functionality that is agreed upon with the customer. There are expectations as to how long it should take to reach that point and how much it will cost. In this case, the added complication of needing to understand the content, prior to putting a page around it, will affect the plan.

You might ask why the content needs to be understood first. Well, perhaps not first, perhaps we don't need a finish-to-start relationship between understanding content and developing the underlying page. Perhaps we can put some of the page in place initially, but we can't finish.

For example, let's say we'll be allowing the user to look at the stock value. Until we know where that value will come from, whether we will present just the value or shares traded and high and low for the day, we won't know how to lay out the page.

So the relationship is more one of finish-to-finish — we can finish a page no earlier than the task of acquiring the content, and once we've finished that development, the cycle begins again if time and money will allow it — keeping the customer "honest."

That's also how the customer will keep you honest — the bait being further funding available for further functionality if you deliver the core functionality in the time and at the cost agreed upon.

So, let's put together a development plan for each of the applications. We're going to include just enough detail to make the plan meaningful here, but more detail would be needed before I'd be comfortable managing this development. The plan can be seen in Figure 4-21.

Each development epoch will take place if the time allows (it's been predetermined that there is sufficient budget to fund the entire evolution), and if not, the minimum acceptable functionality will have been delivered in the first wave.

This brings up an interesting point about project plans. The plan accounts for the amount of effort we believe will be necessary to accomplish a task. We know, however, that stuff happens, gremlins that get into the works — gremlins that have people out sick, cause equipment to stop working properly, cause things to get lost in the mail, etc. How do we account for that in the plan? It's done through adding risk to the plan, and it's best done through associating risk with each task rather than adding a risk item because it's more controllable. For instance, if we determine that a particular type of task takes 25 percent more time than estimated, and we've only added 20 percent risk, then we can make the appropriate changes to that type of task.

It pays to give attention in the planning stage to the confidence you have in the estimates being given, and also to the fact that those estimates

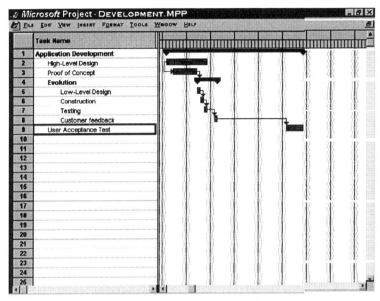

Figure 4-21 Development Plan

will typically not account for any gremlins showing their faces. There are two areas in which to consider this, the task estimates and the task relationships.

When asking for estimates I ask for a best-case and worst-case estimate. I then take a weighted average of the two (see Figure 4-22) and use it. What I've found over the years is that developers tend to be optimistic. If in working with a developer you find his or her estimates to be conservative, a straight average may suffice.

There are two other considerations that must be given to using the Evolutionary methodology.

- The personnel for low-level design, construction, and testing have to be available throughout the evolution. If their calendar shows them being available to you 50 percent of the time, as an example, you're going to lose. Someone who is sharing time will not always be able to give you your 50 percent at the

Best-case estimate	130 hours
Worst-case estimate	160 hours

Scorecard: Optimistic	Scorecard: Realistic	Scorecard:Pessimistic
160	160	160
160	130	130
130		130
----	----	----
450 hours	290 hours	420 hours
3	2	3
----	----	----
150 hours	145 hours	140 hours

Figure 4-22 Weighted Estimates

times best for your team, and if several people are scheduled like that their time will never synch up.

- The customer personnel needed for user acceptance testing will need to be available more flexibly than with other methodologies. You will be coming to them for less contiguous time, but more insertions on their calendar with less lead time, because with each evolution — ranging from a day to a few days — you won't know until a day in advance that you're going to need thirty minutes or an hour of their time. You can't plan it in advance, and if you try to compromise and schedule, say, one hour every other day in the afternoon on their calendar, you risk keeping the entire team twiddling their thumbs if they finish an evolution between those days.

TIP ☞   Be suspicious immediately if a resource is scheduled for more than one activity with the sum of their availability being 100 percent — once you ask someone to juggle activities, part of the 100 percent, at least 10 percent, is given to overhead.

Well, that kicks off the software development cycle as much as we want to at this point (remembering we're in Phase 1, the scoping phase, of a three-phase project). Daniel's almost done with this "discovery" portion of the project. The next thing to tackle is the initial implementation scoping.

4.3 IMPLEMENTATION SCOPING

Isn't it too early to be thinking about implementation? No, otherwise the section heading would be wrong. Seriously, the requirements to be met during implementation can certainly impact or even define the effort that will be required, and thus can certainly impact the cost to an order of magnitude.

How about an example? I want you to install your application on fifty PCs. Okay, now you can sit back and form a picture in your mind of that effort. Part two: I want you to install it on fifty PCs, but they'll be right out of the box (you being the "de-boxer"), and I want them to have "instant ignition" (pre-configured, ready to go just by turning on the power), and I want minimal interruption to my staff.

Whoa. Now we're talking about a whole different level of effort. I mean, does the staff have power receptacles for this stuff? Desk space? Are we using the operating system it comes with, or do I have to install another one?

Well, you get the idea. This is actually more than just an example, this is the implementation requirement for Daniel's team. We'll take a closer look at the logistics later on, but at least we have a feel for our responsibility, and can begin looking at what that means for the time that will be necessary for planning the implementation, because the cost we will incur in Phase 2 is the cost of planning, and the result of that planning will show us the cost of actually implementing in Phase 3, but we don't need to know the implementation cost now.

Well, there's only one thing left to do in Phase 1, and that's to develop a proposal and project plan for Phase 2. We've been through producing a proposal, so let's concentrate on the project plan; it will give us a better idea of what the scope of Phase 2 is.

4.4 PHASE 2 PROJECT PLAN

Phase 2 will be the development phase. We'll be developing the applications, the deployment processes, and the implementation plan. The information Daniel and his team gathered in Phase 1 will facilitate the development of this plan, which is shown in Figure 4-23.

There are very few surprises in this plan. The portions to note are the relationships between task groupings (keep in mind that there will be an evolutionary development cycle of low-level design, construction, testing and acceptance).

- Proof of Concept will occur prior to the start of the first low-level design (that customer feedback can influence the design without the treat of heavy rework).
- Infrastructure development depends on the first wave of low-level application design being completed (so that the data structures and application modules that will drive some of the infrastructure requirements have been designed).
- Deployment planning will occur any time after the first low-level design has been completed, but as late as possible (so that any changes to the initial design will have already occurred).
- Test planning (acceptance, beta, pilots) won't occur until after the deployment planning, not because the content of deployment planning needs to be completed first (although that content will be used), but because some of the same resources are needed for both.

With the plan and proposal completed and delivered, Daniel received word back that Phase 2 was a go. One thing to consider is how did Daniel manage to price construction within the proposal when the design hasn't been done yet? I mean, picture trying to decide how much it will cost to build something for which there is no design.

In this case we're going to do a minimal construction for acceptability, and then will improve it as time and money allow. Nonetheless, if Daniel were not confident in his team's ability to estimate the high-level design (HLD) and minimal low-level design (LLD) and construction, there would be no way to price anything beyond the HLD right now, and

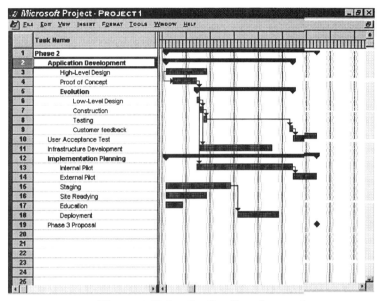

Figure 4-23 Application Development

we'd have to insert another phase. The reason his team was able to provide that estimation is that for them the requirements are nothing out of the ordinary, they have a great deal of experience with the technology and its implementation. If the customer were to be doing this work themselves, or were assembling a team to do it that had similar skills but not direct experience, there would be a great deal of risk in committing to anything beyond the HLD at this point. Even with the team's experience, there is still a fair amount of risk because they have committed to delivering the minimal functionality, and at this point they're basing their understanding of the effort to design, construct, test, and implement that functionality from the requirements and gut instinct.

So let's jump out of Phase 1 and this chapter and start doing the real work. You'll find that the design and implementation effort in the book move much faster than the investigation, just like in a real project.

Chapter 5

I t's time to get to the fun part of the project — the development. Naturally, this part of the project carries higher risk than the investigation, because now we're going to depend on a number of people to produce contractual deliverables; but despite that, this phase typically gives people more of a feeling of accomplishment than the first phase.

There are two things we want to accomplish in this chapter: to understand the scope of a proof of concept exercise, and to move further into the application development cycle. These topics go hand-in-hand because the application development cycle won't proceed beyond the high-level design until we have the feedback from the proof-of-concept. This dependency is shown in Figure 5-1 as a minor alteration to the methodology we looked at earlier.

If we were working with a customer who had more experience with this technology we might have a higher level of confidence in their understanding what they really want at the onset, but because that isn't the case there is a strong possibility that the feedback from the proof-of-concept will cause some minor changes to the high-level design, which would cause turmoil with the low-level design if we were already deep into it.

5.1 HIGH-LEVEL DESIGN

Four main purposes for a high-level design are as follows:

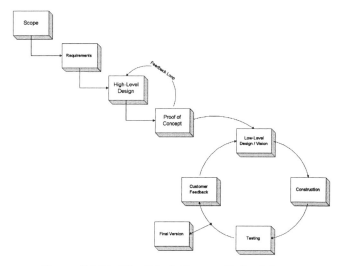

Figure 5-1 Modified Evolutionary Methodology

- to remove a level of abstraction from the scope documentation.
- to provide a vehicle for developing the low-level design.
- to document the business rules to be used in processing.
- to give the customer the opportunity to see their requirement expressed in a manner that allows more visualization than pure scope.

So what do we put in a high-level design? This is a very broad question, so let's tighten it up a bit by describing what we put into a web site high-level design — but let's look at it from the view of what we don't put in.

- Aesthetic components — we're not interested at this point with the banners, logos, image maps, animated images, and other elements that give a web page visual appeal.
- Specific controls — we're not at a point where we care whether, for example, navigation through the web site will be afforded through image maps or individual links.
- Nonfunctional (Web text) Content — there is typically a ratio of 80 percent nonfunctional content to 20 percent functional on each web page. The functional being links or controls, the nonfunctional being everything else including most of the text. We want to account for the functional members only.

So what we want to include is the functionality that will be necessary to deliver what has been defined in the scope. In fact, the "cross totaling" check for our work will be to go through the scope documentation line by line and make sure that each requirement is accounted for in the high-level design. If you have the time, it works well to number each paragraph in the scope documentation, and then whenever a requirement is fulfilled in the design, show the reference paragraph number in parenthesis.

We will also include business rules to be used in performing calculations and processing. At this point those rules need not be expressed as calculations or as pseudo-code (English expression of computer instructions), unless it makes the depiction easier, but we do need to document these rules so that the detailed processing considerations of the LLD can be derived from our HLD document.

The high-level requirements for the Internet application are shown in Figure 5-2; for the intranet application in Figure 5-3.

5.2 PROOF OF CONCEPT

When developing a screenplay with the hopes of having the idea "picked up," one method is the two-page screenplay — the theory being if the plot doesn't work in two pages, it certainly won't in 100, but you'll have expended far less effort to discover it.

The same holds true for implementation. The main reason for a prototype is that if the concept doesn't work in prototype, it won't work later.

Intranet application HLD

1. Hyperlink access to corporate information
2. Employee-specific pages are password protected
3. Background database access to employee ID data
4. Background database access to benefit data (not payroll information)
5. Intranet search page

Figure 5-2 Intranet High Level Design

Internet application HLD

1. Hyperlink access to corporate information
2. "Live" shareholder information
3. Corporate background information
4. Corporate dynamic news
5. Product information
6. Customer access to account information with password barrier
7. Customer ability to order residential add-on services

Figure 5-3 Internet High Level Design

Of course, money can be thrown at a failed prototype to make it work, but the decision should be made beforehand whether this is acceptable, not while under fire.

The problem frequently is that there is insufficient discussion with the customer prior to a proof of concept, and when the time comes to deliver it, the customer's expectations don't match what they're seeing; they've come to see the entire screenplay, not just the two-page version.

Is it possible to give them that? Perhaps, but whether it's worth it is another question. Let's say that we're building an "old west" town, and we're going to do a proof of concept for the customer in the way of a mock-up, much like a Hollywood set. Do we build a set of the entire town instead of one or two buildings? We could, but is the effort worth if? Not if the following conditions are met by showing less:

- The content sufficiently reflects the feasibility of delivering the technology and functionality in the high-level design.
- The content is sufficient to prove the first point to the customer.
- The customer's expectations are met.

The last point is the most important, so it's a good thing that Daniel took the time to sit down with the customer and instill the idea that this is simply a mock-up to give them an understanding of what the environment looks like, and to prove that the technology can deliver the functionality that is needed.

The next thing to consider is the technology. Some people believe that the proof of concept should contain at least one of each piece of hardware, but does that make sense? In our business case, we'll be using a type of technology not previously used by this customer, such as a UNIX server, but if the final configuration is going to use three different models of the same server technology, how many do we need to use in the proof of concept? One. The same goes for the client hardware. Of course, if there is a technological difference between models, and that technology needs to be proved, then you might want to use each. For example, if I have a PC with a CD-ROM drive and another without the drive but with a built-in photo scanner, and the solution makes use of both and we're at the point in time where PC's didn't have a CD-ROM drive or a built-in scanner, then I would want to make use of both in my proof of concept. If, however, CD-ROM drives have been around for awhile, then there's no need to include that technology in the proof of concept (because it's proven technology), unless the customer isn't comfortable with or knowledgeable about the technology.

Networks are another example of this concept. Yes, the client will be on one 'end' of a LAN and the server on the other, and the server will be on one node of a WAN and the corporate mainframe on another — but we're going to be using industry-standard networking here, nothing fancy and nothing proprietary, so we should be able to avoid much of the networking headache in the prototype. Sure, the server-to-mainframe part of the network might need to be included because the customer might not want to take that connectivity as being given, but we still might be able to scale things down.

The last consideration about the scope of the proof of concept is the functionality. The high-level design will have provided us with a list of function points that the application(s) will need. Do we need to prototype all the function points? No way José! Not unless each function point is so technologically different from the other that in proving one we've not proven any other. No, typically we will group the function points by like technology and prove one from each grouping.

So with all that in mind, let's take a look at what our proof of concept will look like. Figure 5-4 lists the function points we will prototype and a list of the technology. We might not specifically prove each technology item, some might be proven indirectly by the fact that a function point is proven. For example, a TCP/IP connection from a client to a server can be proven by successfully competing a client-to-server: you can't log on if there's no connection.

With the functions and technology that we'll be proving listed, let's take a look at what the proof of concept will look like. There's a pleasant side-effect of developing applications for the web, and that is that it's easy to do a mock-up for a proof of concept because the development-to-a-view in this environment is almost immediate, unlike, for example, the mainframe COBOL environment. If we were developing the client applications in compiled programming language, then we could use, in this case, something like Visual Basic for the prototype, because it lends itself to RAP (Rapid Application Prototyping) by requiring very little in the

Proof of Concept Scope

1. PC intranet connection to HP-UX intranet server
2. Web-page-initiated sever database look-up
3. Password barrier to web page
4. PC->modem->Internet connection to ISP
5. Routing of order to remote printer
6. Dynamic web page content

Figure 5-4 Proof of Concept Scope

way of development in order to throw something visible and responsive up on the screen.

The function points that we've listed above will be represented in five different screens. Example:

- a network log-onscreen;
- an intranet form screen;
- an Internet informational screen;
- an Internet navigation screen;
- an Internet order screen.

5.3 LOW-LEVEL DESIGN

The high-level design, modified to accommodate the feedback from the proof of concept, will provide us with the information necessary to create the low-level design. The low-level design will be the last layer of documentation, and the last customer sign-off, prior to code construction beginning.

Where the high-level design simply defined the function points of the application and the business rules to be used with each, the low-level design lays out what form the embodiment of that functionality will take as well as the format of the visual vehicle, be it screen, report or web page. Decisions will be made about the placement of controls and the division of the logical function points into physical presentation. This can be compared to a stage in building a house, as shown in Figure 5-5.

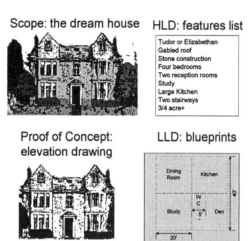

Phases of Building a House

Scope: the dream house   HLD: features list

Tudor or Elizabethan
Gabled roof
Stone construction
Four bedrooms
Two reception rooms
Study
Large Kitchen
Two stairways
3/4 acre+

Proof of Concept: LLD: blueprints
elevation drawing

Figure 5-5 House Construction Analogy

We will have a fairly large low-level design document, but for the sake of brevity, I'll limit our discussion to the functionality we presented in the proof of concept. Remember our methodology: we're going to deliver limited functionality and then move on to another round. The low-level design documentation can be seen in Figures 5-6 through 5-10.

Account Access Form

This page is a form page that accepts information from the user that will be compared to the information on record to verify access to their customer service information.

PAGE LAYOUT

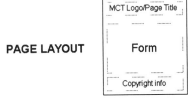

First name [_____]

Last name [_____]

Password [_____]

Enter your area code and phone number in the space provided below.

[___] - [___] - [_____]

[Submit Form]   [Reset Form]

Editing

First name: Initial letter should be forced to uppercase.
Password: Fail if any characters are not alphanumeric.
Phone number: Verify 3-3-4 with no initial 0 or 1 in exchange.
                Validate area code against local area

Functionality

Check phone number and name against customer database
If data matches then
  If password on record then
    If password field not empty then
      If password field matches password then
        Retrieve customer data and proceed to customer page
      Else fail
    Else request password
  Else if password field not empty then
      accept password and proceed to password confirmation
    else request password
else fail

Figure 5-6 Account Access Form LLD

Credit Union Withholding Request

This page is a form page that allows an employee to request the creation of, change to or deletion of a withholding order.

PAGE LAYOUT

Please provide your account information:
First name

Last name

Enter your employee number:

This order:
⦿Is a new withholding order ○Changes an existing order ○Deletes an existing order

Effective date: -- mm/dd/yy

Amount to be withheld? $

Account: ⦿Checking ○Savings ○Loan ○Xmas Club

Submit Form   Reset Form

Editing

First name: Initial letter should be forced to uppercase.
Employee no: Numeric. Pad to 8 digits.
Effective date: Standard date editing. Date >= today.
Amount: 0 if deletion, else >0

Functionality

Check employee number and name against employee database
If data matches then record request in database and route to
Credit Union printer

Figure 5-7 Credit Union Form LLD

Credit Union Withholding Request

This page is a form page that allows an employee to request the creation of, change to or deletion of a withholding order.

PAGE LAYOUT

Functionality

Provide two links:
  To product features
  To service order screen, passing service

Figure 5-8 Product Screen LLD

Service Order Request

This page is a form page that allows a customer to order residential services .

PAGE LAYOUT

Functionality

Poll the database to build a list of available services, then present them left to right, top to bottom with a check box for each. Retrieve the customer record as well. Any service match on the customer record will be reflected by the corresponding boxes being checked. If this form was invoked from a service ordering link then the applicable service will be checked. Submission of this form with any box checked will lead to the confirmation screen.

Figure 5-9 Service Order Screen LLD

Service Order Request

This page is a form page that allows a customer to order residential services .

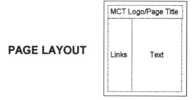

PAGE LAYOUT

Functionality

Three frames, 20% over 80%, 25% left of 75%.

The links section of the page will be a table of contents into the MCT web site. The text will provide a welcome to the site.

Figure 5-10 Home Page LLD

During the low-level design we will naturally have internal design review meetings to ensure the following:

- the design has a homogenized feel — not many individual efforts.
- the detailed design is delivering the promise of the high-level design.
- common design elements or objects are accounted for and assigned.
- all design elements, functional and aesthetic, are accounted for.

5.4 PRECONSTRUCTION

Having completed the low-level design and having received a sign-off on it from the customer, we're ready to move to construction; well, almost ready to move to construction. There are a number of things we need to have prepared in our development environment before we launch into construction. These things don't necessarily need to wait until now, they could have begun as soon as Phase 2 did, but they need to be completed. Let's take a look at the list.

- Clients assembled — the PC's being assembled, plugged in, and connected to power and the network.
- Clients configured — the PC's have had the operating system installed and IP addresses assigned.
- Server assembled.
- Server configured.
- Development software installed — development software installed and configured, as well as the software version control utility.
- Software licenses — accounted for and in place.
- Client and server configurations recorded.
- Web site set up on server — it's best to have the web site set up so that all references to the locations of the web pages in the links, the URL (e.g., http://www.dummy.com/tryme/) can be identical to what they'll be when implemented. If a directory is different or a local file name is used temporarily instead of a URL (e.g., file:///c:\html\temp\tryme.html), it will be too easy to forget to change it later on, and a real pain if we need to make changes later on between the test and live environments.
- Technical support arranged — for the development hardware, operating system software, network hardware, and development software.

5.5 CONSTRUCTION

Okay, now we're ready to move on to the construction phase. We're not going to cover the specifics of code construction, but we do need to make some points about it.

We need to keep our infrastructure team in mind. They were fed the low-level design as soon as we completed it because they need that information for their decisions. Our decision on methodology doesn't make their life easy if any of their answers are tied up in functionality that won't be delivered in the first cycle, so we need to keep them in mind and be as cooperative as possible with them.

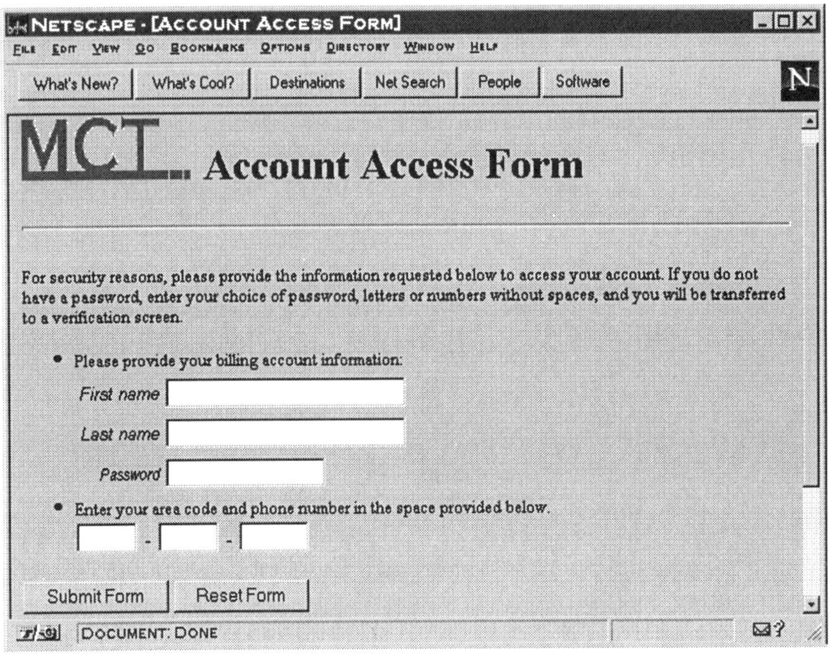

Figure 5-11 Account Access Form

There are going to be code reviews during the construction phase just as there were design reviews during the design phase. We want to make sure that all code is up to snuff and similarly constructed.

The code will of course need to be tested. The user testing will come later, but we will be doing internal testing first. We'll cover that right after taking a look at the fruits of our labors in Figures 5-11 through 5-15.

5.6 INTERNAL TESTING

Unit and system testing, an integral part of the development cycle are often given less attention than necessary, usually due to time constraints, especially when using one of the waterfall methodologies. However, insufficient internal testing can lead to embarrassment, at the least during the subsequent customer testing, as well as an exercise in thrashing

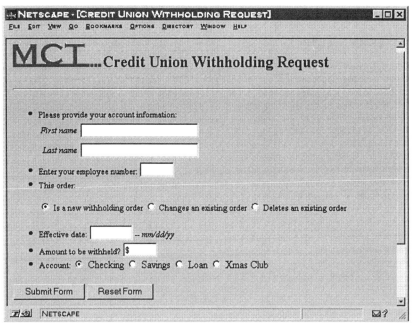

Figure 5-12 Credit Union Form

ɔetween users discovering the errors and the development team needing
:o make quick fixes. No, better to do it right the first time.

A unit test is meant to test that unit of development — whether that
-s a screen, report, web page, or module — and how it works designed
ınto itself, whereas the system test ensures that the unit plays nicely with
ɔther units and/or systems, and allows data to pass through the system so
:hat the end result can be analyzed. Let's look at what we would want to
ıccomplish in each test.

5.61 Unit Testing

Unit testing can be thought of as being introspective. We want to re-
-iew what's within the boundaries of the executable — the application, the
:creen, the web page, etc. — and make sure it's working as described in the
ɔw-level design. Let's take a look at a unit test checklist in Figure 5-16 for
ɔne of the web pages developed by Daniel's team.

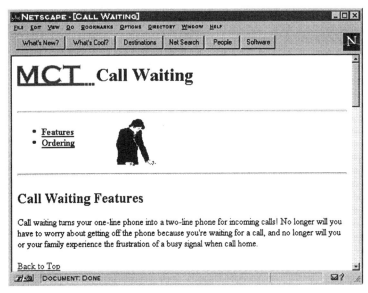

Figure 5-13 Product Page

Many of the normal items that would be tested in unit testing will not be tested here because we have no input fields on this screen. For example:

- Entering numeric or symbolic data into an alpha field triggers an edit message.
- Entering alphabetic or symbolic data into a numeric field triggers an edit message.
- Entering an invalid date into a date field triggers an edit message.
- Entering a valid date into a date field results in the date being formatted with a four-digit year (let's avoid the year 200 'plague').
- Tabbing into a nonempty text field results in the current text string being selected in its entirety.

Unit testing can be done by the coder to cover their own work, and is par for the course in a highly interactive development environment such as MS-Windows where you almost can't help noticing whether something

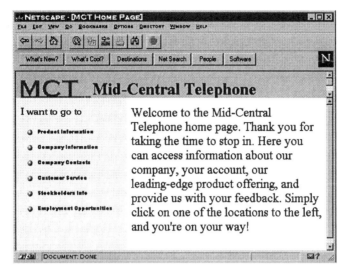

Figure 5-15 MCT Home Page

Unit Testing Checklist

Y	N	
o	o	Web page loads
o	o	Banner graphic loads
o	o	Navigation map loads
o	o	List box loads
o	o	List box responds according to spec
o	o	Program button responds
o	o	Descriptive graphic loads
o	o	Page resizes
o	o	Links affect cursor properly
o	o	Child window loads from button push
o	o	List box-selected image loads in child
o	o	Child window resizes
o	o	Closing child returns to parent
o	o	Audio button plays audio

Figure 5-16 Unit Test Checklist

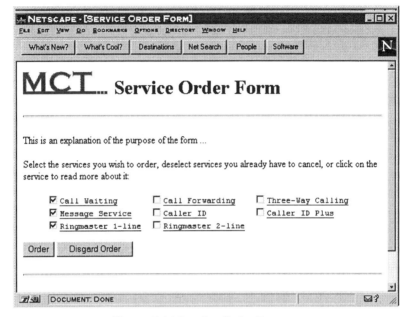

Figure 5-14 Service Order Page

works correctly or not. In some instances you might want to have someone other than the coder unit test and sign off on it, but the opportunity to accomplish the same thing will be given during system testing.

5.62 System Testing

System testing will test much of what unit testing did, but will more importantly test this unit's connection to all of its external connections. If we were testing an application that created or deposited data into a database or something similar, we would check that container to make certain the data is what we're expecting. In the case of this web page, we will not be creating persistent data. So let's create a check list in Figure 5-17 for system testing. This list focuses on functionality as opposed to data flows.

With the internal testing out of the way we want to make sure that the tested environment is on a test system that is sterile and remains ster

System Testing Checklist

Y	N	
o	o	Navigation controls lead where expected
o	o	Links lead where expected
o	o	Order button leads to order screen
o	o	Order button leads to service selected on order screen

Figure 5-17 System Test Checklist

ile; this will be the gold system from which we launch our customer tests. Now it's time to move on to planning the invasion.

Chapter 6

The primary concept of cookie-cutter proliferation is that the implementation be planned and executed correctly once, hopefully the first time, and then re-used without additional overhead. This chapter leads the reader through a proliferation plan, site readiness checklist, data transfer, user education, release synchronization, staging, and support.

6.1 PROLIFERATION PLANNING

Proliferation planning can be viewed as implementation planning with the added dimension of a multiple-instance deployment. When rolling out numerous systems, one left-hook during the implementation can cripple a tightly coupled plan, so the most prudent thing to do is plan the proliferation as thoroughly as possible, more so than normal planning; Let's segue into a visual analogy.

In Delhi, India, driving conditions are horrendous, but driving is an art. On the main roads around the Indian presidential palace and houses of parliament, there are three lanes for travel in each direction. The lanes are filled beyond capacity with trucks, automobiles (some barely fitting the term, three-wheeled taxis, auto-rickshaws, bicycles, scooters (carrying entire families or four), motorcycles, horses, donkeys, cows, water buffalo, oxen and elephants — yes, elephants — and they tend to receive the most right-of-way for obvious reasons. All of these vehicles, including the bicycles, are sharing space, swerving to avoid each other, swerving to avoid cars that have turned to park perpendicular to traffic, and the result of the swerving and jockeying for position is that the six distinct lanes melt into seven or eight or nine, with the two outside lanes sometimes having traffic in both directions.

The amazing thing, what makes the driving an art, is that there is rarely a collision. In the two hours of traveling these roads one rush-hour afternoon, I saw no collisions (and this was not an exception), whereas, for example, on I-285, the perimeter road around Atlanta, Georgia, every rush hour brings what seems like a collision every ten miles every ten minutes. So how do they do it? By taking a completely passive attitude: they assume they are seen by no one. If you assume that, in changing lanes, no one can see you, and that the other guy doing a lane change doesn't see you, then you make the change slowly, leave a little space in case someone is next to you, beep your horn incessantly so that people are aware of your presence, and accept no right-of-way (unless you're an elephant).

In developing a low-risk proliferation plan, you need to take a completely passive attitude — assume nothing. Start with a premise that the system will appear at someone's desk or in what will be used as a computer room, and work backwards. This ground-up format is used very often in other environments, such as woodworking. I want to end up with an object that looks like this, what pieces of wood, cuts, and joins will I need to get there?

Daniel will be doing this with the MCT project team as well as nonteam personnel. The reason for the nonteam personnel is because we want to make sure that any functional group capable of derailing the deployment or of helping to ensure its success are present when we identify the deployment issues. An example might be the purchasing department. We'd hate to have the deployment go down the tubes because we don't have power because we filled out a blue requisition form to bring in an electrician instead of a mauve requisition form.

The process Daniel will use to determine the plan items is quite simplistic. He'll start with, for example, writing on a white-board the premise that a client system is up and running on someone's desk, the final milestone for the client, and will mark that as Item 0. He'll then take a step back, and say that the power cable will be turned on, Item 1, and ask if anyone can think of anything that will stand in the way of that. A partic-

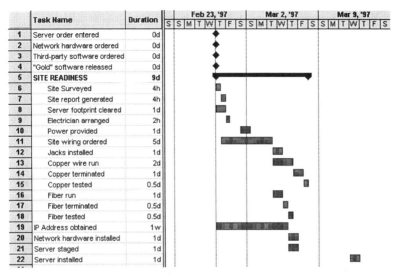

	Task Name	Duration
1	Server order entered	0d
2	Network hardware ordered	0d
3	Third-party software ordered	0d
4	"Gold" software released	0d
5	**SITE READINESS**	**9d**
6	Site Surveyed	4h
7	Site report generated	4h
8	Server footprint cleared	1d
9	Electrician arranged	2h
10	Power provided	1d
11	Site wiring ordered	5d
12	Jacks installed	1d
13	Copper wire run	2d
14	Copper terminated	1d
15	Copper tested	0.5d
16	Fiber run	1d
17	Fiber terminated	0.5d
18	Fiber tested	0.5d
19	IP Address obtained	1w
20	Network hardware installed	1d
21	Server staged	1d
22	Server installed	1d

Figure 6-1 Sample Deployment Plan

ipant might volunteer that some desks will not have an open electrical socket so there will be no power available for the client.

That gets us on our way. Step by step, until the last and final item is planning the deployment, which they are. Let's take a look at a sample deployment plan for the server system in Figure 6-1.

Something to keep in mind here is that prior to the proliferation we will be having a beta test (which will act as the final user-acceptance test), an in-house pilot (which requires limited deployment) and a remote pilot (which requires full deployment), and since success of the deployment logistics are part of the testing, you want to make sure that the logistics necessary for the proliferation represent the same logistics as readying the test sites but in multiple. There might be some umbrella items that occur outside any of the individual boxes, such as site wiring. When you finish the planning, move those items outside on their own as preceding the proliferation phases, then look back at the remaining plan items and ask the gathered masses whether, assuming the independent items and other items are all executed, this plan will work for the pilot site.

Daniel noticed that the staff of the Operations Director, Bryan Spanner, makes up a majority of the attendees. This is typically the part of the project where that group will start making a contribution, and since much of the logistics issues in achieving proliferation will be overcome by Operations, it's a good time for them to be there.

Daniel is careful to watch body language during the discussions. Not everyone contributes in a forum like this for varying reasons.

- fearful of their ideas being rejected
- they aren't in control
- they don't want to be there
- they're there only to be their manager's eyes and ears
- they think the project will fail and don't want to be associated with that
- they think the project will succeed and don't want it to

Daniel is watching the body language to try to determine who isn't contributing and why. At the start of the meeting he had everyone introduce themselves and relate what department they're with, so he's very mindful of whether someone not contributing is thus resulting in their department providing no input, something that needs to be rectified. Daniel's method of going backward through the proliferation might not work if people are fearful of contributing. In that arena each plan item volunteered could result in discussion, positive or negative, and the negative reinforcement is what could keep people from contributing. If the audience seems to be made up of people who aren't contributing or who don't work well together, it might be better to take a two-phased approach.

The first phase would be a brainstorming session. In a brainstorming session you ask everyone to contribute ideas of what is needed for the proliferation to succeed, and what could impede it in a fast-paced forum. The facilitator, in this case Daniel, has two roles. One is to write down the ideas as they're given, and the other is to enforce the rule, which is that at this point there is to be no discussion of or commenting, even regarding the facilitator's spelling, on the ideas. The removal of any potential for negativity will help people to contribute, and the fast pace makes it fun. It should last no more than thirty minutes, fifteen to twenty would be best.

The second phase is to expand on each idea, perhaps get some clarification on those that aren't self-explanatory, to determine which have merit and which don't, and to put them in the proper order, typically what will make sense chronologically. The participants might draw back into their shells somewhat during this discussion, especially as it relates to the appropriateness of an item, but even if they do go quiet on you, you now have the material.

6.2 SITE READINESS CHECKLIST

Keeping the users happy is usually much more important than anyone on the project realizes. More often than not the users report up through a different management chain than the IS department, and the point where the two chains converge, the point at where one person has the responsibility for the users' happiness and the authority to do something about it is higher than you usually want the exposure to be.

The exposure for unhappy users is particularly high when we get to the point where they are disrupted — the installation of their PC or the wiring for it, and at the department or geographic level (depending on how the servers are segregated) the installation of the server(s), network hardware, and cabling. The users will typically forgive a certain amount of disruption, particularly it they're forewarned, but what if we're ready to do the installation, chase the user away from their desk (after having them clean it off perhaps so that we can cover it with a tarp to protect it from ceiling dust), and find that the site isn't ready. Well, aside from the delay to the project and the resulting cost, the user is going to be ticked!

One very simple way to avoid these problems is a site readiness checklist. The contents of the checklist will vary depending on what constitutes 'ready' for that particular site, but a sample is given in Figure 6-21. Checklists such as these come in handy when you'll be asking someone on-site to complete them, or sending someone out to the site to do so. This is material for posting — for putting up in the 'war room' with masking tape.

Site: _____

☐ Site wiring complete

☐ Network hardware environment ready

☐ Environmental - footprint

☐ Environmental - power

☐ Environmental - a/c

☐ Environmental - humidity

☐ Management/staff informed

☐ Security issues resolved

☐ Secure area for storage

Figure 6-2 Site Readiness Checklist

6.3 DATA TRANSFER

Data transfer isn't needed in our business case, but it's an important topic nonetheless. Often this type of project involves installing new hardware in place of old. That isn't necessarily problematic, but if the old hardware has persistent data on it, the potential for heartburn is there.

In one project I managed we had 850 systems to install at separate sites. Perhaps two-thirds of them were going into existing sites, and the existing systems were going to be used up until the minute that the exchange took place. So what was the problem?

- The existing equipment could not be backed-up into a format or media that was readable by the new system.
- The data was too voluminous (at the time) to upload to the corporate server and then download to the new system — the

installation would not fit in the 'opening' in the production window.

- The existing equipment used no standard protocol for data transfer other than Xmodem.
- The cable needed to connect the two systems would be of no use anywhere else and too expensive to produce just to be thrown away later.

The solution in this case was to write a custom script (on each side) that would facilitate the data transfer (which took four to six hours on each system), a utility program that would reformat the data as required (in many cases the data structures on the two systems will be different), and the installer to then either cut off the cable end and re-cable, or if the connector was of the right type, to re-pin it.

The most interesting part of this story is that if not for an aside at one of the planning meetings, the need for this data transfer could have gone completely undiscovered (a good advertisement for having as cross-organizational a planning team as possible).

6.4 USER EDUCATION

By now the questions of budget and content should have been answered, but there are questions remaining.

- How many people will be formally trained?
- Will they be trained in one central location or several locations?
- Will the training be en masse or will there be several classes?
- What equipment is needed for the training? (a training server? Workstations for each student? On a LAN?)
- What materials, presentation, lab and study, need to be developed?

6.5 SOFTWARE RELEASES

Let's look at a hypothetical situation. What if our deployment is going to take several months or longer. During that period, we'll have sites up and running from the start, and the software they'll be running will require maintenance updates like any other software. We'll then.

- Put a moratorium on software updates until the deployment is complete.
- Provide support for more than one version of software during the deployment.
- Push maintenance releases to the installed sites and synchronize the release with staging activities in the remaining deployment.

We're going to discuss quality control in Chapter 8, so for now let's assume that multiple testing iterations is not the issue, but that it is the support of sites on different releases or moving between releases during the deployment. There are then just two questions that need to be answered: Do we have a viable means of pushing out and supporting new releases during the deployment, and is there justification to do so?

Chapter 7

It's been awhile since we checked in with our team members. With the application design available, they have acted on their approach recommendations and have completed their infrastructure design. Let's take a look at each piece.

7.1 NETWORKING

Lindsay Coffee determined that we'll be using networking to provide the following functional connectivity:

- clients to server
- server to mainframe
- server to ISP (Internet Service Provider)

Figure 7.1 shows what the network topology will be.

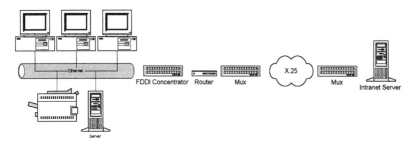

Figure 7-1 Network Topology

This topology will certainly add logistics to the deployment. There's obtaining and configuring network hardware to consider, and site wiring (which we'll see in the next section), the procurement of an ISP and the associated logistics, not a negligible consideration since the ISP will provide the MCT customer's electronic entree into MCT via the web site; responsiveness of the connection and availability are important factors, and not under MCT's control.

7.2 SITE WIRING

Amber Darling has worked with the HP Site Wire personnel to lay out the site wiring design. This work will need to be started as quickly as possible since it is an invasive task. At times it might be delayed because of the needs of various personnel. In one project I managed we did site wiring for over a dozen of the customer's buildings. Many locations could only be wired at night, and sensitive areas like the CEO's office could only be done when that person was going to be out of town, and the wiring contractor had to be accompanied by security.

If you do have a contractor provide the service (and perhaps even you don't), there are a number of gotchas to look out for.

- Is there an easily accessible and secure area for the contractor to store their materials (you'd be amazed how much room spools of wire, junctions boxes, and others can take)? If the contractor can't get to the materials, or materials disappear, your critical path is in jeopardy.
- What is the lead time on the materials? Some times there can be a shortage of things you would never think of, like copper wire or fiber connectors.
- Has the contractor come forward with material that meets the customer's requirements as well as that of the network design (for example, the customer might want two wire pairs run to

each desk instead of one for future expansion, and they might want Category 5 wire even if the design doesn't require it).

- Do the contractors have current blueprints available to them (you'd be surprised how blueprints fall behind much like any other documentation).
- Do the contractors have access to the building(s) after-hours (if after-hours work is needed)?
- Do the contractors have access to the wiring closets? We had a situation where there were thirty-six wiring closets and one person with a key!
- Is there room in each wiring closet for the new panels? I've seen where there wasn't, and what a delay this can cause!
- Has a jack/port numbering scheme been determined? If not, the contractors might use a system that leaves everyone scratching their heads.
- Has the method of "dressing" the wires coming into the panels been agreed upon? If the contractor runs all the wires in from the bottom and terminates them, and the customer says they need to come in from the top — oops!
- Has it been determined how panels, well-mounted and free-standing, will need to be anchored, and who is responsible for this?

And then there's the testing. Wow, the headaches that can come up when discussing testing. Make certain that, in advance, the exact method of testing, equipment to be used, and results to be recorded are agreed upon. The cost of testing can range wildly depending on what equipment is needed, and in some cases the type of testing the customer typically requires might not have a standard yet for the type of equipment being installed (for example, the development of test standards for Category 5 wiring lagged greatly behind the availability and use of the wire).

The wiring specifics for our business case are shown in Figure 7-2.

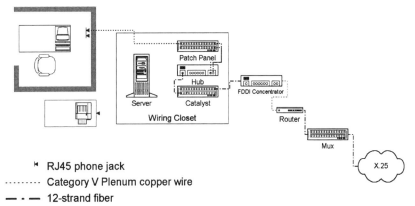

Figure 7-2 Site Wiring

7.3 BACKUP AND RECOVERY

Marguerita Bass has determined the backup and recovery needs for the system. It was actually an easier task than it could have been, primarily because there is little in the way of persistent data.

The backups will not involve the clients as the data on them isn't mission-critical. The server in each office will be backed up centrally from the corporate server via Hewlett-Packard's HP Openview/Omniback® II software, which allows the corporate server to "pull" the backup from each system as shown in Figure 7-3.

As far as the recovery goes, there are no complex transactions being stored. Any customer order consists of one record that is kept on the corporate server in a store-forward arrangement, that is the data is on the server, but is also forwarded on to the mainframe order system, so if the server data is lost there's no concern, particularly since the server data will also be protected via disk mirroring (as discussed in High-availability). The configuring and testing of this solution will need to be accounted for in the implementation.

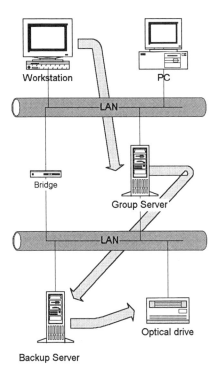

Workstation   PC

Bridge

Group Server

Backup Server

Optical drive

In this example, the backup server backs up the workstation
through the group server to the optical drive

Figure 7-3 Backup

7.4 HIGH AVAILABILITY

Claudia Culbiens developed the high-availability solution, which focuses on the corporate server that will provide data to MCT's web site.
The entire intranet solution, for now, will not be considered a candidate
for a high-availability solution. Perhaps down the road when the services
provided to the employees via the intranet are more critical this feeling
will change.

The high-availability solution for the corporate Internet server will consist of the following:

- Redundant networking between the servers and the ISP.
- Disk arrays with AutoRAID technology and networked disk mirroring to a remote site.

This might seem to be over-the-top for the application, but the customer feels that if their presence were to disappear on the web, that the cost to them would be much more than the cost of the high-availability solution.

The implementation plan needs to account for the testing of this solution. The switch-over testing should be straightforward, but the networked mirroring requires that the network is up and running, not necessarily an issue but certainly a dependency.

7.5 OPERATIONS

Pam Jogger spent time meeting with Kaitlin Still, Bryan Spanner's operations manager, to discuss the operations requirements of the two applications.

The initial considerations were the management of the servers and the new network. Pam had made the recommendation that the systems be managed with HP OpenView IT/Operations® under the umbrella of HP OpenView, which would be used to manage the network. One major benefit of the two applications is that they can manage their charge remotely.

The next consideration was the operational requirements of the applications, such as daily batch processing. The only batch processing necessary for these applications is the feed to and from the Internet database. There is ancillary database maintenance necessary as well, but since the database is not persistent, the maintenance is needed less often and requires no special planning.

7.6 THE INTERNET

Al Ferreman is working on certain portions of the Internet/intranet in advance of the applications being ready. There are a number of things that need to fall into place for this piece of the solution to go smoothly, and Al wants to move ahead with three of them right away.

- Obtaining a Domain Name — when you browse the Web and give your browser an address to go to, for example, www.hp.com, the 'www' portion of the address signifies that it is a world-wide web address (as opposed to another Internet type of connection like 'ftp'), 'com' indicates that this is a commercial location ('edu' for a school, 'net' for a network provider, 'org' for a nonprofit organization, and 'gov' for government), and 'hp' is the domain name. Domain names are worthless unless they're known by the systems that translate domain names into IP addresses and Domain Name Servers (DNS). The propagation of the IP address and its associate domain name to all the DNS' on the Web, and the registration of this name are handled by InterNic. MCT doesn't currently have a domain name, and Al knows that they have a sometimes considerable lead time.

- ISP — MCT will have just about everything they need in the way of hardware, software and networking, except a connection to the Internet. Sure, they can get a dial-up account like everyone else, but that's not what they need. When a customer outside of MCT goes to www.mct.com, there needs to be a location that's on the Web that 'accepts the call' and connects the caller to MCT's server. This is a form of a 'web-hosting' service, where the ISP provides the space on their server for your web site and applications, or a front-end for you.

- Internet connection — the connection from MCT to the ISP will be dedicated; that is, it will always be (as 'always' as 'always' can be in the computer world) up, as opposed to a modem dial-in connection. This type of configuration will typically be a T1 or T3 connection, and since MCT provides this type of line as one of its products, the availability isn't a concern (although the lead time might still be). What is a concern is making sure that visitors to the MCT web server go no further than that server; MCT doesn't want people to use their web server as a gateway to other MCT systems. The way we'll handle this is by putting up a "firewall" — a barrier that prevents unauthorized people from exploring where they shouldn't. It'll take awhile to get the MCT purchase order cut for the software (they need to buy the software so that the license will be in their name), and to get the software installed and configured properly, so Al is starting now.

Well, the infrastructure preparations seem to be in good hands. Let's move on to other things.

Chapter 8

This chapter covers the various application and system testing phases at a high level. The intent is to provide you with an understanding of each phase and how that phase fits into the bigger picture.

The test phases we'll cover are

- Application unit testing
- Application system testing
- System alpha testing
- System beta testing
- User acceptance testing
- Internal pilot testing
- External pilot testing

Keep in mind that the terms above are relative — there's no official text that defines how alpha testing differs from beta testing, so the usage given here will be subjective.

TIP ☞   In woodworking you're told to "measure twice and cut once" — in software development you should test twice and deliver once.

8.1 APPLICATION UNIT TESTING

Unit testing an application is akin to a director initially viewing edited footage; it's the first time it will be looked at as the user will see it. Several mistakes are too often made in this testing phase, the two biggest being the unit coder doing the testing, and the testing being done with no plan.

In the first case, having a coder unit test their code is like having a writer proofread their own work — their closeness to the work, their familiarity, can cause them to unconsciously miss something that someone else, taking nothing for granted, won't. As for the test plan, sure this is only a unit test, how much of a test plan do we need? If you're asking that question, the answer is: more than you think!

There are a number of reasons why a test plan should be used.

- A test plan provides documentation that can be archived.
- A test plan enumerates the unit function points to be tested and thus ensures that all are.
- A test plan, or a part thereof, ensures that all function points common to multiple modules are tested equally.

So, assuming you buy into the fact that a test plan is useful and that it should spell out what needs be tested, we can show a test plan and by doing so explain what unit testing involves (see Figure 8-1).

As you can see from Figure 8-1, unit testing covers five categories.

- Functionality specific to the unit function points as defined in the low-level design. Let's make sure that the application does what the design says it will.
- Screen controls behave as defined as standard (for example, when tabbing into a text box that contains text, the existing text becomes highlighted). This is based on the assumption that you have a standard for screen controls, which you should.
- Local error handling. Entering bad dates, numeric names, and alphanumeric values are handled cleanly.
- Set-up and clean-up function properly (fields are initialized properly with default or required values when entering the

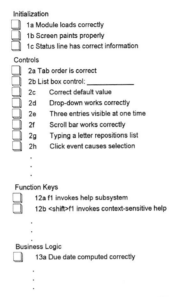

Initialization
☐ 1a Module loads correctly
☐ 1b Screen paints properly
☐ 1c Status line has correct information

Controls
☐ 2a Tab order is correct
☐ 2b List box control: _____
☐ 2c   Correct default value
☐ 2d   Drop-down works correctly
☐ 2e   Three entries visible at one time
☐ 2f   Scroll bar works correctly
☐ 2g   Typing a letter repositions list
☐ 2h   Click event causes selection

Function Keys
☐ 12a f1 invokes help subsystem
☐ 12b <shift>f1 invokes context-sensitive help

Business Logic
☐ 13a Due date computed correctly

Figure 8-1 Application Unit Test

screen, and reset properly when the transaction has been completed or canceled).

- Navigation controls work as defined as standard (tab order, back-tab, function keys, etc.)

What defines 'unit' in unit testing is that the testing is limited to the bounds of the application. That is, if the application interacts with others or networks, etc., that functionality is either stubbed off (the handshaking with external components is faked) or disregarded as much as possible; we will be testing that functionality, but right now we're testing a unit of code.

The standards mentioned above are a necessity. Without the standards every screen could look and behave slightly different than another. The easiest way to maintain a standard in this context is to use object-oriented development, because then each object, kept in a library, is responsible for displaying itself, printing itself, manipulating its data, and responding to queries and updates — the developer simply needs to know

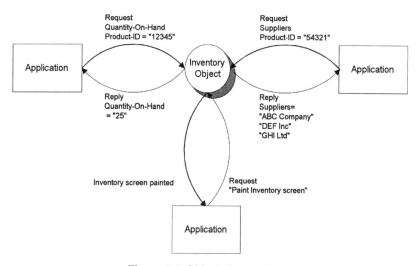

Figure 8-2 Object Technology

what calls to make to the object and what parameters to use and expect. This concept is shown in Figure 8-2. One consideration of the object-oriented approach is that the front-end effort for designing the objects can be considerable and that time might not always be available. Failing the ability to use objects, shared libraries are the next best thing. The developer in this case is responsible for including all the appropriate pieces of code in their application, but that code has been created already. The danger is that the behavior of the object can be altered unintentionally. This approach is shown in Figure 8-3. Lastly, failing the time to develop shared libraries, coding standards are the next best thing, and a sample is shown in Figure 8-4.

As a timeline entry, unit testing is tied to development. Most often the unit testing is taking place simultaneously with the development, especially in an interactive development environment like Visual C++ where the developer can run the application immediately upon adding a new line of code.

Source Code   Code Library

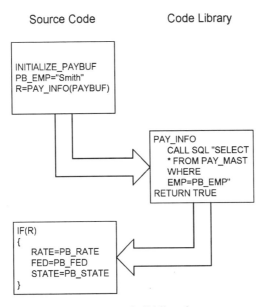

Figure 8-3 Call Libraries

Even so, the unit testing needs to be shown as a separate activity due to resource allocation and sign-offs. There can still be informal interactive testing done by the developer, but it should not be referred to as unit testing, but rather as screen testing or construction debugging. Obviously this activity should be encouraged, because it will reduce the iterations of unit testing that need to take place if bugs have already been identified and remedied.

The problem, though, is in showing the two activities as distinct, how do you account for a return to construction when the unit test fails? It's very easy to show feedback loops and cyclical activities in a diagram, less so in a project plan. One way to do it is to have a final task located within construction that is 'unit test support'. This task would entail the resources you plan to hold onto for bug fixes during unit testing. If the resources are the same as the unit testers, then this task needs no resources assigned to it (they're already accounted for). The trick here is that this task has an end-to-end dependency on the unit testing; that is, the task

1. Text boxes will have the following properites:
   Height: 50 pixels
   Width: (# of characters +2) * 5
   Forecolor: Black
   Justified: Left
   Font: Arial
   Font Size: 10
2. Text boxes will have the following event when receiving the focus
   textbox.SelectText=textbox.Text
   textbox.SelectLen=len(textbox.Text)
   thus having the result, shown below, of selecting the contents of the
box so that upon typing the previous contents of the box are deleted

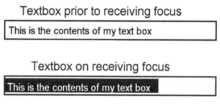

Textbox prior to receiving focus

This is the contents of my text box

Textbox on receiving focus

This is the contents of my text box

Figure 8-4 Coding Standards

can't end until the unit-testing task ends. Your project plan might have each application's unit test as a separate task, but there's no need to do that with the unit test support; instead you would have a group-level task that contains all the unit testing, and assign the dependency to that group item, as shown in Figure 8-3.

The unit testing completed, we should be able to move on to the system testing with confidence that we will receive minimal interruption from unit-level bugs.

8.2 SYSTEM TESTING

System testing differs from unit testing in that the full functionality of the application is tested, and not just each unit. It is essential that a test plan have been created for the system test; the scope of a system test is too complex to rely on instinct.

I wholly support the incorporation of 'use cases' for system testing. 'Use cases' are essentially scripts (the traditional type, not the UNIX type) that present a typical transaction that a user would request of the system. There are two benefits of 'use cases' when they are comprehensive.

- The system tester will not omit a test case because the combination of events didn't occur to him/her.
- The system tester won't waste time testing permutations that won't ever be used.

Following is a hypothetical example of each of these points.

Omission

A new employee timecard system has been system tested and passed, as it has also with UAT (User Acceptance Testing). We've moved on through to production, and the following scenario arises. Leann Grove is on vacation for a half-day. She returns to work at noon, eats a bad piece of cafeteria fudge, and goes home sick at 2 p.m. So her timecard needs to account for vacation time, sick time, and regular time on the same day, but this usage was never tested, and doesn't work.

What happens next is the customer and the contractor go running for the design document to see who is going to lose money on this — had the time and thought been given to extensive 'use cases,' this most likely would have been avoided.

Unnecessary Permutations

It's fairly simple to think of an example here. Following from the example above, we can look at testing a scenario where the employee is out sick for the day in excess of normal working hours. This could be an unnecessary test (and there will be so many that are necessary that we don't want to add needless testing) — then again this might also be a test that you want, not because this scenario can take place, but because it's possible that the data entry clerk can enter a transaction like this erroneously and the application needs to be able to reject it (although, depending on what the application needs to do in order to decide to reject it, this might be a unit test item). The point is that unless we have a test plan we could be performing unnecessary tests and omitting needed ones.

The other critical part of system testing, particularly when it is going to precede a first-time deployment, is that it be done in a sterile environment. If the system testers are sharing the system with the developers, there is too much chance that they will inadvertently end up sharing part of the environment. The environment could therefore change during the testing, and files, needed or unneeded, could be introduced into that environment. If the system testing is done in a sterile environment on a sterile system, there are no concerns about "which version this script is pointing at," etc. The testing completed, the system can be used to generate a "gold system" from which the deployment package can be constructed.

So what differentiates the system testing from the unit testing? The system testing doesn't stop at the unit (typically application) boundary, it tests the programmatic interrelationship between units as well. So if a function key on the customer screen in application A is supposed to launch application B with the current customer as the key, unit testing will ensure that pressing the function key would cause a launch request to take place (the launch itself would be stubbed off, or perhaps a dummy application B used), while the system test will ensure that application B is indeed launched with the proper initialization taking place.

If we have a lengthy deployment, there could be subsequent versions of the same system that require testing. It certainly would be best to schedule the system testing and version releases so that system testing on one version is completed before the next version needs to be tested, but in any case each subsequent version, once installed on the system test machine, should be considered to complete invalidate earlier system testing; that is, the entire system test should be run again even if "we didn't touch those modules," especially if shared code or libraries are used.

What I prefer is to see each module coded with a version number that changes every time the code changes, and the system test results being documented with a build list that shows the version of each module in that build.

What happens if the system test fails? Well, first it needs to be decided what constitutes failure. In the perfect world, if any of the system test items fail, the system test is failed. However, since failing the system test means returning to construction and eventually performing a new system test, we might want to create a list of failure types and ranking values, and only consider the system test a failure if the threshold is passed or certain criteria met, and in other cases document the issues to be addressed in the next version. Figure 8-5 shows a sample of such a punch list.

P/F	Issue Rank	
[ ]	Essential control functionality	1
[ ]	Control aesthetics	5
[ ]	Non-essential control functionality	3
[ ]	Abnormal termination	1
[ ]	Business logic - workaround	2
[ ]	Business logic - no workaround	1
[ ]	Data structure error/misalignment	1
[ ]	Function key (keyboard equivalent)	4
[ ]	Function key (no keyboard equiv.)	1

Figure 8-5 Issure Ranking

8.3 SYSTEM ALPHA AND BETA TESTING

Alpha and Beta testing serve the same purpose as system testing, except there is end-user involvement in the process. We're employing users to hopefully find that the system works as advertised, but more likely to find bugs that slipped through the unit and system testing. Depending on how they're done, these phases can also be considered to be field testing.

The differences between Alpha and Beta testing are

- Alpha testing comes first. Yes, of course, but this also means that the code is more stable when the Beta testing takes place.
- Duration. Since the code isn't supposed to be 'ready for consumption' when the Alpha testing takes place, the Alpha test doesn't last as long as the Beta test.
- Participants. Having a shorter duration than the Beta test and needing less man-hour investment to uncover bugs, the Alpha test requires less participants for less time than the Beta test.

One final distinction. With the Alpha test, there can be an informal method of reporting bugs back to the testing team, but with the Beta test, there should be a more controlled way to pass the data back to the testing team.

Although these are user tests, they are basically bang-and-use tests. There can certainly be prerequisites in selecting users based on what their usage will be, but this isn't the place to introduce a test plan. Within the context of our business case, I would certainly introduce a prerequisite, if the circumstances allow, that the tester be familiar with the technology. The purpose of the Alpha and Beta is to uncover bugs, not to get the users comfortable with the technology; their focus needs to be on the application.

8.4 USER ACCEPTANCE TESTING

Wow. How'd we get here? All the way to the UAT! The good news is that we've come a long way to get here. The bad news is that we've come a long way to get here. Why is that bad news? Because if the users find something wrong in their testing, we've got a big feedback loop. The good news is that the feedback loop is not as big as you might think — unless you've got an exceptional amount of time and money on your hands, we're going to treat any fixes from this point on as minor releases and not run subsequent Alpha and Beta tests. Figure 8-6 shows the cycle.

The users should have an acceptance test plan that has been approved by the customer and you well in advance (you would need this to be able to plan the resources and time to accommodate the testing). The environ-

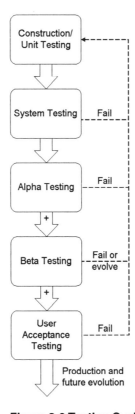

Figure 8-6 Testing Cycle

ment should be set up so that the user can be pointed at the client system, be given the documentation, and run with it.

In our business case, since we're using the Evolutionary Methodology, we'll need to spend more time with the user than UATs in projects using other methodologies because we'll have feedback cycles until the application is fully evolved or we run out of time or money.

There is a painful aspect to the UAT — one of those things that nobody wants to do, but it really needs to be done (like a dose of cod liver oil). It's guaranteed that during the UAT there will be enhancement requests; functionality that isn't in the design. The painful thing is having to turn down the requests, even when they make great sense. That is, unless you're working with the methodology that we're using here, because enhancing is part of the evolutionary process!

When the UAT is complete and signed-off, so is the job of the construction team. From this point on, any bug that arises is going to be treated just as that — a bug to be fixed in the maintenance process and not a challenge for the construction team. Of course a showstopper of a bug can change the formalities suddenly, but we can start by trying to do it right.

8.5 PHASE 3 PROPOSAL

At this point we've looked with a planning eye at everything that needs to happen for deployment. There are a number of items that we'll discuss subsequently in the context of execution, but at this point we'll note them as having been accounted for in our planning.

- Staging
- Command center
- Support desk startup
- Switch over

We need to end this phase by providing MCT with a third and final (for this project) proposal: implementation. This proposal needs to layout the services necessary for deployment and implementation. The same advice given on the initial proposal holds here; identify the services but don't line-item them, otherwise you leave it open for the customer to red-line services they feel they can live without but you know are essential to your and their success. What position would that leave you in? Do without and fail, or tell the customer you can't help them and kill the relationship. I'm sure that some of my colleagues reading this are smirking while thinking "that's easy to say, but if the client insists you line-item then you line-item," and that's true — but it would be easier all around if you can avoid it.

Chapter 9

The deployment is imminent. There are still a number of implementation support components we need to cover, so let's get started.

9.1 STAGING

Staging can be a critical success factor in the deployment, but is often underdone. As a foundation, let's take a look in Figure 9-1 at a list of issues I had installing a friend's computer and printer.

1. The os was incorrectly preinstalled
2. There was no media from which to reinstall
3. The os did not recognize the peripherals
4. The drivers that came with the peripherals were three or four versions old
5. Two peripherals were preset for the same IRQ
6. Two other peripherals wanted the same address
7. Applications he already had would not work with this version of the os

Figure 9-1 PC Installation Woes

The experience was frustrating and time-wasting for me, and I'm sure my friend experienced a range of similar sentiment. Also, although he'd probably deny it, he probably came away with the feeling that I don't know as much as he thought I do. Now, multiply that by a few hundred systems and you begin to understand what we could face if we removed the systems from their boxes at the site and installed them. There are a few dozen things that singularly can go wrong, and almost infinite permutations. And trust me, you don't want that to be Act 1 Scene 1 with the user.

TIP ☞   If you ever want to prove Einstein's theory of super-light-speed travel, watch how fast the discontent of a new user, who is outside the IT organization, travels back up the management chain.

So how do we prevent this opportunity for an implementation maelstrom? By staging the equipment. If you consider the activity that will take place at the user's desk as staging, then you can look at what we're about to discuss as "prestaging," but I'll call it staging — less typing.

I'm a strong advocate of staging because of the experience I had with it. I imagine there are people whose experience with staging wasn't good and thus they aren't advocates. Let me give you a statistic of how things can go when staging is done correctly; then you can decide.

The example I gave earlier of implementation where the data transfer and cable repinning needed to take place was a deployment for a large retail organization. This customer's stores are spread across most of the continental U.S., and in this project we needed to deploy 850 systems, one to each store, in six months.

In those days systems were shipped in multiple boxes because network cards were manufactured in one location, software in another, etc. There were also add-on peripherals that went with each system and custom software. So picture the amount of assembly and installation activity that would need to happen at each site and the resulting room for failure not to mention boxes going missing. Instead of doing this, the HP System Support Organization (now the HP World-Wide Customer Support Organization) created a staging area which has since grown into the HP Americas Integration Center. The functionality of this operation is what will be presented below, but the net-net was that 850 systems arrive at their destination ready to be switched on and used and 849 did so with no difficulty. This is an astounding statistic and explains my enthusiasm for this activity.

It does add a cost to the implementation. It's an activity that should probably be a line-item on the deployment proposal. However, upon investigation the customer should find that the incremental cost is less than what it would cost to do it another way, and less than the intangible cost of dissatisfied users and offset to some extent as well by the intangible revenue of the hum that will come from the a happy grapevine.

Let's take a look at how to make that grapevine hum.

9.2 SCOPING THE STAGING

A staging center is a place where we perform tasks that otherwise would be undertaken on site, and perform these tasks in an assembly line fashion wherever possible. In Figure 9-2 we see a checklist of services that a staging center can perform. The important rule to remember is that any activity the staging center performs needs to be verifiable, otherwise you're not buying yourself anything except potential trouble from yet another source.

Figure 9-3 shows what the staging process might look like.

Aside from identifying the services needed and the requirements of each, there are several things that are very important for staging to be successful.

- How many days prior to the deployment the staging center will receive the equipment?
- What company is running the staging center, and as a result, who is responsible for the equipment while it is there?
- Do the payment terms from the hardware and software manufacturers to the customer begin when the item is shipped to

Staging Center Services

o Write installation scripts
o Write test scripts
o Remove system and components from boxes
o Assemble system
o Install components into system
o Test assembled system
o Assemble external peripherals
o Test assembled peripheral
o Format internal media (hard drive)
o Install operating system (Win95, etc.)
o Apply operating system patches
o Create predefined directory structure
o Install custom / third-party software
o Configure software for customer or site
o Configure network s/w for customer or site
o Configure network h/w for customer or site
o Label (color-code?) ports and cable connectors
o Record asset information (serial number, etc.)
o Apply asset tag
o Perform integrated system test
o Perform communications test or loop-back test
o Affix site-implementation documentation
o Prepare system for shipment (shrink-wrap)

Figure 9-2 Staging Center Services

the staging center, or when the customer receives it from the staging center?

• Same question of timing, but in reference to the warranty, and if the clock doesn't begin ticking until the item reaches th

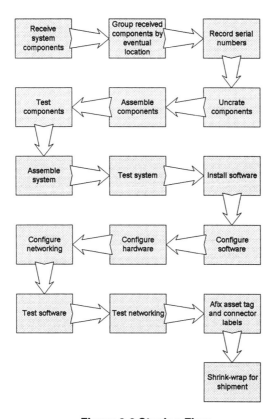

Figure 9-3 Staging Flow

customer (a good thing right?), then what happens if the item doesn't work when the staging center tests it?

- Can the manufacturer's invoicing system handle shipping to one location (staging center) but charging the sales tax based on the final destination (customer site)?
- How should the equipment be shipped from the staging center, and who pays?
- Can a sample configuration (each piece that will be staged to comprise a system) be provided to the staging center in advance so a process and test scripts can be created and tested?

One final piece that is extremely important to plan is the "gold tape" or "gold CD." We'll see more about that in Chapter 10, but at this point it's worth mentioning that depending on the frequency of anticipated updates to the gold system, the timing of when a system is staged as compared to when it is installed could be a consideration; you don't want the system showing up on site with outdated software.

If the timing issues can't be resolved, one way around this dilemma would be to have an Initial Software Pull, that is, when the system is installed on-site and fired up, it can be set up so that the first thing it does is to pull software updates down from the next-level server. Daniel has made this approach part of his plan. He'll bypass the need to update the gold software at the staging center with minor versions by having all installed systems contain a major version (1.0, 1.1, etc.) of the software, and then the most minor releases or patches will be received from the server when the system is installed.

Chapter 10

10.1 PILOTS

If the UAT (User Acceptance Test) goes well, it's a fairly sedate enjoyable experience. If the pilots go well, they are, well tumultuous. The pilot, you see, is the time when we test everything.

- The applications
- Period-end processing (if applicable)
- Communications
- Infrastructure
- Education
- Documentation
- Support

In our business case we'll be doing two pilot tests, one internal and one external. There are various ways in which these can be handled, but the team at MCT has determined that they'll use MCT end-users for both the intranet and Internet internal pilot testing, and the customer community on the external pilot. Typically, the internal pilot is done so that the deployment can be tested without concentrating on the transportation issues and without worrying about everyone tripping over each other in front of the users. Sure, the project team would understand why the Laurel and Hardy antics were happening, and might even have the forethought to forewarn the users, but the user would still look at it as "based on what I've seen this will never work," and bad news travels at Warp 10.

The pilots need to be timed so that if there is any period-end processing (day-end, week-end, month-end, and so on) as many period boundaries are crossed during the testing as is practical.

Another consideration for the pilot is the location to be the external pilot. There needs to be a good representation of transactions, a cooperative manager or supervisor, sufficient staff, and hopefully room for the members of the project team who need to be present during the test. If the sites are geographically dispersed, it usually makes sense to use one near the development location so that support staff can "run over" as needed.

There's an additional consideration with our business case. Part of what we'll be testing is the Internet web site — how are we going to do that? How do we put a site out on the web and limit its audience?

A possible approach would be to have a screen that requests a user ID and password and only grant access to those with the information. The problem with that approach is that we'll lose many of the people because they don't want to register in order to visit the site. Another approach, and the one we'll use, is to create an orphaned page.

Pages at a web site are accessed via links from other pages as shown in Figure 10-1. An orphaned page is a page that is not the main page, which you get to simply by browsing www.mct.com, and is not linked to any other page. Therefore, if no one knows that the page is there, chances are slim to none that they'll stumble across it accidentally.

What we want to accomplish during the pilot is to observe and solicit feedback. The observation is to note what works well and what doesn't and to then try and improve what needs improving. The feedback will be from the user community that are helping with the testing, and they'll give us our first true look at how the user community is going to accept the deliverable.

If the testing is going to include functionality that was already present, either with a different application of different hardware, then the decision needs to be made between a cut over or a parallel test. The consideration is moot if there are technical or personnel reasons that prevent parallel testing from taking place. Otherwise you need to determine

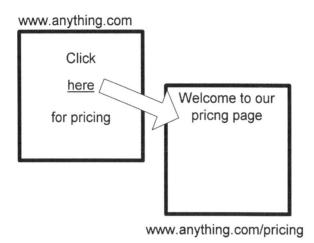

Figure 10-1 Web Page Link

whether it's technically feasible to have a site be two functional sites (one to process transactions on the new equipment and one on the old), and whether there are enough people to enter each transaction twice.

The pilot test is also the place where we first have a strong need for a "gold" system back at the system testing area. Whatever we uncover with the pilot testing, we want to make sure that our version control is not corrupted, and that we adhere to the change management process when the user pommels us with enhancement requests — well, we recognize them as enhancement requests, the user will see them as design deficiencies.

10.2 CHANGE MANAGEMENT

When the project was scoped at the beginning and the contract signed, Daniel and his client agreed that a specific set of deliverables was to be provided at a specific cost in a specific time frame. This is typical with fixed-price contracts. In time and materials contracts payment is based on time spent, so the time frame is not fixed and neither should be the cost of the deliverables.

Three things to watch out for that can impact the timing of the deployment are

- Creeping elegance — the desire to perfect a certain deliverable beyond what is covered by scope. Often introduced by creative or perfectionist members of the project team.
- Scope creep — minor (individually) changes to scope to accommodate changed requirements or requirements that were conveyed poorly originally. Typically introduced by the user for whom the deliverable is earmarked.
- Change of scope — an obvious change to the defined scope.

All three of the above can serve to delay a project at best, and remove any chance of success at worst. Any hint of them or of work being done as a result should be watched for and ceased. The only way to avoid setting a precedent which results immediately or ultimately in irreparable harm being done to the project is to insist that all changes to scope, not just the big ones, are done via change management.

Change management is nothing more than the words imply. If a change is needed, it should be requested in writing, either via a form supplied by the client or the project team. The request should be numbered so that there is an audit trail. When a change request is received, the project managers and appropriate members of the project team need to evaluate the additional effort required to affect the change both for the direct effort required and the effort resulting from any subsequent impact (other development, testing, implementation, etc.). A determination can then be made as to whether the change can be entertained (that is, if it can not be accomplished without delaying the project, it might be rejected) and what price, if any, the client needs to pay for it.

Because change requests need to be evaluated, the requests themselves require an expense of effort. Into each fixed-price contract a risk amount is typically included to provide coverage for such things as third-party labor, unique resources, rate increases, etc. The cost of change management should be anticipated too.

10.3 GOLD MASTER

The development phase is complete, as is the system testing. It's time to install the applications at the customer site and do some testing. You have a tape cut and install it on the customer's machine, but the application won't run. After several hours it's discovered that some of the files that are required were not on the tape, and the reason is that they were located in an obscure directory.

Eventually you get the system running smoothly. Then during testing some defects are discovered in the code. The repairs are made back at the office, and the new version needs to be installed at the customer site. Guess what? The files that were missing last time are not missing now, but the newly installed files don't include the repairs.

How do you avoid these issues that cause delays and a loss of face? It's done with software configuration management and a packaging process. Software configuration management provides a way to ensure that all code being worked on is checked back in to a central library. Daniel and his TSSP team have taken their process a step further — when the code is checked in the programmer is queried by the system to provide a description of the changes made, and the code is then put through a maintainability index generator.

To copy the contents of the system to another, some form of master needs to be created, much like the install programs that come with Microsoft Windows applications. This will ensure that all the files necessary for the application are present. There also needs to be some installation tool so that the files are all put in the correct place, and older versions of the files already present on the system don't prevent the installation of the newer files.

There are enough issues in a development and deployment project to keep everyone hopping; hunting down the oversights that have caused the copying of a system image to fail is not the best use of anyone's time.

Chapter 11

Some final considerations before you deploy. Once we finish this chapter, Daniel will let the team loose, and we'll catch up after the fact.

11.1 THE COMMAND CENTER

Having artfully planned the deployment earlier, we eventually get to the point, here, where we turn the team loose to go forth and deploy. And while the deployment is taking place Daniel can go out and play a round of golf, right?

Okay, so he has more career goals than that. In that case Daniel will need to staff a command center to track the installations and deal with any nonsupport issues that come up (nonsupport because the support is being provided by section 11.2).

I prefer a small, dedicated conference room for prolonged deployments. I want to be able to use the white board, tape flip-chart sheets to the wall, whatever, and not have to worry about taking it all down and cleaning the boards at the end of each day.

The necessary equipment isn't too daunting; a phone line (two would be better), a beeper or voice mail, and some "official" check list on which to check off the installations.

The deployment can be taxing. Despite all the best planning and testing, something can go awry. The challenge is to fix any defects in the deployment plan. If an individual system were to take one day, soup to nuts, to deploy, and the change to the deployment plan were to take one hour to incorporate, there would be little problem in doing so. If, however, there were a 10 day cycle from receiving the hardware from the manufacturer to it being on site for installation, and several systems per day, or per week, were being deployed, any change to the deployment plan could potentially wreak havoc. So, change management will be needed, but it must be a streamlined hit-squad change management process otherwise it can throw off the deployment more than the change that's being managed.

11.2 SUPPORT DESK START-UP

Hopefully, with all the planning that's taken place, everything will go perfectly as planned during the installation. The chances of that are slim and none though, so we need to have a contingency plan, and I prefer the proactive type above the reactive type.

Most companies that have an IT department have some form of help desk, and we want to have one too. There are a number of potential users of the help desk.

- The person doing the on-site installation.
- The pilot test users.
- The staging center.
- Live users.

Since we're launching a new environment here, the call can represent an issue with almost any aspect of that environment. The purpose of the temporary staff is to

- Augment the existing or newly hired help desk staff with people who are familiar with the new environment.
- Provide support for the spike of calls that will occur during the deployment and when going live.
- Provide tier 1 support with the knowledge of where to receive tier 2 support if necessary.

Table 11-1 shows typical call categories and where tier 2 support would come from if required.

CALL	TIER 2 PROVIDER
Hardware problem	Hardware provider
Hardware config	Team/ hardware provider
3rd-party software	Software company
Custom software	Team
Infrastructure	Team
Network hardware	Hardware provider
Network config	Team
Cabling	Site wiring contractor
General environ.	Team

Table 11-1 Typical Support Calls

Aside from taking the calls and providing answers, the support desk personnel need some method of tracking the calls and avoiding investigating answers for questions that were previously answered. The tracking system and query system can be homegrown, or if the customer already has the software, it's probably best to use theirs if it's feasible. In the absence of those circumstances and the time or desire to create one, there are several off-the-shelf applications that will do the job.

11.3 SWITCH-OVER

Switch-over is the last implementation activity to take place. The switch-over consists of all the one-time events that need to take place so that the project can move from "testing" to "live." There are a number of possible events; the list varies greatly from one project to another because the need for these events is typically customer-specific or a combination of customer- and technology-specific. An example of a switch-over event is the reinitialization of a database following testing. It could be that because of the legacy systems that are interfaced and the way that needs to happen, that there can't be more than one environment at one time, so the testing environment needs to be 'refurbished' into a production environment.

Another example is the off-site storage of backup media. This service will typically start at the time that the data is live data. Because many of these events will only happen once, which is at this point, it can be difficult to identify them during the planning stages. One final example, one which applies in our case study, is 'connecting' the world to MCT's web. Make the links that point to the page(s) active, advertise, and go!

11.4 PERFORMANCE TUNING

Once the public has access to the web site, if the site is successful there can be performance issues with the speed of the web server (the machine that provides the web pages to the user), the time to download a page, or both. Periodic analysis of the site should be done, and performance issues addressed.

If a faster or larger web server is needed, there will probably need to be a financial justification, especially if the upgrade is needed before the return on investment for the original server is realized. Performance issues with loading individual web pages may be relieved somewhat by reworking the pages to reduce the number of graphical elements, or to reduce the size of the elements.

Epilogue

Well, it's just about over. It's been a fair-ly smooth ride for Daniel and the team, as projects go. There were tense moments, fire fighting, end-users with design ideas, but these things are typical in a project — the important thing is that everything was installed on-time and under budget, and the users are happy.

TIP ☞   The number one danger of any project is that the client feels, justly or unjustly, that their expectations were not met

Following a successful project of this magnitude it's appropriate to have a party for the participants, so long as the customer is satisfied and the relationship is good. I'll leave the decision as to who pays up to you, but if things did go well you made enough revenue to afford it. The project party is a great venue for awarding recognition to project team members as well as member of the user community. I also try to give out a few hu-morous awards, good-natured, nothing to embarrass or humiliate anyone, but fun, like a plaque for "most tenacious."

There are a few pieces of cleanup needed. You'll need to tidy up the "war room," take all your equipment back to the office, get the final sign-off from the customer. If you have the "keys" for anything, it's time to turn them over to their new owner. And this is the time for the postmortem. No, not for you, for the project!

The one final event that will greatly improve the relationship you have with your customer is a project postmortem. The idea of the postmortem is to cover the project, in chronological order, by phase, and determine what can be done better next time. It can't be stressed enough that this is not to be a finger-pointing session. You're not there to decide who was at fault for anything, but simple to acknowledge things that went wrong and, hopefully, identify recommendations for how to do it better next time.

I tend to do two postmortems. A higher level version for the customer, and then an in-depth session internally. The in-depth session is to go over each unique task in the project plan (if you deploy ten machines, all with the same tasks, you need only review one set). The review is to decide how the actual task compared to the planned task in

- Effort
- Resource allocation
- Cost
- Dependencies

This information is especially useful if you will be doing similar projects in the future, or projects where there are some similar tasks.For example, if in the planning two days of development for training materials were allocated for each day of training delivery, and the actual turns out to be three days, then the next time around you're likely to have a more accurate plan if you use three days for your planning.

You might find that certain tasks could have started earlier than their dependencies indicated, and that some tasks needed some elapsed time between them. For example, if it takes one hour to order an item and two days to receive it, but between the two it's discovered that it takes three days to raise the purchase order, next time (assuming the next client's purchase order cycle is three days) you would want to set up the dependency between order and receipt to be finish-to-start plus three elapsed days of lag time. With a more accurate planning template in hand you'll be ready for the next project.

Remember, learning from your mistakes doesn't do much for you unless you try again. Well, that's it. We hope you enjoyed the book, now go forth and deploy!

Appendix A — Technical Stuff

A.1 CLIENT-SERVER OVERVIEW

"Client-server" is an ambiguous term because it describes a relationship in a very broadbrush fashion. At some point there will need to be a standard developed and applied to the terminology. For now, defining the term and the bounds of its various forms will suffice.

However, even a definition of client-server requires the taking of some latitude. There is no 'official' definition and opinions vary. Here then is one definition; the one that will be used within the context of this text.

```
cli•ent-serv•er adj. 1. A relationship between
computers in which one, the client requests the
other, the server to fulfill a request for ser-
vices.
```

It's important to note that client-server is an adjective. There is no such thing as 'a client-server.' There is a relationship between client and server that exists with client-server applications. This relationship can exist at various levels, which are described in Figure A.

Each instance of client-server functionality in the diagram differs from the next by the amount and type of services provided by the client. Fascinating is that the examples with less client functionality reflect technology from the seventies and eighties.

Yes! And this is one of the reasons that an understanding of client-server technology is imperative before buying or developing it, other-

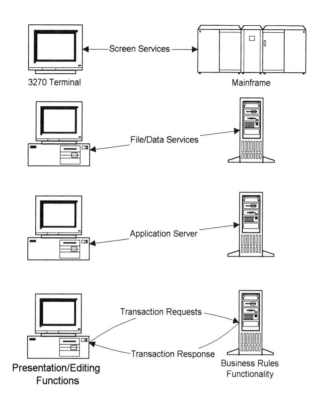

Figure A-1 Client-Server Levels 1- 4

wise you might end up with something that comes no closer to addressing the business issues than what you already have in place. This will become more evident with a practical example of each level in the diagram. The level numbers as presented here are arbitrary and do not correlate to any standard as there is none.

A.2 CLIENT-SERVER SERVICES

There are three major divisions of service in the chart, application, data, and presentation. Let's define these as follows:

- Presentation — The services to display data on a video display device in a manner that facilitates assimilation of the data by the user.
- Data — The services to retrieve data from a data structure such as a file or database.
- Application — The services to perform instructions, subroutines, functions, transactions, or an entire application.

The above services are software-based. This precludes hardware functionality from clouding the model. The level 1 example would be different if the built-in functionality of a 'dumb terminal,' which allows it to display characters, were considered to be presentation services in this context. It would mean that presentation services were being provided by both the client and the server just because the terminal hardware was painting the screen using the control codes sent by the server. While that might technically constitute a client-server relationship, it's not in the context used here, any more than a modem is server to a PC just because it fulfills a request.

Level 1

The best example of this level is a terminal connected to a computer, perhaps by a modem. The person sitting at the terminal presses a key (Enter, Return, PA1, etc.) which, when transmitted to the computer, lets the computer know that the terminal is ready to receive information. The application running on the computer receives the terminal's keystroke and sends the terminal the information needed to format the screen properly as well as the data to display. As mentioned before, this level of functionality is only technically client-server.

Level 2

This level is much like Level 1, except that the client device is providing the presentation services. An example of this is a PC with terminal emulation software, so that the formatting of the screen is not done by the server. This is also a 'push' so far as an example of client-server technology.

Level 3

The first good example of client-server technology, this level has an application on the server providing data to an application on the client for presentation. An example of this is a PC application that accepts then entry of a record, then passes it on to an application on the server for storing. Note that the two applications aren't necessarily integrated. For example, the PC software can pass the entered record on to a mainframe application that stores it in a file for later batch processing.

Level 4

This level represents client-server technology within the context of this book. The client application obtains, manipulates, and presents the local data (data that resides on the client device or a peripheral local to it), and when there is a need, requests data from the server, or provides data to the server for processing. The case study for A Methodology for Developing and Deploying Internet and Intranet Solutions uses the level 4 technology.

Level 5

With this level of functionality the server is an application server (the application is stored on the server and loaded into the client's memory for execution). There does exist the relationship where the client passes some of its processing on to other processors that have available processing cycles. This is known as a peer-to-peer relationship, so the two participants are not client and server, but a server can be used to 'broker' the availability of other processors, which would make them clients.

A.3 CLIENT-SERVER FUNCTIONALITY

Although a definition has been provided for client-server technology, what the definition really means, the application of it, is fairly ambiguous at this point. Figure A-2 will provide a better grasp of this client-server functionality. Again, if you're not a 'technoid,' don't be put off by this discussion. In this example a PC will be used for the client device, but that device can be any workstation or computer up to and including a mainframe or 'super computer.'

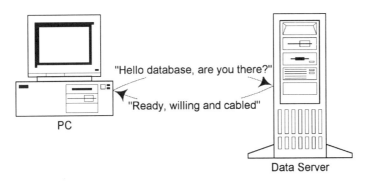

"Hello database, are you there?"

"Ready, willing and cabled"

PC

Data Server

Figure A-2 Client-Server Data Services

In this scenario the user will launch the client application by moving their mouse cursor to the appropriate icon on their screen and double clicking. The initial portion of the application needed for execution will be loaded from disk into the PC's memory, and the first instruction of the program into the instruction register on the chip. If the requested application is stored on another computer's disk (a file server) instead of the user's PC, the transfer of the program from the file server to the client PC is in itself representative of client-server technology.

There are many things that happen when an application begins execution. It looks for its critical files, such as its initialization file and help file, and initializes its variables. The client application has one additional initialization task to perform that is critical: establishing a session with the server. In a client-server application, the client requests some service from the server. The requested service depends on what form of client-server relationship there will be, as shown in Figure A-3. The server might be providing simple data services, or might be doing everything except the actual presentation.

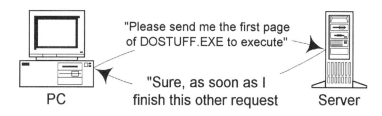

Figure A-3 Client-Server Application Server

Whether the services being provided are application, data or presentation, there are other services that need to be provided as a foundation for the rest, because for the client's request to be received at all by the client there needs to be the means of having a conversation between the client and server. Following is a discussion of these services. I'm going to present it using the analogy of a phone call.

When one person phones another, both have phones with a wire going into the wall, up the road, and to the phone company. That's the physical connection. From one device to the other, there is a physically traceable route. Satellite links make that route somewhat harder to trace, but it's there. The route that connects your phone to Uncle Phil is always there. So why isn't Uncle Phil on the line every time you pick up the phone (yes, it might seem he is)? Because until one person dials the other, who then answers, there is no logical connection established. And having established that logical connection, the next step is to establish a session.

There are many methods of establishing connections and sessions, so a context needs to be established for this discussion. For connections and sessions to be established, services need to be provided to the computer and its user, services such as the presentation of data on the screen (user interface). Each service except the first depends on the success of those before it for its own success, and thus the services are typically presented as layers. The most popular model for presenting the layers is that of the reference model of Open Systems Interconnection (OSI) developed by the International Standards Organization (ISO). In Figure A-4 you can see each layer of the OSI model and how it maps to the physical or logical connection or the session between the client and the server.

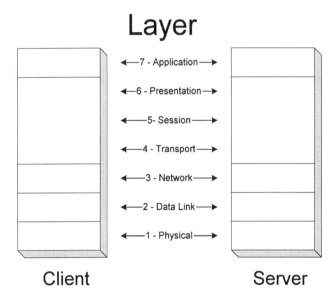

Figure A-4 OSI Layers

Note for future use that each layer on the client communicates with the same layer on the server using a protocol, and that one or more protocols on a client or server is provided by an interface, an example being the parallel interface on your PC and printer. When more than one protocol (thus more than one layer) is provided, the grouping is called a stack.

A.3.1 The Physical Connection

The physical connection comes down to two computers with a bunch of stuff in between, but despite that simplistic view there are issues to be considered with the physical layer just as with subsequent layers (one can only shove so much data through a wire and can only expect it to move so fast). This introduces the first layer of the OSI model.

OSI Physical layerprovides the physical connection. Essentially this layer is made up of the components, hardware and software, that move the bits from one computer to another. It is only concerned with moving them; it has no concern with the meaning of the data.

In this example the rear of a typical PC has card slots for adding functionality, such as a sound card or an internal fax/modem. One such card has been installed in the form of a 802.3 Ethernet LAN adapter. The visible end of the card has two connectors, a RJ45 jack like an office telephone, and a connector for coaxial cable, not unlike the cable that connects a television to the local cable company. The connector is unused, and between the RJ45 jack on the card and its counterpart on the office wall is a Plenum Category 5 copper cable rated at 100 MHz, more than enough bandwidth to support the 100 Mbit network speed. Behind the jack in the wall, another Cat 5 cable leads down to the floor, across to a telecom closet, and to the back of a port on a patch panel. Another copper cable connects the patch panel port to a port on the back of a concentrator, which is connected to a catalyst via a fiber optic cable with a connector on both ends.

Out of another port on the catalyst, a second fiber cable with a coaxial connector extends back to a patch panel and terminates in another connector. The back of that port on the patch panel has a fiber cable which runs to the main telecom room on another floor, to another patch panel and from that patch panel to a router. The router has a fiber cable which runs to a 802.3 connection on the back of a Hewlett-Packard HP9000 K class UNIX server. This description might seem like overkill, but during implementation planning an understanding of details is important; a box full of cables with a ten-day production lead time and the wrong connector can be a show stopper.

The result of all this should be that there is equipment in place that will allow the signal from the client to traverse the geography to the server (1) at an acceptable speed, (2) with minimal errors, and (3) without be lost in a myriad of competing signals.

A.3.2 The Logical Connection

The existence of a physical connection, the method for the signal from one computer to reach another, doesn't imply the existence of a logical connection. When you dial Uncle Phil, a bunch of guys in phone company uniforms don't swarm to his house to connect a bunch of wires, then disconnect them once the call is over. The physical connection should already be present. However to establish the logical connection, you first do what a good modem does and open the line (in your case by picking up the phone), check for a dial tone, and then dial the number. The computer at the phone company is responsible for establishing the logical connection by establishing the switching between your phone and the person you're calling. What this really means is that a logical connection is provided mostly by software, whereas the physical connection is hardware. Sometimes, there can be a need for manual intervention in setting up the logical connection, like getting past the secretary of the person you're calling or having someone put paper in the fax machine so it will answer the phone. Let's discuss the layers that make up the logical connection.

A.3.2.1 OSI Data Link layer

With the physical links in place, this layer enables data transport between them and is responsible for identifying, reporting, and correcting any errors that occur in the transmission of the data. An example of this is a LAN card on the back of a PC. The card has associated software that creates packets of network-compliant outgoing data and plucks packets off the LAN with the card's transceiver (much like watching the luggage go by on the carousel at the airport and plucking yours off). This data can be messages, spreadsheet data, database information, or even program code. The data link layer is typically a mix of hardware and software.

A.3.2.2 OSI Network layer

Although the previous layer moves the data, this layer ensures the protocol necessary for each node (system) on the network to communicate with the next; that is, a system attached to the network expects to be able to identify data in a particular way. Going back to the airport, if the luggage were sent up the conveyer belt to the carousel in sealed containers, you'd have a hard time identifying your luggage. This layer also addresses the data so it gets to the correct place (luggage flight tag), segments it so that it is sent in packets of the correct size over the correct route (baggage handling — but in this case if the baggage gets lost, the layer can simply retransmit it), and controls the congestion through alternative routing.

A.3.2.3 OSI Transport layer

When errors occur in the network layer, the transport layer is responsible for correcting them. It also takes the packets which have been plucked off the network and disassembles them into data the receiving system considers usable. So at this point we have the hardware, software and protocols in place to allow the client and server to connect physically and logically. Now we need a session.

A.3.3 The Session

Let's recap how far our phone call has progressed.

- Physical connection — provided by the phone company.
- Launching logical connection — caller picking up a phone and dialing.
- Establishing logical connection — phone rings at the destination end.

The next step is to establish a session. If Uncle Phil answers the phone, a dialogue has begun. If he receives no reply to his initial "hello," he will terminate the session. Yes, when that happens you and I refer to it as having "lost the connection," but only the logical connection. Now that we have a physical and logical connection, the establishing of a session needs to take place. We left Uncle Phil saying "hello". If we lower our voice and say, "This is the IRS calling. Would you like to participate in our popularity poll?" the session will probably be terminated immediately. If instead we say, "Hi Uncle Phil," the session will hopefully be confirmed so long as there is recognition of the caller (a user or process ID), but perhaps Uncle Phil has many nieces and nephews and needs to perform a security check at the next level: "Do I owe you money?"

So long as Uncle Phil receives acceptable information, he will confirm the session. Let's look at some of the items involved in establishing a session.

- *Initiation* — This again is accomplished by Uncle Phil saying "hello." The server needs to acknowledge the client in order for a session to be activated.
- *Activation* — Uncle Phil being satisfied he doesn't owe you money. The session is activated after some criteria has been met, typically some form of security checking like a 'login' with a password.
- *Synchronization* — Should you and Uncle Phil both start speaking at the same time, you will need to resynchronize the conversation (this happens frequently with overseas calls and conference calls). Sometimes the client system assumes, after some waiting period has elapsed, that the server is not responding to its last request, and retransmits it, and just as it retransmits the request the server transmits a response to the initial request. Synchronization needs to occur at this point.
- *Dialogue Control* — Let's face it, depending on the topic and the personalities, either you or Uncle Phil is going to be in charge of the conversation. The server needs to control the dialogue between it and the server, to make sure that the request-response cycles are in a manner it can deal with.
- *Data transfer* — You've seen 'transfer' before, but that was packet transmission. Once the packets have been disassembled into something meaningful to the client or server, it becomes

data (and once that data becomes something meaningful to you, then and only then does it become information).

- *Termination* — Either party can terminate the phone call for various reasons. The same holds true with the client and server. A clean termination occurs when the client's requests have been fulfilled, and it says 'goodbye' to the server. Factors such as loss of communications (a break in the logical or physical connection) can cause a dirty termination.

The session provides the means for the server to respond to the particular requests of a client, but there are more things that need to take place for the user to recognize the benefits of this interaction.

A.3.4 The Presentation

We'll have to leave the phone call behind at this point as we move on to services that transcend audio. The name of this penultimate layer can be misleading because it doesn't mean the presentation of the data to you but the presentation of the data to the system. It translates the data coming off the network to something meaningful in terms of character code and internal format, and makes sure that the data gets to the right place. The program you have running on your PC has an area of memory assigned to it for the storage of data. When you ask for a customer's payment record, that information is provided by the server, packetized, transported across the network, depacketized, and reassembled, but then what? It needs to be massaged into the format that your application can deal with, and sent to the right place in memory so that your application can find it. The presentation is discussed later.

A.3.5 The Application Layer

On the other layer section headings, I omitted the word 'layer.' I used it here because it's important to note that the application layer does not include the application. The application running on your PC sits above the OSI layers. The application layer provides services to the application such as printing capability, database access, and disk access. The presentation to the user can also be defined in the application layer a a sublayer service instead of in an application-defined user interface. The common PC operating environments, Macintosh, Windows, and OS/2, are a combination of these approaches. They provide user interface services, such as the drawing of the command button, text box, etc., but the application directs where these elements should go, so both are dealing with presentation. The definition gets fairly gray. If you have tons of application code that requests the system (let's say Windows) to draw something for you, is your code not considered presentation layer because it doesn't actually do the drawing? Perhaps, but then again many of the Windows API calls that programmers reference do not actually do the presentation but call other routines that do, so are those initial API routines thus not in the presentation layer? My take on this is — why care? — unless it becomes an issue of ownership, delivery, or resources, a painfully exacting definition won't be important in this context.

A.3.5.1 HTTP

HTTP is the protocol of the Internet. It fulfills the application layer of the OSI model, typically transferring HTML files and requests because HTML is the de facto language of the Internet.

I could make a lot more out of HTTP than I need to, but I won't. HTTP is a typical client-server style of protocol. The client requests something, and the server responds, preferably in a positive way.

A.3.6 TCP/IP

Hopefully, I have given you a passing understanding of the OSI layers and HTTP. While HTTP can be made to run on just about any client-server-friendly protocol, it almost always is found sitting on Transmission Control Protocol/Internet Protocol (TCP/IP) for two reasons: TCP/IP is what the Internet runs on, and TCP/IP guarantees delivery of the HTTP information packets.

In the client-server world, the network and transport layers are usually facilitated by TCP/IP, which was created by the military. Let's return to the luggage analogy to understand the relationship between the OSI model and TCP/IP. The OSI layers define what needs to happen for

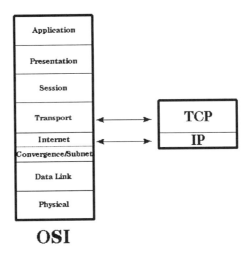

Figure A-5 TCP/IP and the OSI Model

the luggage to go from one place to another, TCP/IP is one method of tagging the bags, routing based on the tags, and providing a facility for quality control of the transfers. Figure A-5 positions the layers of TCP/IP against the OSI model.

As shown in the preceding figure, TCP/IP is a set of services that deal with network and network transport. The OSI network layer is actually divided into three sublayers: Internet, convergence and subnet. It's not important for us to make a distinction between them here aside from pointing IP to the sub-layer on which it operates.

In the OSI model, there is a distinction between 'protocols' and 'services,' and so a definition of protocol is warranted.

```
Pro•to•col   n. 1. Rules or standards governing
the provision of a service.
```

So, TCP/IP provides services based on a set of standards. Just about every aspect of computing either has a number of standards, or there are standards being developed. There are standards for the serial and parallel port communication, the modem, the CD-ROM drive, and even the wire that carries the information. The net of this is protection for the technology investment because older technology can be supplanted by new with less effort if both adhere to the same standard(s).

TCP/IP provides the services that get data, in a 'packetized' form, from one system to another. In doing this it also takes on the responsibility for ensuring that the packets are received error-free, and are disassembled at their destination in the proper order. Why is the order an issue? There is typically more than one physical route between two machines, and the likelihood of this increases as you move the machines farther apart. A packet being sent over the phone from Cincinnati to New York might go via Pittsburgh or Washington, and because of this there is the possibility of packet 2, via Washington, getting to New York before packet 1, via Pittsburgh. And even if packet 1 gets there first, if the packet is diagnosed as having been corrupted during its journey, TCP/IP will have to retransmit it from Cincinnati, and that new packet 1 will probably arrive at its destination after packets 2 and 3. TCP/IP will ensure that the receiving system gets the data in the proper order regardless of the order of arrival, as shown in Figure A-6.

A.3.7 The Client-Server Application

Sitting atop the OSI layers like a penthouse is the client-server application, which is dependent on all the layers under it, a dependency I'll illustrate more in a moment. First, let's take a look at what a client-server application is functionally. What makes it different than a normal application? We'll use a real-world example, an application, CUSTAPP, that manages customer records. Let's start with a one-tier version of the application, one that you would find in a typical mainframe environment.

A.3.7.1 CUSTAPP — Mainframe Version

A user selects CUSTAPP from the menu on the 3270 screen on their PC. A screen full of fields appear. The user enters a customer number, then presses a function key to signify that they are deleting that customer.

Although the user has entered the information using the PC, the application is running on the mainframe down in the computer room. The only application actually running on the PC is an emulation program to allow the PC screen and keyboard to behave like a 3270 terminal. The CUSTAPP application provided the field information to the PC so that it

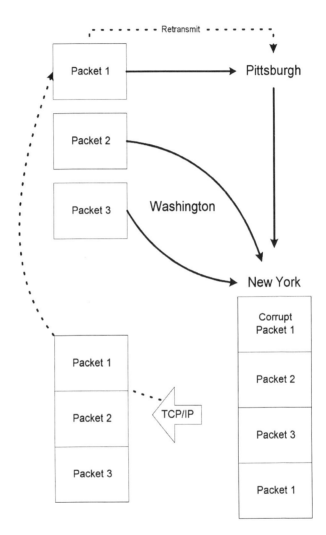

Figure A-6 TCP/IP Services

could draw the customer screen appropriately (the customer field goes i
the top left, the text entered in the state field in the address section shoul
be uppercase, and so on), and in pressing the function key the user h

caused an event to be triggered — the PC emulation application has taken the information from the screen, clumped it together, and transmitted it to the transaction buffer that the mainframe has set aside for this user. The exact method of this transfer depends on many factors such as the type of network and session, but those details are not important to us. What is important is what happens next.

The application first takes notice of the fact that a deletion has been requested. This is not a transaction available to the general population, so a check is done to verify that the user has the authority to perform this type of transaction. Now there are hundreds of subtle variations as to the how the events I've mentioned thus far could be handled functionally. For example, the function key used to request the deletion of a customer might not be enabled on a user's keyboard if they don't have deletion authority. These variations aren't important and I won't make an attempt to cover them as we proceed. At this point, we know that the user has requested a deletion and the system has verified that this user can do that, whatever the method and chronology.

Having validated the user's authority, the system then turns its attention to the fields necessary for this type of transaction. It validates that those fields all contain information, and that the information is of the correct format, such as a date field containing a valid date. Attention next goes to the piece of information around which the transaction centers, the customer number. CUSTAPP takes the customer number and makes a database call, a routine that access the customer database, to retrieve the customer information. If the call is successful, CUSTAPP has verified that the customer exists.

At this point CUSTAPP has verified that the user is entitled to delete a customer and that the customer exists (you can't delete a customer it's not there). So at this point the customer is deleted, right? No. At this point the business rules come into play. With any functional item in an application (deleting a customer, credit authorization, taking an order) there are policies specific to that company which need to be satisfied before the transaction can take place. When accepting an order, if the customer wants five widgets and three are in stock, one company might backorder two widgets and ship three, another might wait until the two back ordered widgets arrive before shipping any, and another company might not take the order at all because they, or that specific customer, don't accept backorders.

CUSTAPP first queries the accounts receivable database. Does this customer owe us money? It wouldn't be a good long-term strategy to allow the deletion of customers with open accounts. No, the customer is all paid up, but we're not done yet. On to the order database — does the customer have an open order pending? No, but we may still not be done. Depending on our business rules, we might not allow the deletion of customers to whom we have made sales in the last six months (still a candidate for business), or to whom we have ever made a sale until three years have passed since the last activity. Only if all of these rules are satisfied can the customer be deleted.

Now that we've deleted the customer, there are two important things to note.

While everything in the third block is taking place, the user is idle experiencing 'wait time' in computer parlance; also, all the programming code resides in one application — the field checking, the accounts receivable checking, the order file checking — all in the customer delete program. This latter point probably needs further clarification if your background is not in software. There are two drawbacks to having these diverse functions in one application. First, any time one of the business rules change, the application needs to change. For example, if the requirement for retaining a customer record after a sale changes from six months to nine months, the application deleting the customer needs to be changed to reflect that. If there are other applications that use the retention rule then they must be changed as well. Second, other applications might need to be changed to reflect changes to the customer deletion program. For example, if there is the possibility that the SALESHIST program can display sales history but not find the customer record because it's been deleted, the SALESHIST program needs to know that.

If the user could be making modifications to the program while idle waiting for their transaction to finish it would be a perfect world, but that's not usually the case. There are a number of places where we could focus attention to improve things, with the two major ones being

- minimize the need to change multiple applications when business rules change.
- reduce the user's 'wait time.'

These issues lend themselves to client-server technology as a solution. Let's take a look at why that is.

A.3.7.2 CUSTAPP — Client-Server Version

A user clicks on the CUSTAPP icon on their PC screen. A screen appears with a number of menu items across the top, from which the user selects CUSTOMER MAINTENANCE with a mouse cursor. This action causes a second menu, a drop-down menu, to appear, from which the user selects DELETE CUSTOMER. Had the user not been entitled to delete a customer, the menu item would be disabled or 'grayed' and not selectable.

A smaller screen containing a number of fields appears within the first one (see Figure A-7). The first field is CUSTOMER, and next to it a horizontal rectangle at the end of which is an arrow pointing down. When the user clicks on the arrow, a list of customers appears from which the user selects the one to be deleted. Some additional information appears on the screen so that the user can be certain that this is the correct customer. The user then verifies that the deletion should take place.

In many ways the objects on the screen interact with the user, that is the click of the menu causes a submenu to appear, and the click of the list box causes further data to be displayed. The reason this is possible is that everything the user has seen up to clicking the CUSTOMER list box has been provided by the client system, the PC. The Graphical User Interface (GUI), the presentation on the screen, is available because it is provided by the local, and powerful, client. If the GUI had to be provided by a remote system, it could not be as elaborate. The ability to segregate functionality so that it is provided in the most effective way, such as a local system providing the presentation services, is one of the benefits of the

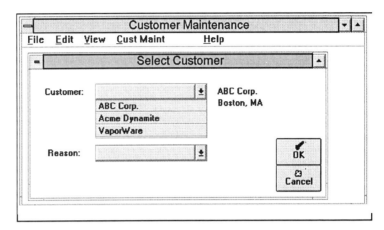

Figure A-7 Customer Select Screen

client-server approach. Of course, the entire application, not just the presentation services, could be provided by the client. There are instances where that makes sense, but this isn't one, and the reasons why lead us further into client-server functionality.

There are actually three client-server exchanges during this scenario. The first is when the user starts the application. The application requests a session (see section A.3.3) with the server system in anticipation of the services that the PC will be requesting from the server. The second exchange occurs when the user clicks on the list box and receives a list of customers, and this second exchange is a splendid example of why this application would not be a good candidate for being a pure client application. If the application were purely a client application, then the customer database would need to be located on the user's PC. If there are several users who work with customers, each would need a copy of the customer database on their PC. The salespeople who book orders need access to the customer database, so each of them would need a copy of the database on their PC. Having put a copy on each PC, what happens when one user makes a change to the customer's address and a user down the hall enters an order for that customer? The order won't reflect the correct address because that copy of the database hasn't been changed. Aside from the integrity benefits to be gained from having one copy of the data, there are security and storage considerations as well. Let's say that user X isn't entitled to see a customer's credit limit. Do you create a database for their PC that doesn't include that information? If so, then most likely every user will have a different database to suit their functionality, and the programs necessary to maintain and account for those differences would be a nightmare. If you don't create a database without that information, then even though the user doesn't have access to it through CUSTAPP, the data is still on their PC and thus providing a security risk — after all, PC data is very difficult to secure.

So let's go with one customer database sitting on a file sever. When the user clicks on the arrow on the list box, the application says, "Aha" (yes, it really does, but it says it very quietly in computer-speak). The application recognizes that it needs data which resides somewhere else and uses TCP/IP to send a message to the server saying, "Hey, send me a current sorted list of customer names." The server validates the request that the underlying security requirements have been met (just because it agreed to a session doesn't mean the user has Carte Blanche), accesses the customer database, and provides the data to TCP/IP which shoves it in a packets, wraps them and puts bows on them, sends them to the PC, yanks the data out of the packets (after neatly folding the wrapping paper for later use), and sticks it in a buffer for the application to use. The application now takes the data and sticks it in an array which is presented to the user in the form of items in a menu that drops down from the list box that was clicked. Whew. All of this only took a moment. In fact if everything went well the list box dropped as soon as the user clicked it with no indication that all of this was going on behind the scenes. Making sure that all the pieces are in place so that this can happen seamlessly and immediately will be addressed throughout the book, because the irony is that a tremendous amount of planning and effort need to occur for the user to notice nothing.

The user having acknowledged the deletion, the system then turns its attention to the fields necessary for this type of transaction. It validates that those fields all contain information, and that the information is of the correct format, such as a date field containing a valid date. This validation is all done by the client. Attention next goes to the piece of information around which the transaction centers, the customer number. CUSTAPP takes the customer number and makes a database call, a routine that access the customer database, to retrieve the customer information. If the call is successful, CUSTAPP has verified that the customer exists. Now you might think that this is a wasted step — why validate the customer since the user is selecting it from a list provided by the server? The reason is that between the time the user received the list and acknowledged the deletion, someone else might have already deleted that customer.

At this point CUSTAPP has verified that the user is entitled to delete a customer (DELETE would not have been selectable from the menu otherwise) and that the customer exists (you can't delete a customer if it's not there). We're up to the business rules again, and this is the third client-server exchange and one of the major benefits of client-server design.

The client application (CUSTAPP) now sends a parcel of information to the server. There are many different forms this information can take based on how the application is written and the type of networking, but an example that will suit our purposes is shown in Figure A-8. What the parcel needs to contain is all the information required by the server application to perform a specific function. Now, I just passed some 'subliminal' information past you, and need to take it step by step. I mentioned 'server application.' The server system is running a separate application from the client. We're not in an environment now where the client is merely a terminal to an application running on a larger machine. The fact that the server is running a separate application in and of itself is of no benefit to us. The server application could have the same name as the client application, but that would introduce unnecessary confusion, so we'll call the server application TRANSAPP. The function of TRANSAPP is to provide data services to CUSTAPP, and other client applications as well. CUSTAPP sits around and waits for the arrival of a parcel containing information, formatted in the expected way, which tells TRANSAPP what type of information or service is being requested. Time for another analogy.

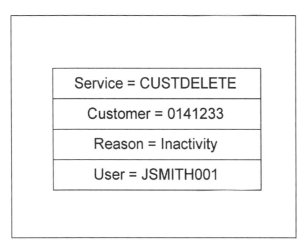

Figure A-8 Customer Transaction

Picture making a catalog merchandise order. You're not interested in where the warehouse is, what the receptionist's name is, or how their dental plan works. You don't want a phone number or directions. You mail the catalog company the information they require to process your order: your name, address, phone number, and credit card information and the items you want to purchase. In order to ensure the information they required is provided, and provided in a format that expedites their ability to process it, they provide you with a form. Once you have sent the form in you get on with your life. You don't worry about Phil on the loading dock complaining that he can't find the item on his picking list because it's in the wrong bin. If all goes well, the items you ordered will appear on your doorstep, otherwise you'll get a letter letting you know that the form was not completed properly, that the items are back ordered, or, gulp, discontinued.

Okay, back to client-server design. CUSTAPP wants CUSTTRANS to delete a customer, so it bundles the request and pertinent information in the format which CUSTTRANS understands. Once the request is made, CUSTTRANS and the user don't care how the server goes about deciding if the customer can be deleted, and while that decision is being made, the CUSTTRANS user can be doing something else. Eventually, perhaps immediately, a message will come back from the server saying either that the customer was indeed deleted, or that it wasn't along with the reason why. This segregation of functionality between the client and server provides benefits beyond freeing up the user while the transaction is being completed, it allows the design of the server hardware to become more specialized for the jobs it needs to do instead of having to provide a least common denominator so that it can handle the GUI and cosmetic editing services as well. Also, any client application that can establish the proper session with the server can request the same services in the same way without having to build the logic into the client application. Any time the code that accomplishes the services needs to be modified due to rules changes or other reasons, the changes are made in one place, not 100 different applications. As long as the format of the information needed for the transaction doesn't change, neither does the client application. A lesser-functionality example of this is a routine for checking that a date is valid.

Every programmer who's ever lived has written a function to validate a string of characters containing a proper date. Many of these routines use a date of the format mm/dd/yy where mm is a two-digit month, dd is a two-digit date, and yy is a two-digit year. To calculate how overdue your payment is, the date the payment is due is put in the form of yymmdd as is the date the payment is received, and one is compared to the other. If the format wasn't changed, comparing a January 1 due date to a December 25 payment would be comparing 01011995 to 12251994. The second date would be considered greater even though it isn't. In changing the format you compare 19950101 to 19941225, thus giving the correct result. The problem comes when you reach the year 2000. On January 1, 2000 (which by the way, is NOT the new century — it begins a year later) a zillion date routines will blow up because the system won't know January 1, 2000 from January 1, 1900 (both are 01/01/00), and they'll all have to be tracked down and changed (not before you get bills showing you're 99 years overdue).

"So what?" you ask. The "Y2000 problem," as it is known, represents over a billion dollars in expense to correct. Think of all the applications that need to be changed, the data record definitions, the database schemas, the unloading, correcting, and reloading of data. Having the code in one place facilitates making changes more easily.

At the higher end of functionality is OOP. No, not a descendant of Alley Oop, but an acronym for Object Oriented Programming. Objects allow the functionality to be completely self-contained. For example, a customer record can be an object. The oCUST object would contain many internal processes that it hides from the public, such as its method of determining whether a customer can be deleted and how it prints itself. To the public, oCUST would provide entry points such as the method for requesting the deletion of a customer. The only thing the user needs to know about the object is the entry point (function or subroutine name) and the parameters that need to be provided. Any time code needs to be changed with regards to the functionality of maintaining customer records, it's easy to find because it's all in one place, in the object, and isolated from all of the applications that request the services.

A.3.8 The Internet

Wow. As you can probably guess by looking at the bookshelves, this is a topic unto itself. What I'll provide here is a snapshot of what it's all about. Additional information can be found in the glossary at the end of the book.

'The Internet' is different than 'an internet.' The two are gradually losing their distinction though (in fact my word processor's spelling checker doesn't recognize the lower-case form). An internet is two or more networks connected together, while The Internet is the current interconnection of over 100,000 independent networks that has evolved from its beginnings as the Department of Defense's ARPANet in the late 1960s/early 1970s.

So you have all of these networks connected together, via TCP/IP by the way. What do you do with it? You provide or gather information! Each network that's part of the Internet provides a portion of the information it contains as public information. This information could be as diverse as a software upgrade, or an article on the mating habits of the anopheles mosquito. The concepts of the Internet that seem to creep into the morning coffee-machine talk represent different technologies under the covers, but simply a varying manner in which the information is stored and presented on the surface.

A.3.8.1 World-Wide Web

The World-Wide Web, or WWW, or 'the Web,' are the hypertext servers on the Internet which allow the displaying of hypertext markup language (HTML), 'pages' of information, like an electronic book, with interactive cross-references. These 'pages' can contain text, graphics, table data, sound, video, etc., so that you have a multimedia approach to displaying information, and an easy one at that. Let's take an old-world example, Hello World.

I think every programming language I ever undertook began with an example of the smallest functional program possible in that language, a program that would print the message "Hello World." Several examples are presented below.

C "Hello World"

```
main (argc, argv)
{
  printf('Hello World');
}
```

BASIC "Hello World"

```
print "Hello World"
end
```

I won't bother with the COBOL example, as it's a half-page in length. You get the general idea. So, what does a "Hello World" example look like for HTML, the language of a web page?

HTML "Hello World"

```
<TITLE>Hello World</title>
<BODY>
Hello World
</body>
```

"Wow," you exclaim, "is that all there is to it?" Well, yes. The big difference is what you have to do to go a step further. Let's say you want the text to be bold and red, and want an electronic movie of a rotating earth displayed alongside it. If you're lucky you'll have a wonderful call library available to you as a BASIC or C programmer, as that's the only way you're going to accomplish this with those languages — they have nothing in their syntax to cover this requirement. With HTML though, the power is in the program used to view the "web page," the browser.

HTML "Hello World"

```
<TITLE>Hello World</title>
<BODY>
<IMG SOURCE="earth.mpg" ALIGN=left>
<FONT color="red"><B>Hello World</b></font>
</body>
```

Now that's impressive. This assumes of course that you have the MPEG file of the rotating earth, and that the person viewing the web page has a browser that understands what a .mpg file is, and that it is configured with a "helper application" that knows how to display the image. So a "web browser" is an application which uses its understanding of the principles of the communications protocol used for the Web, HyperText Transport Protocol (HTTP), to access a remote machine and ask for the contents of a particular page, and then uses its understanding of the

HTML code it is sent to display the text and graphics appropriately on your screen. A screen shot of the Navigator browser displaying a web page is shown in Figure A-9.

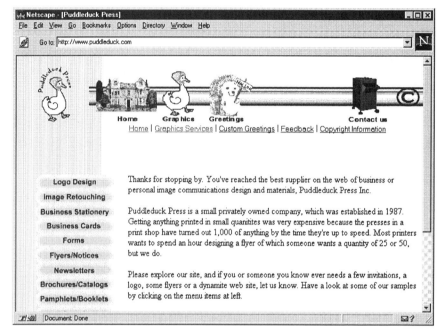

Figure A-9 A Web Page

The protocol behind web pages had been that whatever was contained on the page first had to be fully downloaded from where it resided to your computer before it was displayed. This made the displaying of graphics tedious with slow modems, and the displaying of video and sound almost unbearable. Advances in technology have made it possible now for "streaming" this information that is to be displaying the video, sound, or graphics while they are downloading. For example, when someone leaves you a voice-mail message, you can't listen to it until the message has been completed, but when speaking to someone on the phone, you hear their "message" as they are saying it.

The streaming opened the way for web pages with increased content. So now in addition to displaying formatted text and graphics, sound and video could be displayed too. But this still left the web page as little more than a display device — what about increasing its functionality (and business value)?

Sun Microsystems was the first to hop on that. They developed a scripting language, Java, that allows the web page developer to describe, via a small program called a script, an action that part of the web page should perform so long as the web browser being used supports Java. At first this functionality was limited to minor activities or applets such as animated icons, but streaming technology is quickly coming to Java and its counterparts as well so that fully functional applications will soon be possible.

A.3.8.2 FTP

Let's say you want to obtain the MPEG file from the above example to display, and someone on another network connected to the Internet has thoughtfully made it available (see Figure A-10). The tool for downloading that file to your system is FTP (File Transfer Protocol). Given the IP (Internet Protocol) address of the other person's machine (sort of like an Internet phone number), and a friendly FTP application, you can connect to their machine as an "Anonymous" user, and copy the file as if it were just in another directory on your machine.

Now what if you know there's a file out "somewhere on the 'net" that you need, but don't know what machine it's on. There are additional tools that work in conjunction with FTP to make life a lot easier, and make searching for the files possible.

There are applications that go forth on the 'net at night with the mission of compiling a list of all information out there. A daunting task, but the result is the ability to maintain an index of that information which can be searched by filename or topic. The search is presented in menu format, and the type of application that allows you to search is called a "gopher."

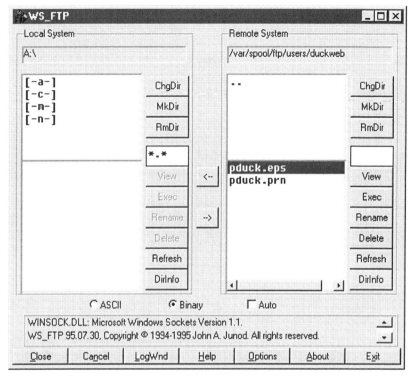

Figure A-10 WS-FTP

With the billions of pages of information available in FTP directories on the 'net, searching "gopher-space" can be quite disconcerting. The University of Nevada came to the rescue by developing a method of indexing gopher entries and allowing these indices to be searched. This database is called VERONICA (Very Easy Rodent-Oriented Netwide Index to Computerized Archives) ["rodent" referring to "gopher"]. If you know the actual filename that you're searching for, or a subset of it you can search for it by using another tool, named, yup — "Archie."

A.3.8.3 Newsgroups

The easiest way to describe a newsgroup is to make an analogy to e-mail. If your e-mail system were to allow you to define a mailing list for your department (and it may), imagine sending out a message to that mailing list. Everyone on the list receives the message. Now imagine that one of the people who receives the message composes a reply, but that instead of the reply being solely to you it is to everyone on the original mailing list. So now everyone on the list has seen your original message and the reply. Let's say that the reply has resulted in one of the other parties on the list sending a further reply. You get the idea.

The thing about the newsgroup is that it is topical (a newsgroup on authoring computer books, for example) and that everyone who joins the newsgroup can see all existing messages, even ones that were posted prior to their joining. Good news reader software will present you with a list of new message topics, called headers, for each newsgroup to which you subscribe, and present you with the option of obtaining the text of any of the messages, message bodies, which interest you. The arrangement used by a good news reader, an example of which is shown below, is helpful as well. A new message will be grouped with all subsequent messages of the same topic, and this grouping is referred to as a "thread."

The typical options give to you within the news reader are

- obtain new message headers for the newsgroup.
- obtain message bodies for any selected, or "marked", headers.
- post a message to begin a new "thread."
- reply to a message; add to an existing "thread."
- post an e-mail reply to the author of a posting.

Thus, the newsgroup is a wonderful forum for discussions on various topics. Each topic discussed becomes a "thread," with responses to each part of the thread being indented below the original message in the list of messages.

Mutual Fund Newsgroup

<->Consolidated Widgets	Joe	3/24
Con. Widgets - nah	Bob	3/25
Con. Wid. is great	Sheila	3/26
You're nuts	Bob	3/26
<->New 401K Legislation	Phil	3/25

Appendix B – Project Management

Since much of this book deals with the management of technology implementation, we need a common platform of project management understanding to build on. To keep this book of manageable size, I'll have to assume that anyone managing a project of this type has a grasp of basic project management skills, despite my having experience for myself that this is not always true. For example, I won't discuss the method of developing a Gantt chart in this book, but I will discuss the understanding and planning that need to go into developing a Gantt chart, the items that have to be on it, and how to determine if the project is straying from the plan in time to remedy the situation. What I want to discuss here is some of the basic terminology of project management so that I can use it freely later on.

B.1 WORK BREAKDOWN STRUCTURE

The WBS is a way of enumerating the steps necessary to get from point a to point b. The ultimate goal is divided into a number of items of equivalent importance that need to happen in order for the goal to be realized. The items from the first subdivision are typically considered to be milestones. Every item that needs to happen during the project is then grouped along with the most appropriate milestone and becomes a task. The tasks are listed without consideration (at this point) of chronology, responsibilities and dependencies; the object of the WBS is to provide a framework for developing the Gantt chart which does make those considerations. At this point, as seen in figure B-1, all we're interested in are the tasks. You can think of the WBS development process as listing tasks on yellow 'stickies' and pasting them on the wall.

Figure B-1 Card Shopping Task List

B.2 NETWORK DIAGRAM

The network diagram gives a visual representation of the tasks from the WBS in chronological order with dependencies considered. Having stuck the tasks on the wall, we now want to give consideration to the order in which they need to occur and the dependencies between them. We need to arrange the 'stickies' from left to right, start to finish. When we get to a point where more than one task can occur simultaneously, this is represented by those tasks being stacked.

A dependency is a relationship between two tasks where the successor task's completion is governed by the predecessor task in some way. Let's take a look at the types of dependencies.

B.2.1 Finish -> Start

When Task B can't start until Task A has been completed, there is a Finish->Start relationship between the two tasks. For example, if picking up this book and opening it were two tasks, the second can't happen until the first has. If we add a third task, reading the introduction, we can see that there is a Finish->Start relationship between opening the book and reading the introduction.

B.2.2 Start -> Start

If Task B can't begin until Task A begins, there is a Start->Start relationship. This implies that with regards to Task B, we don't care if or when Task A completes as long as it has started. For example, in transcribing a conversation, as soon as the conversation starts, so can the transcribing. In this instance, as in many Start->Start relationships, there is also an Finish->Finish relationship between the two tasks.

B.2.3 Finish ->Finish

In the example above, we pointed out that the transcribing of a conversation doesn't start until the conversation does. Likewise, the transcribing does not end until the conversation ends. This means that the finish of Task B is dependant on the finish of Task A. This is a Finish -> Finish relationship. It's typical for a Finish->Finish relationship to have a lag time defined. Lag can be specified with any relationship. Staying with the transcription example, let's assume that once the conversation ends there will be ten minutes needed to review the transcript. Now it's very unusual to specify task durations down to the minute, but we'll assume that in this case we're planning out our morning. The relationship would then be Task B Finish = Task A Finish + 10 minutes, so that we have a Finish->Finish dependency with lag.

The dependencies in Figure B-2 are shown by connecting each of the 'stickies' with an arrow, from the left side of a task to denote the start, or the right side of the task to denote the finish. Not all relationships are shown though. If Task 3 can't happen until Task 2 is completed, and Task 2 can't happen until Task 1 is completed, then there is an implicit Finish->Start dependency between Task 1 and Task 3. Think of a family tree. A line is drawn from you to your parents, and from your parents to their parent, but not from you to your grandparents — that relationship is implied. This avoidance of representing all nexuses is necessary in order to avoid an unruly mess of arrows, after all, the idea of a network diagram, or any diagram, is to relay a more immediate understanding than could be had nongraphically. If you had to 'untangle' the diagram, it would be of no use.

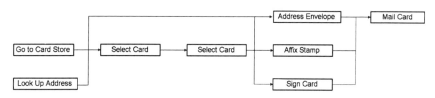

Figure B-2 Card Shopping Network Diagram

So let's take Figure B-2 task by task so that you can understand how dependencies were derived from assumptions.

- Going to the Card Shop — For the sake of brevity, we're putting the beginning of the time line immediately to the left of this task and say that it depends on nothing to be done, otherwise we'd be dealing with the need for a card, the need for a card shop having been built, etc.

- Select Card — Hopefully it's obvious that we can't select a card unless we're at the card shop. Let's take a somewhat closer look though. I've found that many people learning English have a hard time with the nuances of the timing built into our conjugations, for example, run, ran, have run, am running, have been running, and will have been running. There are nuances in task timing that need to be resolved in determining dependencies. Knowing that Task 2 depends on Task 1 is a start, but we need to know what state Task 1 needs to be in to satisfy the dependency. So let's answer some basic questions.

- If Task 2 has begun, does its completion in any way depend on Task 1? If the answer is 'no', which it is, then the dependency is not of the->FINISH type because the FINISH of Task 2, the task on the right-hand side of the arrow, is not dependent on Task 1.

- Does the start of Task 2 depend in any way on Task 1? If so, which is the case here, then we have a ->START dependency; the start of Task 2 is dependent on Task 1. Now we need to fill in the left-hand side of the arrow.

- Can Task 2 start while Task 1 is in progress or does Task 1 have to be completed? In this case Task 1 needs to have been completed first: We can't select a card if we're 'almost' at the card shop. The dependency is thus a FINISH->START: The second task can't begin until the first task finishes.

- Buy Card — It's apparent that we can't purchase a card until it's been selected. Having said that I'll contradict myself with a hypothetical situation. If all the cards in the shop, or in the category from which we are making our selection, are of the same price, then there exists the potential to prepurchase the card, that is to be, for example, fifty percent through the selection process and then purchase the card before we have finished selection. Yes, it's a stretch in this situation (and there's no good reason to do it), but keep it in mind, because that is an example of collapsing tasks. If you find yourself at a point where you're behind schedule, one method of making up time is to find tasks scheduled as FINISH->START where the second task can begin during the course of the preceding task instead of waiting until the absolute completion of the preceding task, an example being coding and documentation. In this case, though, the dependency is clearly FINISH->START.

- Look up Address — What needs to happen before we can look up the address? Within the bounds of this example, nothing. We can look up the address at any time, so this step has no dependency and no predecessor.

- Address Envelope — It's fairly straightforward that we can't address the envelope until we look up the address, right? Wrong. We can put our return address on the envelope at any time after having bought the card (assuming we're using the envelope that comes with the card — we could be putting it in a larger envelope with other things. We won't get caught up in this, but again, keep it in mind when the importance and scale of the tasks are greater). So, buying the card needs to have been completed before we can address the envelope, a FINISH->START dependency, and looking up the address needs to have completed before we can complete the addressing of the envelope, a FINISH->FINISH relationship.

- Affix Stamp — No surprises here, I think. The stamp can be affixed so long as we have the envelope. There are no other dependencies. Most of us affix a stamp after we have addressed the envelope, but that is not a requirement. Thus the dependency here is a FINISH->START between the tasks of Buy Card and Affix Stamp.

- Sign Card — No surprises here either. There is no relationship between the signing of the card and the addressing or stamping of the envelope. We can sign the card as soon as we own it, so the tasks Buy Card and Sign Card have a FINISH->START dependency.

- Mail Card — This final step is typical in having many dependencies because there are parallel actions taking place, all which need to be completed prior to this final task being completed. The card cannot be mailed until the envelope is addressed, so there is one FINISH->START dependency. The card cannot be mailed until the stamp is affixed to the envelope, another FINISH->START dependency. And finally the card can not be mailed until it is signed, another FINISH-START dependency. Now keep in mind that technically this step can begin without those three predecessors completing (we can walk to the mailbox and open the flap), so the dependencies can be shown as FINISH->FINISH. However, we'll do what is often done in these circumstances. FINISH->START dependencies are the least complicated and most prevalent, and unless there exists a threat of not completing this task on time, there is no reason to collapse it and start it prior to its predecessors ending.

B.3 GANTT CHART

Having laid out the tasks in the network diagram, the next step toward creating a time line is to assign resources. Resources can be money, people, or materials. Once we have determined what resources are required by, and available for, each task we can see how their availability impacts the timing and plan accordingly. In Figure B-3 the second Gantt chart shows the same tasks as the first with the following factors being considered:

- the card store is closed on Sunday.
- no time is available on Monday to purchase a stamp.
- a half-day to purchase stamps due to the limited availability of those with the new rate.

You can see how some minor obstructions can change the schedule. Breaking a complete project down into a structure can be a daunting process.

One thing worth mentioning here is duration and effort. When looking a how long a task will take you need to consider if it would take any less time were you to increase the number of people working on it. If not, then the task should be measured in elapsed time, an example being the nine months it takes to have a baby. If you know that, for example, the task requires one individual to do six hours work, but it will take them a day to do that work, then the duration of the task is one day, but the effort is six hours. The distinction is made by many project management software packages, showing you a duration column but having a distinct effort column elsewhere, and knowing the distinction will help you figure out why the bar on the Gantt chart for a particular task is longer than you think it should be.

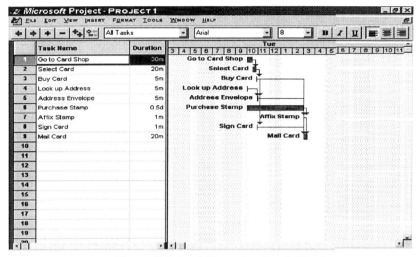

Figure B-3 Card Shopping Gantt Chart

There is another reason to understand the difference — so that you can better measure variance. Identifying variance and accounting for it is critical to a project being successful. Listed here are the important aspects to managing variance.

- Create the project plan before the project begins. This might sound obvious, but many times the entry of the plan and adjustment of the dependencies spill over into the beginning of the project. The problem is at that point you've probably altered data on the initial tasks before freezing the baseline. If you don't have a baseline to compare to, you can't measure variance.
- Indirect causal variance — variance that results from something other than the estimate being incorrect. For example, a task is scheduled as fifteen hours of effort over three calendar days (the resource is available five hours per day). On the second day a construction crew cuts through a cable and power to the building is lost. That task is now late, but not because

the estimated effort is incorrect, yet some subsequent tasks will need to be collapsed to still come in on-time.

- Direct causal variance — variance resulting from estimated effort not matching the actual effort for whatever reason. It might be that it just plain took longer to do it than estimated, or that the resource was tired and couldn't put in that twelve-hour day, or that supporting variables, such as a PC being ready, didn't happen.

The most important thing about variance is identifying it quickly and making necessary adjustments. In some cases the adjustment might be an additional resource (hopefully, there were risk dollars built into the project pricing), or it could mean realizing that all subsequent estimates by that person or relating to that activity need to be adjusted. The adjustment(s) could then push the end-date of the project out unless tasks could be collapsed to avoid that.

Glossary

ARPA	Advance Research Projects Agency
BASIC	A programming language
C++	An object-oriented programming language
CAD	Computer aided design
CAE	Computer aided engineering
CAM	Computer aided modeling
CBT	Computer-based training
CEO	Chief Executive Officer
CFO	Chief Financial Officer
CGI	Common Gateway Interface
CIO	Chief Information Officer
COBOL	COmmon Business Oriented Language
COO	Chief Operating Officer
CPLC	Customer Project Life Cycle
DB2	A database environment
DNS	Domain Name Server
DRP	Disaster Recovery Planning
FTP	File Transfer Protocol
Gantt	A charting methodology for timelines
GUI	Graphical User Interface
High-Availability	Software and hardware used to assure that a computer system is available a high percentage of the time
HLD	High-level design
HTML	Hyper Text Markup Language
HTTP	Hyper Text Transfer Protocol
Internet	A worldwide network of computer systems

intranet	A proprietary network of computer systems
IP	Internet Protocol
IS/IT	Information Services / Information Technology
ISP	Internet Service Provider
ITSM	Information Technology Service Management
LAN	Local Area Network
LLD	Low Level Design
LU6.2	The protocol for System Network Architecture
MFLOPS	Millions of FLOating Point instructions per Second
NSM	Network System Management
OS	Operating System
PL/1	Program Language 1
PM	Project Manager
PPP	Point-to-Point Protocol
RACI	Responsible-Accountable-Consulted-Informed
RAP	Rapid Application Prototyping
ROI	Return On Investment
RTF	Rich Text Format
SEPC	Software Engineering Process Consultant
SME	Subject Matter Expert
SNA	System Network Architecture
TCP	Transmissions Control Protocol
TPS	Transactions Per Second
UAT	User Acceptance Testing
UNIX	A computer operating system
URL	Universal Resource Locator
Visual C++	A programming environment and language
WAN	Wide-Area Network
WBS	Work Breakdown Structure
WWW	World-Wide Web

Index

317

also see Disaster Recovery Planning
duration 105, 250

E
expectations 17, 18, 19, 29, 66, 84, 89

G
Gantt chart 12, 93, 94, 99, 112, 114, 305, 311
GUI 16, 291, 296

H
HTML 56, 158, 285, 298, 299, 300

I
infrastructure 1, 2, 3, 17, 39, 41, 42, 51, 53, 57, 59, 61, 64, 72, 81, 83, 89, 108, 129, 140, 145, 167, 176, 187, 217, 233, 240
Internet 1, 2, 47, 55, 56, 81, 148, 158, 177, 179, 180, 181, 182, 207 211, 233, 238, 239, 259, 260, 285, 286, 297, 298, 301
intranet 1, 2, 47, 55, 56, 158, 177, 179, 181, 207, 211, 237, 238, 259

J
Java 149, 158, 180, 301

L
LAN 55, 56, 72, 149, 156, 157, 210, 231, 280, 281
Level 5 276
Local Area Network 55, 56, 72, 149, 156, 157, 210, 231, 280, 281

M
methodology
Cascading Waterfall 185
CPLC 30, 52